W9-BWG-109

THE TIMELESS WAY OF BUILDING

The Timeless Way of Building is the first in a series of books which describe an entirely new attitude to architecture and planning. The books are intended to provide a complete working alternative to our present ideas about architecture, building, and planning—an alternative which will, we hope, gradually replace current ideas and practices.

volume 1 THE TIMELESS WAY OF BUILDING

volume 2 A PATTERN LANGUAGE

volume 3 THE OREGON EXPERIMENT

Center for Environmental Structure

BERKELEY, CALIFORNIA

THE

TIMELESS WAY

OF BUILDING

Christopher Alexander

with love and thanks
to Ingrid, Sara, and Peter

NEW YORK

OXFORD UNIVERSITY PRESS

1979

Library of Congress Cataloging in Publication Data

Alexander, Christopher.
  The timeless way of building.
  1. Architecture. 2. Pattern perception. I. Title.

NA2500.A45   720'.1   76-42650
ISBN 0-19-502248-3

Copyright © 1979 by Christopher Alexander

Printed in the United States of America

To you, mind of no mind, in whom
the timeless way was born.

ON READING THIS BOOK

What lies in this book is perhaps more important as a whole than in its details. If you only have an hour to spend on it, it makes much more sense to read the whole book roughly in that hour, than to read only the first two chapters in detail. For this reason, I have arranged each chapter in such a way that you can read the whole chapter in a couple of minutes, simply by reading the headlines which are in italics. If you read the beginning and end of every chapter, and the italic headlines that lie between them, turning the pages almost as fast as you can, you will be able to get the overall structure of the book in less than an hour.

Then, if you want to go into detail, you will know where to go, but always in the context of the whole.

CONTENTS

THE TIMELESS WAY

THE QUALITY

THE GATE

CONTENTS

THE WAY

THE KERNEL OF THE WAY

DETAILED TABLE OF CONTENTS

THE TIMELESS WAY

A building or a town will only be alive to the extent that it is governed by the timeless way.

1. It is a process which brings order out of nothing but ourselves; it cannot be attained, but it will happen of its own accord, if we will only let it.

THE QUALITY

To seek the timeless way we must first know the quality without a name.

2. There is a central quality which is the root criterion of life and spirit in a man, a town, a building, or a wilderness. This quality is objective and precise, but it cannot be named.

3. The search which we make for this quality, in our

own lives, is the central search of any person, and the crux of any individual person's story. It is the search for those moments and situations when we are most alive.

4. In order to define this quality in buildings and in towns, we must begin by understanding that every place is given its character by certain patterns of events that keep on happening there.

5. These patterns of events are always interlocked with certain geometric patterns in the space. Indeed, as we shall see, each building and each town is ultimately made out of these patterns in the space, and out of nothing else: they are the atoms and the molecules from which a building or a town is made.

6. The specific patterns out of which a building or a town is made may be alive or dead. To the extent they are alive, they let our inner forces loose, and set us free; but when they are dead, they keep us locked in inner conflict.

7. The more living patterns there are in a place— a room, a building, or a town—the more it comes to life as an entirety, the more it glows, the more it has that self-maintaining fire which is the quality without a name.

8. And when a building has this fire, then it becomes a part of nature. Like ocean waves, or blades of grass, its parts are governed by the endless play of repetition and variety created in the presence of the fact that all things pass. This is the quality itself.

THE GATE

To reach the quality without a name we must then build a living pattern language as a gate.

9. This quality in buildings and in towns cannot be made, but only generated, indirectly, by the ordinary actions of the people, just as a flower cannot be made, but only generated from the seed.

10. The people can shape buildings for themselves, and have done it for centuries, by using languages which I call pattern languages. A pattern language gives each person who uses it the power to create an infinite variety of new and unique buildings, just as his ordinary language gives him the power to create an infinite variety of sentences.

11. These pattern languages are not confined to villages and farm society. All acts of building are governed by a pattern language of some sort, and the patterns in the world are there, entirely because they are created by the pattern languages which people use.

12. And, beyond that, it is not just the shape of towns and buildings which comes from pattern languages—it is their quality as well. Even the life and beauty of the most awe-inspiring great religious buildings came from the languages their builders used.

13. But in our time the languages have broken down. Since they are no longer shared, the processes which keep them deep have broken down; and it is therefore virtually impossible for anybody, in our time, to make a building live.

14. To work our way towards a shared and living language once again, we must first learn how to discover patterns which are deep, and capable of generating life.

15. We may then gradually improve these patterns which we share, by testing them against experience: we can determine, very simply, whether these patterns make our surroundings live, or not, by recognizing how they make us feel.

16. Once we have understood how to discover individual patterns which are alive, we may then make a language for ourselves for any building task we face. The structure of the language is created by the network of connections among individual patterns: and the language lives, or not, as a totality, to the degree these patterns form a whole.

THE KERNEL OF THE WAY

And yet the timeless way is not complete, and will not fully generate the quality without a name, until we leave the gate behind.

THE
TIMELESS
WAY

A building or a town will only be
alive to the extent that it is governed
by the timeless way.

.

CHAPTER I

THE TIMELESS WAY

*It is a process which brings order out of
nothing but ourselves; it cannot be
attained, but it will happen of its own
accord, if we will only let it.*

There is one timeless way of building.

It is thousands of years old, and the same today as it has always been.

The great traditional buildings of the past, the villages and tents and temples in which man feels at home, have always been made by people who were very close to the center of this way. It is not possible to make great buildings, or great towns, beautiful places, places where you feel yourself, places where you feel alive, except by following this way. And, as you will see, this way will lead anyone who looks for it to buildings which are themselves as ancient in their form, as the trees and hills, and as our faces are.

It is a process through which the order of a building or a town grows out directly from the inner nature of the people, and the animals, and plants, and matter which are in it.

It is a process which allows the life inside a person, or a family, or a town, to flourish, openly, in freedom, so vividly that it gives birth, of its own accord, to the natural order which is needed to sustain this life.

It is so powerful and fundamental that with its help you can make any building in the world as beautiful as any place that you have ever seen.

Once you understand this way, you will be able to make your room alive; you will be able to design a house together with your family; a garden for your children;

7

places where you can work; beautiful terraces where you can sit and dream.

It is so powerful, that with its help hundreds of people together can create a town, which is alive and vibrant, peaceful and relaxed, a town as beautiful as any town in history.

Without the help of architects or planners, if you are working in the timeless way, a town will grow under your hands, as steady as the flowers in your garden.

And there is no other way in which a building or a town which lives can possibly be made.

This does not mean that all ways of making buildings are identical. It means that at the core of all successful acts of building and at the core of all successful processes of growth, even though there are a million different versions of these acts and processes, there is one fundamental invariant feature, which is responsible for their success. Although this way has taken on a thousand different forms at different times, in different places, still, there is an unavoidable, invariant core to all of them.

Look at the buildings in the photographs which start this chapter.

They are alive. They have that sleepy, awkward grace which comes from perfect ease.

And the Alhambra, some tiny gothic church, an old

8

New England house, an Alpine hill village, an ancient Zen temple, a seat by a mountain stream, a courtyard filled with blue and yellow tiles among the earth. What is it they have in common? They are beautiful, ordered, harmonious—yes, all these things. But especially, and what strikes to the heart, they live.

Each one of us wants to be able to bring a building or part of a town to life like this.

It is a fundamental human instinct, as much a part of our desire as the desire for children. It is, quite simply, the desire to make a part of nature, to complete a world which is already made of mountains, streams, snowdrops, and stones, with something made by us, as much a part of nature, and a part of our immediate surroundings.

Each one of us has, somewhere in his heart, the dream to make a living world, a universe.

Those of us who have been trained as architects have this desire perhaps at the very center of our lives: that one day, somewhere, somehow, we shall build one building which is wonderful, beautiful, breathtaking, a place where people can walk and dream for centuries.

In some form, every person has some version of this dream: whoever you are, you may have the dream of one day building a most beautiful house for your family, a garden, a fountain, a fishpond, a big room with soft light, flowers outside and the smell of new grass.

In some less clear fashion, anyone who is concerned

9

with towns has this same dream, perhaps, for an entire town.

And there is a way that a building or a town can actually be brought to life like this.

There is a definable sequence of activities which are at the heart of all acts of building, and it is possible to specify, precisely, under what conditions these activities will generate a building which is alive. All this can be made so explicit that anyone can do it.

And just so, the process by which a group of independent people make part of a town alive can equally be made precise. Again, there is a definable sequence of activities, more complex in this case, which are at the heart of all collective building processes, and it is possible to specify exactly when these processes will bring things to life. And, once again, these processes can be made so explicit, and so clear, that any group of people can make use of them.

This one way of building has always existed.

It is behind the building of traditional villages in Africa, and India, and Japan. It was behind the building of the great religious buildings: the mosques of Islam, the monasteries of the middle ages, and the temples of Japan. It was behind the building of the simple benches, and cloisters and arcades of English country towns; of the mountain huts of Norway and Austria; the roof tiles on the walls of castles and palaces; the bridges of the Italian middle ages; the cathedral of Pisa.

In an unconscious form, this way has been behind almost all ways of building for thousands of years.

But it has become possible to identify it, only now, by going to a level of analysis which is deep enough to show what is invariant in all the different versions of this way.

This hinges on a form of representation which reveals all possible construction processes, as versions of one deeper process.

First, we have a way of looking at the ultimate constituents of the environment: the ultimate "things" which a building or a town is made of. As we shall see, in chapters 4 and 5, every building, every town, is made of certain entities which I call patterns: and once we understand buildings in terms of their patterns, we have a way of looking at them, which makes all buildings, all parts of a town similar, all members of the same class of physical structures.

Second, we have a way of understanding the generative processes which give rise to these patterns: in short, the source from which the ultimate constituents of building come. As we shall see in chapters 10, 11, and 12, these patterns always come from certain combinatory processes, which are different in the specific patterns which they generate, but always similar in their overall structure, and in the way they work. They are essentially like languages. And again, in terms of these pattern languages, all the different ways of building, although different in detail, become similar in general outline.

At this level of analysis, we can compare many different building processes.

Then, once we see their differences clearly, it becomes possible to define the difference between those processes which make buildings live, and those which make them dead.

And it turns out that, invariant, behind all processes which allow us to make buildings live, there is a single common process.

This single process is operational and precise. It is not merely a vague idea, or a class of processes which we can understand: it is concrete enough and specific enough, so that it functions practically. It gives us the power to make towns and buildings live, as concretely as a match gives us the power to make a flame. It is a method or a discipline, which teaches us precisely what we have to do to make our buildings live.

But though this method is precise, it cannot be used mechanically.

The fact is, that even when we have seen deep into the processes by which it is possible to make a building or a town alive, in the end, it turns out that this knowledge only brings us back to that part of ourselves which is forgotten.

Although the process is precise, and can be defined in exact scientific terms, finally it becomes valuable, not so much because it shows us things which we don't know, but instead, because it shows us what we know already, only daren't admit because it seems so childish, and so primitive.

Indeed it turns out, in the end, that what this method does is simply free us from all method.

The more we learn to use this method, the more we find that what it does is not so much to teach us processes we did not know before, but rather opens up a process in us, which was part of us already.

We find out that we already know how to make buildings live, but that the power has been frozen in us: that we have it, but are afraid to use it: that we are crippled by our fears; and crippled by the methods and the images which we use to overcome these fears.

And what happens finally, is that we learn to overcome our fears, and reach that portion of our selves which knows exactly how to make a building live, instinctively. But we learn too, that this capacity in us is not accessible, until we first go through the discipline which teaches us to let go of our fears.

And that is why the timeless way is, in the end, a timeless one.

13

It is not an external method, which can be imposed on things. It is instead a process which lies deep in us: and only needs to be released.

The power to make buildings beautiful lies in each of us already.

It is a core so simple, and so deep, that we are born with it. This is no metaphor. I mean it literally. Imagine the greatest possible beauty and harmony in the world—the most beautiful place that you have ever seen or dreamt of. You have the power to create it, at this very moment, just as you are.

And this power we have is so firmly rooted and coherent in every one of us that once it is liberated, it will allow us, by our individual, unconnected acts, to make a town, without the slightest need for plans, because, like every living process, it is a process which builds order out of nothing.

But as things are, we have so far beset ourselves with rules, and concepts, and ideas of what must be done to make a building or a town alive, that we have become afraid of what will happen naturally, and convinced that we must work within a "system" and with "methods" since without them our surroundings will come tumbling down in chaos.

We are afraid, perhaps, that without images and methods, chaos will break loose; worse still, that unless we use images of some kind, ourselves, our own creation will itself be chaos. And why are we afraid of that? Is it because people will laugh at us, if we make chaos? Or is it, perhaps, that we are most afraid of all that if we do make chaos, when we hope to create art, we will ourselves be chaos, hollow, nothing?

This is why it is so easy for others to play on our fears. They can persuade us that we must have more method, and more system, because we are afraid of our own chaos. Without method and more method, we are afraid the chaos which is in us will reveal itself. And yet these methods only make things worse.

The thoughts and fears which feed these methods are illusions.

It is the fears which these illusions have created in us, that make places which are dead and lifeless and artificial. And—greatest irony of all—it is the very methods we invent to free us from our fears which are themselves the chains whose grip on us creates our difficulties.

For the fact is, that this seeming chaos which is in us is a rich, rolling, swelling, dying, lilting, singing, laughing, shouting, crying, sleeping *order*. If we will only let this order guide our acts of building, the buildings that we make, the towns we help to make, will be the forests and the meadows of the human heart.

To purge ourselves of these illusions, to become free of all the artificial images of order which distort the nature that is in us, we must first learn a discipline which teaches us the true relationship between ourselves and our surroundings.

Then, once this discipline has done its work, and pricked the bubbles of illusion which we cling to now, we will be ready to give up the discipline, and act as nature does.

This is the timeless way of building: learning the discipline—and shedding it.

THE QUALITY

To seek the timeless way we must
first know the quality without a
name.

CHAPTER 2

THE QUALITY WITHOUT A NAME

*There is a central quality which is the
root criterion of life and spirit in a man,
a town, a building, or a wilderness. This
quality is objective and precise, but it
cannot be named.*

We have been taught that there is no objective differ-ence between good buildings and bad, good towns and bad.

The fact is that the difference between a good build-ing and a bad building, between a good town and a bad town, is an objective matter. It is the difference between health and sickness, wholeness and divided-ness, self-maintenance and self-destruction. In a world which is healthy, whole, alive, and self-maintaining, people themselves can be alive and self-creating. In a world which is unwhole and self-destroying, people cannot be alive: they will inevitably themselves be self-destroying, and miserable.

But it is easy to understand why people believe so firmly that there is no single, solid basis for the difference between good building and bad.

It happens because the single central quality which makes the difference cannot be named.

The first place I think of, when I try to tell someone about this quality, is a corner of an English country gar-den, where a peach tree grows against a wall.

The wall runs east to west; the peach tree grows flat against its southern side. The sun shines on the tree and as it warms the bricks behind the tree, the warm bricks themselves warm the peaches on the tree. It has a slightly dozy quality. The tree, carefully tied to grow flat against the wall; warming the bricks; the peaches growing in the sun; the wild grass growing around the roots of the tree, in the angle where the earth and roots and wall all meet.

This quality is the most fundamental quality there is in anything.

It is never twice the same, because it always takes its shape from the particular place in which it occurs.

In one place it is calm, in another it is stormy; in one person it is tidy; in another it is careless; in one house it is light; in another it is dark; in one room it is soft and quiet; in another it is yellow. In one family it is a love of picnics; in another dancing; in another playing poker; in another group of people it is not family life at all.

It is a subtle kind of freedom from inner contradictions.

A system has this quality when it is at one with itself; it lacks it when it is divided.

It has it when it is true to its own inner forces; lacks it when it is untrue to its own inner forces.

It has it when it is at peace with itself; and lacks it when it is at war with itself.

You already know this quality. The feeling for it is the most primitive feeling which an animal or a man can have. The feeling for it is as primitive as the feeling for our own well-being, for our own health, as primitive as the intuition which tells us when something is false or true.

But to grasp it fully you must overcome the prejudice

of physics which tells us that all things are equally alive and real.

In physics and chemistry there is no sense in which one system can be more at one with itself than another.

And no sense at all in which what a system "ought to be" grows naturally from "what it is." Take, for example, the atoms which a physicist deals with. An atom is so simple that there is never any question whether it is true to its own nature. Atoms are all true to their own natures; they are all equally real; they simply exist. An atom cannot be more true to itself, or less true to itself. And because physics has concentrated on very simple systems, like atoms, we have been led to believe that what something "is," is an entirely separate question from what it "ought to be"; and that science and ethics can't be mixed.

But the view of the world which physics teaches, powerful and wonderful as it is, is limited by this very blindness.

In the world of complex systems it is not so. Most men are not fully true to their own inner natures or fully "real." In fact, for many people, the effort to become true to themselves is the central problem of life. When you meet a person who is true to himself, you feel at once that he is "more real" than other people are. At the human level of complexity, then, there is a distinction between systems which are true to their "inner nature," and those which aren't. Not all of us are equally true to our inner nature, or equally real, or equally whole.

And exactly the same is true in those larger systems, outside us, which we call our world. Not all parts of the world are equally true to themselves, equally real, equally whole. In the world of physics, any system which is self-destroying simply ceases to exist. But in the world of complex systems this is not so.

Indeed, this subtle and complex freedom from inner contradictions is just the very quality which makes things live.

In the world of living things, every system can be more real or less real, more true to itself or less true to itself. It cannot become more true to itself by copying any externally imposed criterion of what it ought to be. But it is possible to define a process which will tell you how the system can become more true to itself, in short what it "ought to be," only according to what it is.

This oneness, or the lack of it, is the fundamental quality for any thing. Whether it is in a poem, or a man, or in a building full of people, or in a forest, or a city, everything that matters stems from it. It embodies everything.

Yet still this quality cannot be named.

The fact that this quality cannot be named does not mean that it is vague or imprecise. It is impossible to name because it is unerringly precise. Words fail to capture it because it is much more precise than any word. The quality itself is sharp, exact, with no looseness in it whatsoever. But each word you choose to capture it has fuzzy edges and extensions which blur the central meaning of the quality.

I shall try to show you now, why words can never capture it, by circling round it, through the medium of half a dozen words.

The word which we most often use to talk about the quality without a name is the word "alive."

There is a sense in which the distinction between something alive and something lifeless is much more general, and far more profound, than the distinction between living things and nonliving things, or between life and death. Things which are living may be lifeless; nonliving things may be alive. A man who is walking and talking can be alive; or he can be lifeless. Beethoven's last quartets are alive; so are the waves at the ocean shore; so is a candle flame; a tiger may be more alive, because more in tune with its own inner forces, than a man.

A well-made fire is alive. There is a world of difference between a fire which is a pile of burning logs, and a fire which is made by someone who really understands a fire. He places each log exactly to make the air between

29

the logs just right. He doesn't stir the logs with a poker, but while they are burning, grasps each one, and places it again, perhaps only an inch from where it was before. The logs are so exactly placed that they form channels for the draft. Waves of liquid yellow flame run up the logs when the draft blows. Each log glows with full intensity. The fire, watched, burns so intensely and so steadily, that when it dies, finally, it burns to nothing; when the last glow dies, there is nothing but a little dust left in the fireplace.

But the very beauty of the word "alive" is just its weakness.

The overwhelming thing that stays with you is that the fire lives. And yet this is a metaphor. Literally, we know that plants and animals are alive, and fire and music are not alive. If we are pressed to explain why we call one fire alive and another dead, then we are at a loss. The metaphor makes us believe that we have found a word to grasp the quality without a name. But we can only use the word to name the quality, when we already understand the quality.

Another word we often use to talk about the quality without a name is "whole."

A thing is whole according to how free it is of inner contradictions. When it is at war with itself, and gives rise to forces which act to tear it down, it is unwhole. The more

free it is of its own inner contradictions, the more whole
and healthy and wholehearted it becomes.

Compare the trees along a wild and windblown lake,
with an eroded gully. These trees and branches are so
made that when the wind blows they all bend, and all
the forces in the system, even the violent forces of the
wind, are still in balance when the trees are bent; and because they are in balance, they do no harm, they do no
violence. The configuration of the bending trees makes
them self-maintaining.

But think about a piece of land that is very steep, and
where erosion is taking place. There aren't enough tree
roots to hold the earth together, let's say; the rain falls,
in torrents, and carries the earth down streams which
form gullies; again, the earth is still not bound together
because there aren't enough plants there; the wind
blows; the erosion goes further; next time the water
comes, it runs in the very same gullies, and deepens
them; and widens them. The configuration of this system is such that the forces which it gives birth to, which
arise in it, in the long run act to destroy the system. The
system is self-destroying; it does not have the capacity to
contain the forces which arise within it.

The system of the trees and wind is whole; the system
of the gully and the rain is unwhole.

But the word "whole" is too enclosed.

It suggests closure, containment, finiteness. When you
call a thing whole, it makes you think that it is whole

unto itself, and isolated from the world around it. But a lung is whole, only so long as it is breathing oxygen from the air outside the organism; a person is whole only so long as he is a member of some human group; a town is whole only so long as it is in balance with the surrounding countryside.

The word carries a subtle hint of self-containment. And self-containment always undermines the quality which has no name. For this reason, the word "whole" can never perfectly describe this quality.

Another facet of the quality which has no name is caught by the word "comfortable."

The word "comfortable" is more profound than people usually realize. The mystery of genuine comfort goes far beyond the simple idea that the word first seems to mean. Places which are comfortable are comfortable because they have no inner contradictions, because there is no little restlessness disturbing them.

Imagine yourself on a winter afternoon with a pot of tea, a book, a reading light, and two or three huge pillows to lean back against. Now make yourself comfortable. Not in some way which you can show to other people, and say how much you like it. I mean so that you *really* like it, for *yourself*.

You put the tea where you can reach it: but in a place where you can't possibly knock it over. You pull the light down, to shine on the book, but not too brightly, and so that you can't see the naked bulb. You put the cushions behind you, and place them, carefully, one by one, just where you want them, to support your back, your neck, your arm: so that you are supported just comfortably, just as you want to sip your tea, and read, and dream.

When you take the trouble to do all that, and you do it carefully, with much attention, then it may begin to have the quality which has no name.

Yet the word "comfortable" is easy to misuse, and has too many other meanings.

There are kinds of comfort which stultify and deaden too. It is too easy to use the word for situations which have no life in them because they are too sheltered.

A family with too much money, a bed which is too soft, a room which always has an even temperature, a covered path on which you never have to walk out in the rain, these are all "comfortable" in a more stupid sense, and so distort the central meaning of the word.

A word which overcomes the lack of openness in the words "whole" and "comfortable," is the word "free."

The quality without a name is never calculated, never perfect; that subtle balance of forces only happens when the ideas and images are left behind; and created with abandon.

Think of a truck, filled with bags of cement. If the bags are stacked perfectly, in lines, it may be careful, and intelligent, and quite precise. But it will not begin to have the quality without a name, until there is a certain freedom there: the men who piled the bags, running, and throwing them, forgetting themselves, throwing themselves into it, lost, wild. . . .

And a steel mill too can have this quality because its freedom and its wildness show there, blazing in the night.

And yet, of course, this freedom can be too theatrical: a pose, a form, a manner.

A building which has a "free" form—a shape without roots in the forces or materials it is made of—is like a man whose gestures have no roots in his own nature. Its shape is borrowed, artificial, forced, contrived, made to copy outside images, not generated by the forces inside.

That kind of so-called freedom is opposite to the quality which has no name.

A word which helps restore the balance is the word "exact."

The word "exact" helps to counterbalance the impression of other words like "comfortable" and "free." These words suggest that the quality without a name is somehow inexact. And it is true that it is loose and fluid and relaxed. But it is never inexact. The forces in a situation are real forces. There is no getting round them. If the adaptation to the forces is not perfectly exact, there can be no comfort, and no freedom, because the small forces which have been left out will always work to make the system fail.

34

Suppose that I am trying to make a table for the blackbirds in my garden. In winter, when the snow is on the ground, and the blackbirds are short of food, I will put food out for them on the table. So I build the table; and dream about the clusters of blackbirds which will come flocking to the table in the snow.

But it is not so easy to build a table that will really work. The birds follow their own laws; and if I don't understand them, they just won't come. If I put the table too low, the birds won't fly down to it, because they don't like to swoop too close to the ground. If it is too high in the air, or too exposed, the wind won't let them settle on it. If it is near a laundry line, blowing in the wind, they will be frightened by the moving line. Most of the places where I put the table actually don't work.

I slowly learn that blackbirds have a million subtle forces guiding them in their behavior. If I don't understand these forces, there is simply nothing I can do to make the table come to life. So long as the placing of the table is inexact, my image of the blackbirds flocked around the table eating, is just wishful thinking. To make the table live, I must take these forces seriously, and place the table in a position which is perfectly exact.

And, yet, of course, the word "exact" does not describe it properly.

It has no sense of freedom in it; and it is too reminiscent of those other things which are exact in an entirely different sense.

Usually, when we say something is exact, we mean

that it fits some abstract image perfectly. If I cut a square of cardboard, and make it perfectly exact, it means that I have made the cardboard perfectly square: its sides are exactly equal: and its angles are exactly ninety degrees. I have matched an image perfectly.

The meaning of the word "exact" which I use here is almost opposite. A thing which has the quality without a name never fits any image exactly. What is exact is its adaptation to the forces which are in it. But this exactness requires that it be loose and fluid in its form.

A word which goes much deeper than the word "exact" is "egoless."

When a place is lifeless or unreal, there is almost always a mastermind behind it. It is so filled with the will of its maker that there is no room for its own nature.

Think, by contrast, of the decoration on an old bench —small hearts carved in it; simple holes, cut out while it was being put together—these can be egoless.

They are not carved according to some plan. They are carefree, carved into it, wherever there seems to be a gap. It is not in the least contrived; there is no effort in the decoration; it does not seek to express the personality of the man who carved it. It is so natural, that it almost seems as though the bench itself cried out for it: and the carver simply did what was required.

And yet, although the old bench and its carving may be egoless, this word is also not quite right.

36

It does not mean, for instance, that the man who made it left his own person out of it. It was part of his person that he liked the bench, and wanted to carve hearts in it. Perhaps he made it for his favorite girl.

It is perfectly possible to make a thing which has the quality which has no name, and still let it reflect your personality. Your person, and the likes and dislikes which are part of you, are themselves forces in your garden, and your garden must reflect those forces just as it reflects the other forces which make leaves grow and birds sing.

But if you use the word "ego" to mean the center of a person's character, then the idea of making something egoless can sound as though you want the person to efface himself completely. That is not what the word means at all; and yet because of it, the word is not quite right.

A last word which can help to catch the quality without a name is the word "eternal."

All things and people and places which have the quality without a name, reach into the realm of the eternal.

Some are eternal in almost a literal sense: they are so strong, so balanced, so strongly self-maintaining, that they are not easily disturbed, almost imperishable. Others reach the quality for no more than an instant, and then fall back into the lesser state, where inner contradictions rule.

The word "eternal" describes them both. For the instant that they have this quality, they reach into the realm of eternal truth. At that moment when they are free from inner contradictions, they take their place among the order of things which stand outside of time.

I once saw a simple fish pond in a Japanese village which was perhaps eternal.

A farmer made it for his farm. The pond was a simple rectangle, about 6 feet wide, and 8 feet long; opening off a little irrigation stream. At one end, a bush of flowers hung over the water. At the other end, under the water, was a circle of wood, its top perhaps 12 inches below the surface of the water. In the pond there were eight great ancient carp, each maybe 18 inches long, orange, gold, purple, and black: the oldest one had been there eighty years. The eight fish swam, slowly, slowly, in circles—often within the wooden circle. The whole world was in that pond. Every day the farmer sat by it for a few minutes. I was there only one day and I sat by it all afternoon. Even now, I cannot think of it without tears. Those ancient fish had been swimming, slowly, in that pond for eighty years. It was so true to the nature of the fish, and flowers, and the water, and the farmers, that it had sustained itself for all that time, endlessly repeating, always different. There is no degree of wholeness or reality which can be reached beyond that simple pond.

And yet, like all the other words, this word confuses more than it explains.

It hints at a religious quality. The hint is accurate. And yet it makes it seem as though the quality which that pond has is a mysterious one. It is not mysterious. It is above all ordinary. What makes it eternal is its ordinariness. The word "eternal" cannot capture that.

And so you see, in spite of every effort to give this quality a name, there is no single name which captures it.

Imagine the quality without a name as a point, and each of the words which we have tried as an ellipse. Each ellipse includes this point. But each ellipse also covers many other meanings, which are distant from this point.

Since every word is always an ellipse like this—then every word will always be too broad, too vague, too large in scope to refer only and exactly to the quality which is the point. No word can ever catch the quality without a name because the quality is too particular, and words too broad. And yet it is the most important quality there is, in anyone, or anything.

It is not only simple beauty of form and color. Man can make that without making nature. It is not only fitness to purpose. Man can make that too, without making nature. And it is not only the spiritual quality of beautiful music or of a quiet mosque, that comes from faith. Man can make that too, without making nature.

The quality which has no name includes these simpler sweeter qualities. But it is so ordinary as well, that it somehow reminds us of the passing of our life.

It is a slightly bitter quality.

CHAPTER 3

BEING ALIVE

*The search which we make for this
quality, in our own lives, is the central
search of any person, and the crux of any
individual person's story. It is the search
for those moments and situations when
we are most alive.*

We know, now, what the quality without a name is like, in feeling and in character. But so far, concretely, we have not seen this quality in any system larger than a tree, a pond, a bench. Yet it can be in anything—in buildings, animals, plants, cities, streets, the wilderness—and in ourselves. We shall begin to understand it concretely, in all these larger pieces of the world, only when we first understand it in ourselves.

It is, for instance, the wild smile of the gypsies dancing in the road.

The broad brim of the big hat, like arms spread wide, open to the world, confident, huge, . . . The embrace of the child's arms about the grass. . . . It is the solid and entrenched repose of the old man lighting a cigarette: hands on his knees, solid, resting, waiting, listening.

In our lives, this quality without a name is the most precious thing we ever have.

And I am free to the extent I have this quality in me.

One man is free at that one instant when you see in him a certain smile and you know he is himself, and perfectly at home within himself. Imagine him especially, perhaps, wearing a great wide hat, his arm flung out in an expansive gesture, singing perhaps and for one instant utterly oblivious to everything but what is in him and around him at that second.

47

This wild freedom, this passion, comes into our lives in the instant we let go.

It is when all our forces can move freely in us. In nature, this quality is almost automatic, because there are no images to interfere with natural processes of making things. But in all of our creations, the possibility occurs that images can interfere with the natural, necessary order of a thing. And, most of all, this way that images distort the things we make, is familiar in ourselves. For we ourselves are, like our works, the products of our own creation. And we are only free, and have the quality without a name in us, when we give up the images which guide our lives.

Yet each of us faces the fear of letting go. The fear of being just exactly what one is, of letting the forces flow freely; of letting the configuration of one's person adjust truly to these forces.

Our letting go is stifled, all the time, so long as we have ideas and opinions about ourselves, which make us hug too tightly to our images of how to live, and bottle up these forces.

So long as we are still bottled up, like this, there is a tightness about the mouth, a nervous tension in the eyes, a stiffness and a brittleness in the way we walk, the way we move.

And yet, until one does let go, it is impossible to be alive. The stereotypes are restricted; there are very different configurations. The infinite variety of actual people, with their vastly and utterly different forces, require a huge creation, to find the resolution of the person: and in finding this resolution truly, one must above all be free of the stereotypes.

The great film, Ikiru—*to live*—*describes it in the life of an old man.*

He has sat for thirty years behind a counter, preventing things from happening. And then he finds out that he is to die of cancer of the stomach, in six months. He tries to live; he seeks enjoyment; it doesn't amount to much. And finally, against all obstacles, he helps to make a park in a dirty slum of Tokyo. He has lost his fear, because he knows that he is going to die; he works and works and works, there is no stopping him, because he is no longer afraid of anyone, or anything. He has no longer anything to lose, and so in this short time gains everything; and then dies, in the snow, swinging on a child's swing in the park which he has made, and singing.

Each of us lives most fully "on the wire," in the face of death, daring to do the very thing which fear prevents us from.

A few years ago a family of high wire artists had a terrible fall from the high wire, in the middle of their performance. All of them were killed or maimed, except the father, who escaped with broken legs. But even after losing his children in the fall, a few months later he was back to work, in the circus, on the wire again.

Someone asked him in an interview, how he could bring himself to do it, after such a terrible accident. He answered: "On the wire, that's living . . . all the rest is waiting."

Of course for most of us it is not quite so literal.

The fear which prevents us from being ourselves, from being that one person unique in all the world, from coming to life—that may mean nothing greater than the fear of giving up the image of a certain job, an image of a certain kind of family life.

One man can be as free in lighting up a cigarette, as that old man dancing on the wire. Another traveling with the gypsies. A handkerchief around your head; a horse-drawn yellow caravan, pulled up in a field; a rabbit stew, simmering and bubbling on the fire otuside the caravan; licking and sucking your fingers as you eat spoonfuls of the stew.

It has above all to do with the elements.

The wind, the soft rain; sitting on the back of an old truck moving clothes and baskets of possessions while the gentle rain is falling, laughing, crouching under a shawl to keep from getting wet, but getting wet. Eating a loaf of bread, torn in pieces, hunks of cheese cut crudely with a hatchet which is lying in the corner; red flowers glistening in the rain along the roadside; banging on the window of the truck to shout some joke.

Nothing to keep, nothing to lose. No possessions, no security, no concern about possessions, and no concern about security: in this mood it is possible to do exactly what makes sense, and nothing else: there are no hidden fears, no morals, no rules, no undercurrent of constraint, no subtle sense of concern for the form of what the people round about you are doing, and above all no concern for what you are yourself, no subtle fear of other people's ridicule, no subtle train of fears which can connect the smallest triviality with bankruptcy and loss of love and loss of friends and death, no ties, no suits, no outward elements of majesty at all. Only the laughter and the rain.

And it happens when our inner forces are resolved.

And when a person's forces are resolved, it makes us feel at home, because we know, by some sixth sense, that there are no other unexpected forces lurking underground. He acts according to the nature of the situations he is in, without distorting them. There are no guiding images in his behavior, no hidden forces; he is simply free. And so, we feel relaxed and peaceful in his company.

Of course, in practice we often don't know just what our inner forces are.

We live, for months, for years, acting in a certain way, not knowing whether we are free or not, doubting, not even sure when we are successfully resolved, and when we aren't.

Yet still there are those special secret moments in our lives, when we smile unexpectedly—when all our forces are resolved.

A woman can often see these moments in us, better than a man, better than we ourselves even. When we know those moments, when we smile, when we let go, when we are not on guard at all—these are the moments when our most important forces show themselves; whatever you are doing at such a moment, hold on to it, repeat it— for that certain smile is the best knowledge that we ever have of what our hidden forces are, and where they lie, and how they can be loosed.

We cannot be aware of these most precious moments when they are actually happening.

In fact, the conscious effort to attain this quality, or to be free, or to be anything, the glance which this creates, will always spoil it.

It is, instead, when we forget ourselves completely: playing the fool perhaps among a group of friends, or swimming out to sea, or walking simply, or trying to finish something late at night over a table with a group of friends, cigarette stuck to lower lip, eyes tired, earnest concentration.

All these moments in my own life—I only know them now, in retrospect.

Yet each of us knows from experience the feeling which this quality creates in us.

It is the time when we are most right, most just, most sad, and most hilarious.

And for this reason, each one of us can also recognize this quality when it occurs in buildings.

We can identify the towns and buildings, streets and gardens, flower beds, chairs, tables, tablecloths, wine bottles, garden seats, and kitchen sinks which have this quality—simply by asking whether they are like us when we are free.

We need only ask ourselves which places—which towns, which buildings, which rooms, have made us feel like this—which of them have that breath of sudden passion in them, which whispers to us, and lets us recall those moments when we were ourselves.

And the connection between the two—between this quality in our own lives, and the same quality in our surroundings—is not just an analogy, or similarity. The fact is that each one creates the other.

Places which have this quality, invite this quality to come to life in us. And when we have this quality in us, we tend to make it come to life in towns and buildings which we help to build. It is a self-

supporting, self-maintaining, generating quality. It is the quality of life. And we must seek it, for our own sakes, in our surroundings, simply in order that we can ourselves become alive.

That is the central scientific fact in all that follows.

CHAPTER 4

PATTERNS OF EVENTS

In order to define this quality in build-
ings and in towns, we must begin by
understanding that every place is given
its character by certain patterns of events
that keep on happening there.

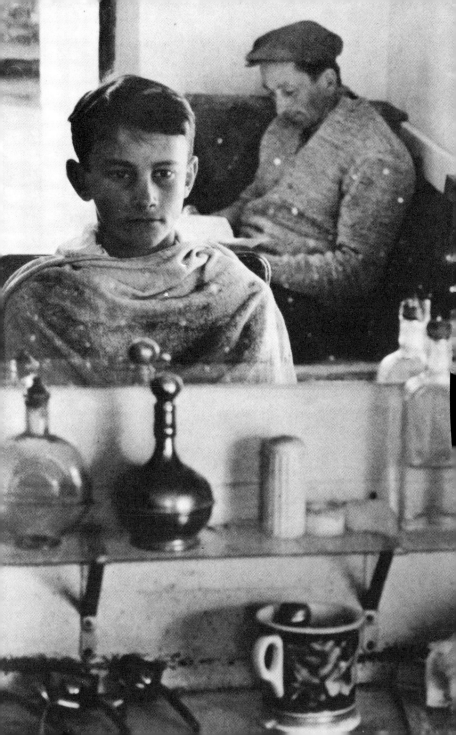

We know what the quality without a name is like in our own lives.

As we shall see in the next few chapters, this quality can only come to life in us when it exists within the world that we are part of. We can come alive only to the extent the buildings and towns we live in are alive. The quality without a name is circular: it exists in us, when it exists in our buildings; and it only exists in our buildings, when we have it in ourselves.

To understand this clearly, we must first recognize that what a town or building is, is governed, above all, by what is happening there.

I mean this in the most general sense.

Activities; events; forces; situations; lightning strikes; fish die; water flows; lovers quarrel; a cake burns; cats chase each other; a hummingbird sits outside my window; friends come by; my car breaks down; lovers' reunion; children born; grandparents go broke. . . .

My life is made of episodes like this.

The life of every person, animal, plant, creature, is made of similar episodes.

The character of a place, then, is given to it by the episodes which happen there.

Those of us who are concerned with buildings tend to forget too easily that all the life and soul of a place, all of our experiences there, depend not simply on the physical environment, but on the patterns of events which we experience there.

What is Lima—what is most memorable there—eating anticuchos in the street; small pieces of beef heart, on sticks, cooked over open coals, with hot sauce on them; the dark, badly lit night streets of Lima, small carts with the flickering fire of the hot coals, the faces of the sellers, shadowy figures gathered round, to eat the beef hearts.

Or in Geneva—chestnuts, hot, in small paper bags, eaten in the autumn mist, warming the fingers.

And, what is it about the California coast—the shock of the waves, the hiss of the surf, standing on a rock while the white water hisses in, runs out, a dash across the wet sand to the rock, before the sea comes in again.

And it is just the same indoors. Think of a big room, vast, huge windows, big empty fireplace, completely empty, no furniture at all, except an easel and a chair—Picasso's studio. Is this not made entirely of the situations, the forces let loose by the configuration of events?

And what of a party around a kitchen table, people drinking together, cooking together, drinking wine, eating grapes, together preparing a stew of beef and wine and garlic and tomatoes which takes four hours to cook—and while it cooks, we drink, and then, at last we eat it.

What of the kind of moment we remember most of all: the flickering candles on the Christmas tree, the small bell ringing, the children waiting, hour by hour, outside the door, peeping through the crack, and finally rushing in, when they hear the tinkling of that small bell, and see the tree there, lit, with fifty white and red candles, burning, and the smell of singed pine needles where a twig caught fire while the candles were being lit.

What of the process of scrubbing the floor, working the stiff bristles of the brush, and the pail of water, over the soft boards, with fibers breaking loose, and the smell of the soap that stays in the wood.

Or saying goodbye, at a train, leaning through the window of the train, waving, kissing, as the train pulls out, running along the platform. . . .

Or, taking the Sunday walk, a family, abreast, in twos and threes, walking along the road, pushing the smallest child perhaps, the others lagging behind to look at frogs, and an old shoe.

These patterns of events which create the character of a place are not necessarily human events.

The sunshine shining on the windowsill, the wind blowing in the grass are events too—they affect us just as much as social events.

Any combination of events, which has a bearing on our lives—an actual physical effect on us—affects our lives.

If, for example, there is a stream bed gouged in the rock outside my house, which fills each time it rains, this is a situation which has a powerful effect on the character of the environment, yet is not a human situation at all.

Compare the power and importance of these events with the other purely geometrical aspects of the environment, which architects concern themselves with.

Compare, for instance, two ways of including water in a building.

Suppose, on the one hand, that there is a concrete reflecting pool outside your room—with no purpose except to reflect the sky.

And suppose, on the other hand, that there is a stream outside your room, with a small rowing boat on it, where you can go, to row, lie on the water, struggle against the stream, tip over . . . .

Which of these two makes the most difference to the building? The rowing boat, of course, because it alters the entire experience of the building.

It is the action of these moments, the people involved in them, and the peculiar situations, which make the impression on our lives.

The life of a house, or of a town, is not given to it, directly, by the shape of its buildings, or by the ornament and plan—it is given to them by the quality of the events and situations we encounter there. Always it is our situations which allow us to be what we are.

It is the people around us, and the most common ways we have of meeting them, of being with them, it is, in short, the ways of being which exist in our world, that make it possible for us to be alive.

We know, then, that what matters in a building or a town is not its outward shape, its physical geometry alone, but the events that happen there.

It is all the events which happen there—the human events given by the situations which are repeated, the mechanical events, the rush of trains, the fall of water, the slow cracking of structures, the growing of the grass, the melting of the snow, the rusting of iron, the flowering of roses, the heat of a summer's day, the cooking, loving, playing, dying, and not only of ourselves, but of the animals, and plants, and even of the inorganic processes which make the whole.

Of course, some events happen once in a lifetime; others happen more often; and some happen very often indeed. But although it is true that a unique event can sometimes change our lives completely, or leave its mark on us, it is not too much to say that, by and large, the overall character of our lives is given by those events which keep on recurring over and over again.

And, by the same token, it is roughly true that any system, any aspect of the life of a part of the world, is essentially governed by those situations, human or non-human—which keep on repeating there.

A building or a town is given its character, essentially, by those events which keep on happening there most often.

A field of grass is given its character, essentially, by those events which happen over and over again—millions upon millions of times. The germination of the grass seed, the blowing wind, the flowering of the grass, the movement of the worms, the hatching of the insects . . . .

A car is given its character by the events which keep on happening there—the rolling of the wheels, the movement of the pistons in the cylinders, the limited to and fro of the steering wheel and axle, as the car changes direction.

A family is given its character by the particular events which keep on happening there—the small affections, kisses, breakfast, the particular kinds of arguments which keep on happening, the way these arguments resolve themselves, the idiosyncrasies of people, both together and alone, which make us love them . . . .

And just the same is true in any person's individual life.

If I consider my life honestly, I see that it is governed by a certain very small number of patterns of events which I take part in over and over again.

Being in bed, having a shower, having breakfast in the kitchen, sitting in my study writing, walking in the garden, cooking and eating our common lunch at my office with my friends, going to the movies, taking my family to eat at a restaurant, having a drink at a friend's house, driving on the freeway, going to bed again. There are a few more.

There are surprisingly few of these patterns of events in any one person's way of life, perhaps no more than a dozen. Look at your own life and you will find the same. It is shocking at first, to see that there are so few patterns of events open to me.

Not that I want more of them. But when I see how very few of them there are, I begin to understand what huge effect these few patterns have on my life, on my capacity to live. If these few patterns are good for me, I can live well. If they are bad for me, I can't.

Of course, the standard patterns of events vary very much from person to person, and from culture to culture.

For a teenage boy, at high school in Los Angeles, his situations include hanging out in the corridor with other boys; watching television; sitting in a car with his girlfriend at a drive-in restaurant eating coke and hamburgers. For an old woman, in a European mountain village, her situations include scrubbing her front doorstep, lighting a candle in the local church, stopping at the market to buy fresh vegetables, walking five miles across the mountains to visit her grandson.

But each town, each neighborhood, each building, has a particular set of these patterns of events according to its prevailing culture.

A person can modify his immediate situations. He can move, change his life, and so on. In exceptional cases he can even change them almost wholly. But it is not possible to go beyond the bounds of the collection of events and pattern of events which our culture makes available to us.

We have a glimpse, then, of the fact that our world has a structure, in the simple fact that certain patterns of events—both human and nonhuman—keep repeating, and account, essentially, for much the greater part of the events which happen there.

Our individual lives are made from them . . . so are our lives together . . . they are the rules, through which our culture maintains itself, keeps itself alive, and it is by building our lives, out of these patterns of events, that we are people of our culture . . . .

There is no aspect of our lives which is not governed by these patterns of events. And if the quality without a name can come into our lives at all, it is clear that it depends entirely on the specific nature of these patterns of events from which our world is made.

And indeed, the world does have a structure, just because these patterns of events which repeat themselves are always anchored in the space.

I cannot imagine any pattern of events without imagining a place where it is happening. I cannot think of sleeping, without imagining myself sleeping *somewhere.* Of course, I can imagine myself sleeping in many different kinds of places—but these places all have at least certain physical geometrical characteristics in common. And I cannot think about the place without also knowing, or imagining, what happens there. I cannot think of a bedroom, without imagining the bed, lovemaking, sleeping, dressing perhaps, waking up . . . breakfast in bed . . . .

Consider, for example, the pattern of events which we might call "watching the world go by."

We sit, perhaps slightly raised, on the front porch, or on some steps in a park, or on a café terrace, with a more or less protected, sheltered, partly private place behind us, looking out into a more public place, slightly raised above it, watching the world go by.

I cannot separate it from the porch where it occurs.

The action and the space are indivisible. The action is supported by this kind of space. The space supports this kind of action. The two form a unit, a pattern of events in space.

The same in a barbershop. Inside, barbers, customers sitting in a row along one side, chairs for haircuts in another row, widely spaced, facing the mirrors, the barber idly talking while he cuts your hair, bottles of pomade around, hair dryer lying on the table, a basin in front for rinsing, a strop hanging on the wall, for stropping the razors . . . . Again, the activity and its physical space are one. There is no separating them.

*Indeed, a culture always defines its pattern of events
by referring to the names of the physical elements of
space which are "standard" in that culture.*

If you look back at the patterns of events that I have
mentioned, each one is almost completely defined by the
spatial character of the place where it occurs.

The barbershop, the porch, the shower, the study with
its writing desk, the garden with its path, the bed, the
communal lunch table, the cinema, the freeway, the high
school corridor, the television set, the drive-in restaurant,
the front doorstep, the candlestand at the back of the
church, the market with its vegetable stalls, the mountain
path. Each of these elements defines a pattern of events.

*And the mere list of elements which are typical in a
given town tells us the way of life of people there.*

When you think of Los Angeles, you think of freeways,
drive-ins, suburbs, airports, gas stations, shopping centers,
swimming pools, hamburger joints, parking lots, beaches,
billboards, supermarkets, free-standing one-family houses,
front yards, traffic lights . . . .

When you think of a medieval European town, you
think of the church, the marketplace, the town square, the
wall around the town, the town gates, narrow winding
streets and lanes, rows of attached houses, each one containing an extended family, rooftops, alleys, blacksmiths,
alehouses . . . .

In each case the simple list of elements is intensely evocative. The elements are not just dead pieces of architecture and building—each one has an entire life associated with it. The names of the elements make us imagine and remember what people are doing in those elements, and what life is like in an environment which has those elements.

This does not mean that space creates events, or that it causes them.

For example, in a modern town, the concrete spatial pattern of a sidewalk does not "cause" the kinds of human behavior which happens there.

What happens is much more complex. The people on the sidewalk, being culture-bound, know that the space which they are part of is a sidewalk, and, as part of their culture, they have the pattern of a sidewalk in their minds. It is this pattern in their minds which causes them to behave the way that people do behave on sidewalks, not the purely spatial aspect of the concrete and the walls and curbs.

And this means, of course, that in two cultures, people may see sidewalks differently, that is, they may have different patterns in their minds—and, that they will, as a result, act differently on the sidewalks. For example, in New York, a sidewalk is mainly a place for walking, jostling, moving fast. And by comparison, in Jamaica, or India, a sidewalk is a place to sit, to talk, perhaps to play music, even to sleep.

It is not correct to interpret this by saying that the two sidewalks are the same.

It simply means that a pattern of events cannot be separated from the space where it occurs.

Each sidewalk is a unitary system, which includes *both* the field of geometrical relationships which define its concrete geometry, *and* the field of human actions and events, which are associated with it.

So when we see that a sidewalk in Bombay is used by people sleeping, or for parking cars . . . and that in New York it is used only for walking—we cannot interpret this correctly as a single sidewalk pattern, with two different uses. The Bombay sidewalk (space + events) is one pattern; the New York sidewalk (space + events) is another pattern. They are two entirely different patterns.

This close connection between patterns of events and space is commonplace in nature.

The word "stream" describes a pattern of physical space and a pattern of events, at the same time.

We do not separate the stream bed from the stream. There is no distinction in our minds between the bed of the stream, its banks, its winding configuration in the land, and the rushing of the water, the growth of plants, the swimming of the fish.

And, in the same way, the patterns of events which govern life in buildings and in towns cannot be separated from the space where they occur.

Each one is a living thing, a pattern of events in space,

73

just like a stream, a waterfall, a fire, a storm—a thing which happens, over and again, and is exactly one of the elements from which the world is made.

And it is therefore clear that we can only understand these patterns of events by seeing them as living elements of space themselves.

It is the space itself which lives and breathes; it is the space which is the walking, jostling sidewalk in New York; it is the space we call the porch, which is the pattern of events we also call watching the world go by.

The life which happens in a building or a town is not merely anchored in the space but made up from the space itself.

For since space is made up of these living elements, these labeled patterns of events in space, we see that what seems at first sight like the dead geometry we call a building or a town is indeed a quick thing, a living system, a collection of interacting, and adjacent, patterns of events in space, each one repeating certain events over and over again, yet always anchored by its place in space. And, if we hope to understand the life which happens in a building or a town, we must therefore try to understand the structure of the space itself.

We shall now try to find some way of understanding space which yields its patterns of events in a completely natural way, so that we can succeed in seeing patterns of events, and space, as one.

74

CHAPTER 5

PATTERNS OF SPACE

These patterns of events are always interlocked with certain geometric patterns in the space. Indeed, as we shall see, each building and each town is ultimately made out of these patterns in the space, and out of nothing else: they are the atoms and the molecules from which a building or a town is made.

We are now ready to come to grips with the most basic problem of a building or a town: What is it made of? What is its structure? What is its physical essence? What are the building blocks of which its space is made?

We know, from chapter 4, that any town and any building gets its character from those events and patterns of events which keep on happening there the most; and that the patterns of events are linked, somehow, to space.

So far, though, we do not know just what aspect of the space it is that correlates with the events. We do not have a picture of a building or a town which shows us how its obvious outward structure—the way it looks, its physical geometry—is interlocked with these events.

Suppose I want to understand the "structure" of something. Just what exactly does this mean?

It means, of course, that I want to make a simple picture of it, which lets me grasp it as a whole.

And it means, too, that as far as possible, I want to paint this simple picture out of as few elements as possible. The fewer elements there are, the richer the relationships between them, and the more of the picture lies in the "structure" of these relationships.

And finally, of course, I want to paint a picture which allows me to understand the patterns of events which keep on happening in the thing whose structure I seek. In other words, I hope to find a picture, or a structure, which will, in some rather obvious and simple sense, account for the outward properties, for the pattern of events of the thing which I am studying.

What then, is the fundamental "structure" of a building or a town?

In the crudest sense, we know from the last chapter roughly what the structure of a town or building is.

It is made up of certain concrete elements, with every element associated with a certain pattern of events.

On the geometric level, we see certain physical elements repeating endlessly, combined in an almost endless variety of combinations.

A town is made of houses, gardens, streets, sidewalks, shopping centers, shops, workplaces, factories, perhaps a river, sportgrounds, parking . . .

A building is made up of walls, windows, doors, rooms, ceilings, nooks, stairs, staircase treads, doorhandles, terraces, counter tops, flowerpots . . . repeated over and again.

A gothic cathedral is made of a nave, aisles, west door, transept, choir, apse, ambulatory, columns, windows, buttresses, vaults, ribs, window tracery.

A modern metropolitan region in the United States is made of industrial areas, freeways, central business districts, supermarkets, parks, single-family houses, gardens, high-rise housing, streets, arteries, traffic lights, sidewalks.

And each of these elements has a specific pattern of events associated with it.

Families living in the houses, cars and buses driving in the streets, flowers growing in the flower pots, people walking through the doors, opening and closing them, traffic lights changing, people gathering for mass on Sundays in the nave of the cathedral, forces acting on the vaults, when the wind sways the building, light coming through the windows, people sitting at the windows in their living rooms and looking at the view . . . .

But this picture of space does not explain how—or why—these elements associate themselves with definite and quite specific patterns of events.

What is the relation between a church, say, taken as an element—and the pattern of events which happens in the church? It is all very well to say that they are connected. But unless we can see some kind of common sense in the connection, it explains nothing.

It is certainly not enough merely to say glibly that every pattern of events resides in space. That is obvious, and not very interesting. What we want to know is just how the structure of the space supports the patterns of events it does, in such a way that if we change the structure of the space, we shall be able to predict what kinds of changes in the patterns of events this change will generate.

In short, we want a theory which presents the interaction

of the space and the events, in a clear and unambiguous way.

Further, it is very puzzling to realize that the "elements," which seem like elementary building blocks, keep varying, and are different every time that they occur.

For among the endless repetition of elements we also see an almost endless variation. Each church has a slightly different nave, the aisles are different, the west door is different . . . and in the nave, the various bays are usually different, the individual columns are different; each vault has slightly different ribs; each window has a slightly different tracery and different glass.

And just so in an urban region. Each industrial area is different; each freeway is different; each park is different; each supermarket is different—even the smaller individual elements like traffic lights and stop signs, although very similar, are never quite the same—and there is always a variety of types.

If the elements are different every time that they occur, evidently then, it cannot be the elements themselves which are repeating in a building or a town: these so-called elements cannot be the ultimate "atomic" constituents of space.

Since every church is different, the so-called element we call "church" is not constant at all. Giving it a name only deepens the puzzle. If every church is different, what is it that remains the same, from church to church, that we call "church"?

When we say that matter is made of electrons, protons, and so forth, this is a satisfying way of understanding things, because these electrons seem, indeed, to be the same each time that they occur, and it therefore makes sense to show how matter can be built up from combinations of these "elements," because the elements are truly elementary.

But if the so-called elements of which a building or a town is made—the houses, streets, windows, doors—are merely names, and the underlying things which they refer to keep on changing, then we have no solidity at all in our picture, and we need to find some other elements which truly are invariant throughout the variation, in a way that we can understand a building or a town as a structure made up by combination of these elements.

Let us therefore look more carefully at the structure of the space from which a building or a town is made, to find out what it really is that is repeating there.

We may notice first that over and above the elements, there are relationships between the elements which keep repeating too, just as the elements themselves repeat. . . .

Beyond its elements each building is defined by certain patterns of relationships among the elements.

85

In a gothic cathedral, the nave is *flanked by* aisles which run parallel to it. The transept is at *right angles* to the nave and aisles; the ambulatory is *wrapped around* the outside of the apse; the columns are *vertical, on the line separating* nave from aisle, *spaced at equal intervals*. Each vault connects *four* columns, and has a characteristic shape, *cross-like* in plan, *concave* in space. The buttresses are run down the outside of the aisles, on the same lines as the columns, supporting the load from the vaults. The nave is always a *long thin rectangle*—its *ratio may vary between 1:3 and 1:6, but is never 1:2 or 1:20.* The aisles are always *narrower* than the nave.

And each urban region, too, is defined by certain patterns of relationships among its elements.

Consider a typical mid-twentieth-century American metropolitan region. Somewhere *towards the center* of the region, there is a central business district, which contains a *very high density* office block; near these there are *high density* apartments. The overall density of the region *slopes off with distance from the center, according to an exponential law; periodically there are again peaks* of higher density, but smaller than the central ones; and *subsidiary* to these *smaller* peaks, there are still smaller peaks. Each of these peaks of density *contains* stores and offices *surrounded by* higher density housing. *Towards the outer fringe* of the metropolis there are *large* areas of *freestanding* one-family houses; *the farther out from the center they are, the larger* their gardens. The region is served by a *network* of freeways. These freeways are *closer together* at the center. Independent of the freeways, there is a *roughly regular two-dimensional network* of streets. *Every five or ten* streets, there is a larger one, which functions as an artery. A few of the arteries are even bigger than the others: these tend to be arranged *radially, branching out* from the center in a *star-shaped fashion.* Where an artery meets a freeway, there is a characteristic *cloverleaf arrangement of connecting lanes. Where* two arteries *intersect,* there is a traffic light; *where* a local street *meets* an artery, there is a stop sign. The major commercial areas, which *coincide with* the high density peaks in the density distribution, all fall on the major arteries. Industrial areas all fall *within half a mile* of a freeway; and the older ones are also *close to* at least one major artery.

Evidently, then, a large part of the "structure" of a building or a town consists of patterns of relationships.

For both the city of Los Angeles and the medieval church get their respective characters as much from these repeating patterns of relationships, as they do from the elements themselves

At first sight, it seems as though these patterns of relationships are separate from the elements.

Think of the aisle of the cathedral. It is parallel to the nave, and next to it, it shares columns with the nave, it

87

runs east-west, like the church itself, it contains columns, on its inner wall, and windows on its outer wall. At first sight, it seems that these relationships are "extra," over and above the fact of its being an aisle.

When we look closer, we realize that these relationships are not extra, but necessary to the elements, indeed a part of them.

We realize, for instance, that if an aisle were not parallel to the nave, were not next to it, were not narrower than the nave, did not share columns with the nave, did not run east to west, . . . that it would not be an "aisle" at all. It would be merely a rectangle of space, in gothic construction, floating free . . . and what makes it an aisle, specifically, is just the pattern of relationships which it has to the nave, and other elements around it.

When we look closer still, we realize that even this view is still not very accurate. For it is not merely true that the relationships are attached to the elements: the fact is that the elements themselves *are patterns of relationships.*

For, once we recognize that much of what we think of as an "element" in fact lies in the pattern of relationships between this thing and the things in the world around it, we then come to the second even greater realization, that the so-called element is itself nothing but a myth, and that indeed, the element itself is not just embedded in a

88

pattern of relationships, but is *itself* entirely a pattern of relationships, and nothing else.

In short, the aisle, which needs the pattern of relationships to the nave and the east window to define it, is *itself* also a pattern of relationships between its length, its width, the columns which lie on the boundary with the nave, the windows which lie on the outer boundary . . . .

And finally, the things which seem like elements dissolve, and leave a fabric of relationships behind, which is the stuff that actually repeats itself, and gives the structure to a building or a town.

In short, we may forget about the idea that the building is made up of elements entirely, and recognize instead, the deeper fact that all these so-called elements are only labels for the patterns of relationships which really do repeat.

The freeway, as a whole, does not repeat. But the fact that there are cloverleafs which connect the freeway to roads at certain intervals—that *does* repeat. There is a certain relationship between the freeway and its crossing arteries and cloverleafs, which does repeat.

But once again, the cloverleaf *itself* does not repeat. Each cloverleaf is different. What does repeat is that each lane forms a continuously curving off ramp to the right—there is a relationship between its radius, its tangency, the fact that it is banked, which does repeat.

Yet once again the "lane" which figures in this pattern of relationships does not repeat. What we call a lane is itself a relationship among still smaller so-called elements—the edges of the road, the surface, the lines which form the edge . . . and these again, although they function temporarily as elements, in order to make these relations clear, themselves evaporate when we look closely at them.

Each one of these patterns is a morphological law, which establishes a set of relationships in space.

This morphological law can always be expressed in the same general form:

   $X \rightarrow r \ (A, B, \ . \ . \ . \ )$, which means:

   Within a context of type X, the parts A, B, . . . are related by the relationship r.

Thus, for example:

   Within a gothic cathedral $\rightarrow$ the nave is flanked on both sides by parallel aisles.

or:

   Where a freeway meets an artery $\rightarrow$ the access ramps of the interchange take the rough form of a cloverleaf.

And each law or pattern is itself a pattern of relationships among still other laws, which are themselves just patterns of relationships again.

For though each pattern is itself apparently composed of smaller things which look like parts, of course, when we look closely at them, we see that these apparent "parts" are patterns too.

Consider, for example, the pattern we call a door. This pattern is a relationship among the frame, the hinges, and the door itself: and these parts in turn are made of smaller parts: the frame is made of uprights, a crosspiece, and cover mouldings over joints; the door is made of uprights, crosspieces and panels; the hinge is made of leaves and a pin. Yet any one of these things we call its "parts" are themselves in fact also patterns, each one of which may take an almost infinite variety of shapes, and color and exact size—without once losing the essential field of relationships which make it what it is.

The patterns are not just patterns of relationships, but patterns of relationships among other smaller patterns, which themselves have still other patterns hooking them together—and we see finally, that the world is entirely made of all these interhooking, interlocking nonmaterial patterns.

Further, each pattern in the space has a pattern of events associated with it.

For instance, the pattern of the freeway contains a certain fabric of events, defined by rules: drivers drive at certain speeds; there are rules governing the way that people may change lanes; the cars all face the same way; there are certain kinds of overtaking; people drive a little slower on the entrances and exits . . . .

And the pattern of a kitchen, in any given culture, also contains a very definite pattern of events: the way that people use the kitchen, the way that food is prepared, the fact that people eat there, or don't eat there, the fact that they wash the dishes standing at the sink . . . and on and on . . .

Of course, the pattern of space, does not "cause" the pattern of events.

Neither does the pattern of events "cause" the pattern in the space. The total pattern, space and events together, is an element of people's culture. It is invented by culture, transmitted by culture, and merely anchored in space.

But there is a fundamental inner connection between each pattern of events, and the pattern of space in which it happens.

For the pattern in the space is, precisely, the precondition, the requirement, which allows the pattern of events to happen. In this sense, it plays a fundamental role in making sure that just this pattern of events keeps on repeating over and over again, throughout the space, and that it is, therefore, one of the things which gives a certain building, or a certain town, its character.

Go back, for example, to the porch of chapter 4, and the pattern of events we may call "sitting on the porch, watching the world go by."

What aspect of the space is it which is connected to this pattern of events? Certainly it is not the whole porch,

in its entirety: it is instead, just certain specific relationships.

For instance, in order for the pattern of events "watching the world go by" to happen, it is essential that the
porch should be a little raised above the level of the
street; it is essential that the porch be deep enough, to let
a group of people sit there comfortably; and it is essential,
of course, that the front of the porch be open, pierced
with openings, and that the roof is therefore supported on
columns.

*It is this bundle of relationships which is essential, be-
cause these are the ones which are directly congruent
with the pattern of events.*

By contrast, the length of the porch, its height, its color,
the materials of which it is made, the height of the side
walls, the way the porch connects up with the inside of
the house, are less essential—so they can vary, without
altering the fundamental and essential nature of the
porch.

*And in this same sense, each pattern of relationships
in space is congruent with some specific pattern of
events.*

The pattern of relationships we call a "freeway" is just
that pattern of relationships required by the process of
driving fast with limited access to and from side roads: in
short the pattern of events.

The pattern of relationships we call a Chinese "kitchen" is just that pattern of relationships required for cooking Chinese food: again the underlying pattern of events.

And insofar as there are different "kinds" of kitchens, there are different patterns of relationships, responsible for slightly different patterns of events, in different cultures, which have different patterns of cooking.

In every case the pattern of relationships in space is that invariant which must repeat itself with some pattern of events, because it is exactly these relationships which are required to sustain that pattern of events.

We realize then that it is just the patterns of events in space which are repeating in the building or the town: and nothing else.

Nothing of any importance happens in a building or a town except what is defined within the patterns which repeat themselves.

For what the patterns do is at the same time seize the outward physical geometry, and also seize what happens there.

They account entirely for its geometrical structure: they are the visible, coherent stuff that is repeating, and coherent there: they are the background of the variation, which makes each concrete element a little different.

And, at the same time, they are also responsible for those events which keep repeating there, and therefore do the most to give the building or a town its character . . .

Each building gets its character from just the patterns which keep on repeating there.

This is not only true of general patterns; it is true of the entire building: all its details; the shape of rooms, the character of ornament, the kind of windowpanes it has, the boards of which the floor is made, the handles on the doors, the light, the height, the way the ceilings vary, the relationship of windows to the ceiling, the connection of the building to the garden and the street, and to the spaces and the paths and to the detailed seats, and walls which are around it. . . .

Each neighborhood is defined, too, in everything that matters, by the patterns which keep on repeating there.

Again, it is just those details which give the neighborhood a "character" which are defined by patterns: the kind of streets which it has, the kind of lots the houses are; the typical size of houses, the way that the houses are connected or distinct. . . .

Isn't it true that the features which you remember in a place are not so much peculiarities, but rather the typical, the recurrent, the characteristic features: the canals of Venice, the flat roofs of a Moroccan town, the even spacing of the fruit trees in an orchard, the slope of a beach towards the sea, the umbrellas of an Italian beach, the wide sidewalks, sidewalk cafés, cylindrical poster boardings and pissoirs of Paris, the porch which goes all the way around a plantation house in Louisiana. . . .

The qualities which make Paris a special place, which make Broadway and Times Square exciting, the qualities which make Venice special, the qualities which make an eighteenth-century London square so peaceful and refreshing—indeed, the qualities in any environment which give it the character you like it for—are its patterns.

A barn gets its structure from its patterns.

It has a certain overall shape, roughly a long rectangle; there is a central portion where the hay is stored, with aisles along the sides where the cows stand; there is a row of columns between the center and the aisle; along these columns are the feeding troughs where the cows feed; there are great doors or double doors at one end; perhaps smaller doors at the other end, in the aisle, for cattle to pass in and out. . . .

And an expensive restaurant gets its structure and character from its peculiar patterns too.

Small tables, each one with a few chairs; small individual lights at the tables; the head waiter's desk at the entrance, with a light and a place for his reception book. Dark perhaps inside, reds, deep colors, often no windows. A swinging door leading to the kitchen . . .

Venice gets its life and structure from its patterns.

96

A large number of islands, typically about 1000 feet across, packed together houses, 3–5 stories, built right up to the canals; each island with a small square in the middle of it, the square usually with a church; narrow, irregular paths cutting across the islands; hump-backed bridges where these paths cross canals; houses opening onto the canals and onto the streets; steps at the canal entrance (to take care of variations in water level) . . .

Venice is the special place it is, only because it has those patterns of events in it, which happen to be congruent with all these patterns in the space.

London gets its life and structure from its patterns too.

First at the regional scale: the characteristic conglomeration of boroughs, the characteristic location of major railway stations on an inner ring, with the railways radiating outwards, the characteristic location of industry at the periphery. Then at the next smaller scale there are the characteristic rows of semi-detached "villas," the characteristic inside details of the railway stations, the characteristic squares, with oval or rectangular green parks in the center, the use of roundabouts, traffic moving on the left. Then to more detail: the interior layout of a typical row house, the particular English character of "filling" stations, the London club, Lyons and Marks and Spencers, the shape and height and placing of advertisement boardings on bridges and outside railway stations, and their particular characteristic shape and height. Then to more detail: the special kind of staircase baluster, the use of two-inch bricks in Georgian houses, the ratio of bathroom area to house area, compared with that typical of an American house, the use of flagstones on the sidewalks. Then down to the tiniest details of all—the special shape of English faucets, the kinds of handles on an English metal window, the shape of the insulators on a telegraph pole.

Again, in each case the patterns define all the typical events which happen there. So "London," as a way of life, lies there completely in these patterns which the Londoners create, and fill with the events that are exactly congruent with them.

And, what is most remarkable of all, the number of the patterns out of which a building or a town is made is rather small.

One might imagine that a building has a thousand different patterns in it; or that a town has tens of thousands. . . .

But the fact is that a building is defined, in its essentials, by a few dozen patterns. And, a vast town like London, or Paris, is defined, in its essence, by a few hundred patterns at the most.

In short, the patterns have enormous power and depth; they have the power to create an almost endless variety, they are so deep, so general, that they can combine in millions upon millions of different ways, to such an extent, that when we walk through Paris we are mainly overwhelmed by the variety; and the fact that there are these deep invariants, lying behind the vast variety, and generating it, is really an amazing shock. . . .

In this sense, the patterns are perhaps still deeper and more powerful than the discussion has made clear so far. From a handful of patterns, a vast, almost incalculable variety can be made: and a building, with all of its complexity and variety, is generated, actually, by a small number of them.

They are the atoms of our man-made universe.

In chemistry we learn that the world, in all of its complexity, is made up from combinations of some 92 elements, or atoms. This is an extraordinary fact, amazing to a person who learns chemistry for the first time. It is true that our conception of these atoms has changed repeatedly— far from being the little billiard balls we once thought, we know that they are shifting patterns of particles and waves—and that even the most "elementary" particle— the electron—is itself a ripple in the stuff of the universe, not a "thing." However, all these changing views do not alter the fact that at the level of scale where atoms occur, they do occur, as identifiable recurrent entities. And even if vast changes occur in physics, and we one day recognize that these so-called atoms are also merely ripples in a deeper field, the fact that there are entities of some kind which correspond to the things we once called atoms will remain.

Just so, we realize now, that at the larger scale of towns and buildings, the world is also made of certain fundamental "atoms"—that each place is made from a few hundred patterns—and that all of its incredible complexity comes, in the end, simply from the combinations of these few patterns.

Of course the patterns vary from place to place, from culture to culture, from age to age; they are all manmade, they all depend on culture. But still, in every age and every place the structure of our world is given to it, essentially, by some collection of patterns which keeps on repeating over and over and over again.

These patterns are not concrete elements, like bricks and doors—they are much deeper and more fluid—and yet they are the solid substance, underneath the surface, out of which a building or a town is always made.

CHAPTER 6

PATTERNS WHICH ARE ALIVE

The specific patterns out of which a
building or a town is made may be alive
or dead. To the extent they are alive,
they let our inner forces loose, and set
us free; but when they are dead they
keep us locked in inner conflict.

We know now, that every building and every town is made of patterns which repeat themselves throughout its fabric, and that it gets its character from just those patterns of which it is made.

Yet it is obvious, intuitively, that some towns and buildings are more full of life: and others less. If they all get their character from the patterns they are made of, then somehow the greater sense of life which fills one place, and which is missing from another, must be created by these patterns too.

In this chapter, and the next, we shall see just how certain patterns do create this special sense of life.

They create it in the first place, by liberating man. They create life, by allowing people to release their energy, by allowing people, themselves, to become alive. Or, in other places, they prevent it, they destroy the sense of life, they destroy the very possibility of life, by creating conditions under which people cannot possibly be free.

Let us now try to understand the mechanism by which this works.

A man is alive when he is wholehearted, true to himself, true to his own inner forces, and able to act freely according to the nature of the situations he is in.

This is the central kernel of truth already expressed in chapter 3.

To be happy, and to be alive, in this sense, are almost the same. Of course, a man who is alive, is not always happy in the sense of feeling pleasant; experiences of joy are balanced by experiences of sorrow. But the experiences are all deeply felt; and above all, the man is whole; and conscious of being real.

To be alive, in this sense, is not a matter of suppressing some forces or tendencies, at the expense of others; it is a state of being in which all forces which arise in a man can find expression; he lives in balance among the forces which arise in him; he is unique as the pattern of forces which arises is unique; he is at peace, since there are no disturbances created by underground forces which have no outlet, at one with himself and his surroundings.

This state cannot be reached merely by inner work.

There is a myth, sometimes widespread, that a person need do only inner work, in order to be alive like this; that a man is entirely responsible for his own problems; and that to cure himself, he need only change himself. This teaching has some value, since it is so easy for a man to imagine that his problems are caused by "others." But it is a one-sided and mistaken view which also maintains the arrogance of the belief that the individual is self-sufficient, and not dependent in any essential way on his surroundings.

The fact is, a person is so far formed by his surroundings, that his state of harmony depends entirely on his harmony with his surroundings.

Some kinds of physical and social circumstances help a person come to life. Others make it very difficult.

For instance, in some towns, the pattern of relationships between workplaces and families helps us to come to life.

Workshops mix with houses, children run around the places where the work is going on, the members of the family help in the work, the family may possibly eat lunch together, or eat lunch together with the people who are working there.

The fact that family and play are part of one continuous stream, helps nourish everyone. Children see how work happens, they learn what it is that makes the adult world function, they get an overall coherent view of things; men are able to connect the possibility of play and laughter, and attention to children, without having to separate them sharply in their minds, from work. Men and women are able to work, and to pay attention to their families more or less equally, as they wish to; love and work are connected, able to be one, understood and felt as coherent by the people who are living there.

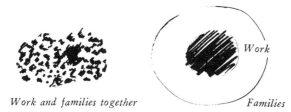

Work and families together   *Work*

Families

In other towns where work and family life are physi-

*cally separate, people are harassed by inner conflicts
which they can't escape.*

A man wants to live in his work and he wants to be close
to his family; but in a town where work and family are
physically separate, he is forced to make impossible choices
among these desires. He is exposed to the greatest emo-
tional pressure from his family, at that moment when he
is most tired—when he just comes home from work. He
is confused by a subtle identification of his wife and
children with "leisure," "weekends," and hence not the
daily stuff of life.

A woman wants to be a loving woman, sustaining to her
children; and also to take part in the outer business of
the world; to have relationships with "what is going on."
But, in a town where work and family are completely
separate, she is forced to make another impossible choice.
She either has to become a stereotyped "housewife," or a
stereotyped masculine "working woman." The possibility of both realizing her feminine nature, and also
having a place in the world beyond her family, is all but
lost to her.

A young boy wants to be close to his family, and to
understand the workings of the world and to explore
them. But, in a town where work and family are
separated, he, too, is forced to make impossible choices.
He has to choose to be either loving to his family, or to
be a truant who can experience the world. There is no
way he can reconcile his two opposing needs; and he is
likely to end up either as a juvenile delinquent, who has
torn himself entirely from his family's love, or as a child
who clings too tightly to his mother's skirts.

In the same way, a courtyard which is properly formed, helps people come to life in it.

Consider the forces at work in a courtyard. Most fundamental of all, people seek some kind of private outdoor space, where they can sit under the sky, see the stars, enjoy the sun, perhaps plant flowers. This is obvious. But there are more subtle forces too. For instance, when a courtyard is too tightly enclosed, has no view out, people feel uncomfortable, and tend to stay away . . . they need to see out into some larger and more distant space. Or again, people are creatures of habit. If they pass in and out of the courtyard, every day, in the course of their normal lives, the courtyard becomes familiar, a natural place to go . . . and it is used. But a courtyard with only one way in, a place you only go when you "want" to go there, is an unfamiliar place, tends to stay unused . . . people go more often to places which are familiar. Or again, there is a certain abruptness about suddenly stepping out, from the inside, directly to the outside . . . it is subtle, but enough to inhibit you. If there is a transitional space, a porch or a veranda, under cover, but open to the air, this is psychologically half way between indoors and outdoors, and makes it much easier, more simple, to take each of the smaller steps that brings you out into the courtyard . . .

When a courtyard has a view out to a larger space, has crossing paths from different rooms, and has a veranda or a porch, these forces can resolve themselves. The view out makes it comfortable, the crossing paths help generate a sense of habit there, the porch makes it easier to go out more often . . . and gradually the courtyard becomes a pleasant customary place to be.

*But in a courtyard where the pattern of the opening
and veranda and crossing paths is missing, there are
forces which conflict in such a way that no one can
resolve them for himself.*

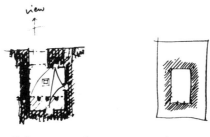

A living courtyard   Dead courtyard

Consider, for example, dead courtyard surrounded by
walls on all sides, with no porch or halfway space between the indoors and the outdoors, and with no more
than one path leading out to it.

In this place, the forces are in conflict. People want to
go out, but their timidity, which makes them seek a
place halfway to the outdoors, prevents them. They
want to stay out, but the claustrophobic quality, and the
enclosure, sends them back inside again. They hope to be
there, but the lack of paths across the courtyard make it a
dead and rarely visited place, which does not beckon
them, and which instead tends to be filled with dead
leaves, and forgotten plants. This does not help them come
to life—instead it only causes tension, and frustrates them,
and perpetuates their conflicts.

And the same can happen even in a window: A window with a "window place" helps a person come to life.

Everyone knows how beautiful a room is when it has a bay window in it, or a window seat, or a special ledge next to the window, or a small alcove which is entirely glassed. The feeling that rooms with these kinds of places in them are especially beautiful is not merely whimsy. It has a fundamental organic reason behind it.

When you are in a living room for any length of time, two of the many forces acting on you are the following:

1. You have a tendency to go towards the light. People are phototropic, biologically, so that it is often comfortable to place yourself where the light is.

2. If you are in the room for any length of time, you probably want to sit down, and make yourself comfortable.

In a room which has at least one window that is a "place"—a window seat, a bay window, a window with a wide low windowsill that invites you to pull your favorite chair over to it because you can see out so easily, a special ledge next to the window, or a small alcove which is entirely glassed—in this room you can give in to both forces: you can resolve the conflict for yourself.

In short, you can be comfortable.

But a room which has no window place, in which the windows are just "holes," sets up a hopeless inner conflict in me which I can't resolve.

A window place *Holes in the wall*

If the windows are just holes in the wall, and there are
no places where the windows are, one force pulls me
towards the window; but another force pulls me toward
the natural "places" in the room, where the comfortable
chairs and tables are. So long as I am in this room, I am
pushed and pulled by these two forces; there is nothing I
can do to prevent the inner conflict they create in me.

The instinctive knowledge that a room is beautiful when
it has a window place in it, is thus not an aesthetic whim.
It is an instinctive expression of the fact that a room without a window place is filled with actual, palpable organic
tension; and that a room which has one lacks this tension,
and is, from a simple organic point of view, a better place
to live.

*In each of these cases we have an example of a pat-
tern which helps us resolve our conflicts, and an example of a pattern which prevents us.*

In each case, the first pattern allows us to resolve our
forces for ourselves. It imposes nothing on us: but merely
allows us to resolve our forces, as they are.

On the other hand, the second pattern prevents us from
resolving our forces for ourselves. It makes it impossible
for us to find an activity which will allow us to resolve our

inner forces, and to make ourselves whole. We turn this way, then that way, rats in a trap, searching for some activity by which we can make ourselves whole. But there are none. We cannot find a way of work which keeps us at one with our family; we cannot enjoy our presence in the courtyard; and in the room without a window place, we cannot even wholeheartedly sit down. These surroundings will not let us take the steps we want to take, to be at peace with ourselves. We experience constant stress.

Of course, stress and conflict are a normal and healthy part of human life.

We constantly meet conflicts, or problems, during the course of the day: and each time, the body goes into a state of "stress" to mobilize itself, to deal with the conflict, to resolve the conflict.

This effect is physiological. We have, within our bodies, a specific physiological mechanism which produces stress. It produces, within us, a highly mobilized state of readiness, a state in which we have extra adrenalin, more alertness, faster heartbeat, higher muscle tone, more blood to the brain, more mental alertness . . . this highly alerted state, which is the state that we call "stress," arises whenever we encounter difficulty, or conflict . . . any situation in which we have to react, to solve a problem, meet a challenge . . .

Under normal conditions, when we solve the difficulty, cope with the threat, resolve the conflict, the stress then disappears, and all goes back to normal. In this normal sense, stress and conflict are an ordinary healthy part of everyday life. An organism could only exist without stress in an environment in which there were no conflicts or challenges at all—and under such circumstances the organism would atrophy and die.

But a pattern which prevents us from resolving our conflicting forces, leaves us almost perpetually in a state of tension.

For, if we live in a world where work is separated from family life, or where courtyards turn us away, or where windows are merely holes in the wall, we experience the stress of these inner and conflicting forces constantly. We can never come to rest. We are living then, in a world so made, so patterned, that we cannot, by any stratagem, defeat the tension, solve the problem, or resolve the conflict. In this kind of world the conflicts do not go away. They stay within us, nagging, tense . . . The build-up of stress, however minor, stays within us. We live in a state of heightened alertness, higher stress, more adrenalin, *all the time.*

This stress is then no longer functional at all. It becomes a huge drain on the system. Since the organism's capacity to enter the stressed state is already partly "used up" because it is perpetually in this state, our capacity to react to real new problems, dangers, and conflicts goes down, because the organism is contantly exhausted by the perpetual state of stress.

And so the "bad" patterns—the window which doesn't work, the dead courtyard, the badly located workplace—

these stress us, undermine us, affect us continuously. Indeed, in this fashion, each bad pattern in our environment constantly reduces us, cuts us down, reduces our ability to meet new challenges, reduces our capacity to live, and helps to make us dead . . .

While, on the other hand, the corresponding "good" patterns, when they are correctly made, help us to be alive, because they allow us to resolve our conflicts for ourselves. As we encounter them, we are always fresh, in the face of new encounters, new problems . . . and we are continuously renewed, and made alive . . .

It is therefore clear that patterns play a concrete and objective role in determining the extent to which we come to life in any given place.

Each pattern that creates conditions in which people can resolve the conflicts they experience, for themselves, reduces people's inner conflict, helps to put them in a state where they can meet more new challenges, and helps them to be more alive.

On the other hand, each pattern that creates conditions in which people experience conflicts which they cannot resolve for themselves, increases their inner stress, reduces their capacity to resolve other conflicts and meet other challenges, and therefore makes them less alive, more dead.

But, beyond that, patterns are not merely instruments which help us live: they are themselves alive or dead.

For, valuable as it is, the concept of patterns as life-giving or life-destroying does not go far enough. The arguments of the last few pages could make it seem as though a good pattern is merely one which is good for *us*. Yet this view, in its simple form, would lead to the same anthropo-centric view of the world which has done so much damage in the past. And above all, it would lead, in the end, to the question—well, if it is to be good for us, then we must decide what we want—and all the arbitrariness which that entails.

It is time now, to recognize that this quality without a name in our surroundings which lets us become ourselves, is not, and cannot be created there, by any effort to make it "for" man.

Good patterns are good because to some extent each one of them reaches the quality without a name itself.

After all, the criterion of being good for *us* could never be a general criterion for patterns—because obviously, there are many patterns, essential to the harmonious on-going life of the seas, the deserts, the forests—which are not directly good for us at all.

If the only criterion for a good pattern were its goodness for *us*, we should be forced to judge the ripples in a pond, or the crash of an ocean wave, according to whether we could get nice fish from it, or whether we liked the sound—and this would be ridiculous.

Certain patterns are simply resolved within themselves, within their proper contexts—in these contexts they are intrinsically alive—and it is this which makes them good.

And this is as true for the pattern of an ocean wave as it is for the pattern of a courtyard in a house.

Consider the ripples in a patch of wind-blown sand.

When the wind blows, at any given speed, it picks up grains of sand, and carries them a few inches. It carries the smaller grains slightly farther, and the bigger grains not so far. Now, in any patch of sand, there are always a few irregularities—places where the sand is a little higher—and of course, as the wind sweeps over the sand, it is just the grains on these little ridges which get picked up and blown. Since, for any given wind speed the wind carries all the grains roughly the same distance, the blowing wind now gradually deposits a second ridge a certain fixed distance from the first, and parallel to it. This second ridge, as it builds up, is also especially vulnerable, so the grains from its top, once again, get blown on to form another ridge, the same distance again, and so on . . . .

This pattern is a recognizable and constant pattern, because it is a truth about the laws which govern sand and wind.

Within the proper context, this pattern creates and re-creates itself over and over again. It creates and re-creates itself whenever the wind blows on the sand.

Its goodness comes from the fact that it is true to its own inner forces, not from any special sense of purpose.

117

The same can happen in a garden, where the plants, and wind, and animals are perfectly in balance.

Consider, for example, a corner of an orchard, where the sun warms the ground, the marrows grow, the bees pollinate the apple blossom, the worms bring air to the soil, the apple leaves fertilize the soil . . . . This pattern repeats itself, hundreds of times, in a thousand different gardens, and is always a source of life.

But the life of the pattern does not depend on the fact that it does something for "us"—but simply on the self-sustaining harmony, in which each process helps sustain the other processes, and in which the whole system of forces and processes keeps itself going, over and again, without creating extra forces that will tear it down.

In short, saying these patterns are alive is more or less the same as saying they are stable.

Compare the eroding gully, of chapter 2, with these patterns. The gully is unstable. It destroys itself. Its own action, gradually tears it down. These patterns on the other hand, have the quality, that their own action helps keep them alive.

You may wonder: what about cancer. Cancer is stable. It maintains itself. And "in the small" this is true. But it only maintains *itself*. Since, in order to maintain itself, it must in the end destroy what is around it—the very organism where it lives—it ultimately too destroys itself, by helping to destroy its surroundings.

And although it is true that nothing is perfectly stable,

and true that everything changes in the end, there are still great differences of degree. The patterns which are alive maintain themselves in the long run, because they do nothing to destroy their own immediate surroundings, and they do nothing drastic, in the short run, to destroy themselves. As far as it is ever possible, they are alive, because they are so much in harmony, that they support themselves, and keep themselves alive, through their own inner structure.

And just this also happens in patterns from the human realm. Their quality does not depend on purpose, but on their intrinsic stability.

Consider two human patterns. On the one hand, consider the fact that certain Greek village streets have a band of whitewash, four or five feet wide, outside every house, so that people can pull their chairs out into the street, into a realm which is half theirs, half street, and so contribute to the life around them.

And on the other hand, consider the fact that cafés in Los Angeles are indoors, away from the sidewalk, in order to prevent the food from being contaminated.

Both these patterns have a purpose. One has the purpose of allowing people to contribute to the street life and to be part of it—to the extent they desire—by marking a domain which makes it possible. The other has the purpose of keeping people healthy, by making sure that they will not eat food that has dust particles on it. Yet one is alive; the other dead.

One, like the ripples in the sand, sustains itself and heals itself because it is in harmony with its own forces. The other one can only be maintained by force of law.

The whitewashed band is so congruent with the forces in people's lives and with their feelings that it sustains itself— when the whitewash gets dirty or worn people take care of it themselves because the pattern is deeply connected to their own experience. From outside, it seems as though the whitewash maintains itself almost as if by magic.

The indoor café in Los Angeles is almost opposite: it has no such congruence with people's inner forces. It has to be maintained by force, by force of law—because, under the impact of its own forces, it would gradually deteriorate, and disappear. People want to be outdoors on a spring day, want to drink their beer or coffee in the open, to watch the world go by, but they are imprisoned in the café by the laws of public health. The situation is self-destroying, not only because it will change as soon as the law which upholds it disappears, but also in the more subtle sense that it is continuously creating just those inner conflicts, just those reservoirs of stress I spoke of earlier which will, unsatisfied, soon well up like a gigantic boil and leak out in some other form of destruction or refusal to cooperate with the situation.

In short, a pattern lives when it allows its own internal forces to resolve themselves.

And a pattern dies when it fails to provide a framework in

which forces can resolve themselves, so that instead, the action of the forces, unresolved, works to destroy the pattern.

That is the distinction between the two patterns in the last example. The fact that both of them are based on human "purposes" is quite irrelevant.

And this explains the importance of the courtyard pattern which inspires use.

It is the self-sustaining character the living courtyard has, which is the essence of its life.

As time goes on, the courtyard which lives is also growing. More and more happens there. Because people enjoy being there, they plant flowers there, and look after them; they keep the garden furniture painted; and even if you go there when no one else is there, you can "feel" the presence of life there, because you can sense that people are taking care of it.

But the other lifeless courtyard, as time goes on, becomes more and more forgotten. No one enjoys going out there—so the paint is peeling; the gravel has weeds in it; even the sculpture standing there somehow looks abandoned. The courtyard which is whole, becomes richer and more whole; the courtyard which is unwhole slowly fades away and dies.

And so we see the wholeness of the living courtyard does not depend on any human values, external to the courtyard, invented by you, or by me, or by the people who live there. It is a fact intrinsic to its own organization.

And now we see just how the circle of the argument completes itself.

In our own lives, we have the quality without a name when we are most intense, most happy, most wholehearted.

This comes about when we allow the forces we experience to run freely in us, to fly past each other, when we are able to allow our forces to escape the locked-in conflict which oppresses us.

But this freedom, this limpidity, occurs in us most easily when we are in a world whose patterns also let their forces loose . . . because, just as we are free when our own forces run most freely within us, so the places we are in are also free when their own forces (which include the forces that arise in us) themselves run free, and are themselves resolved . . .

The quality without a name in us, our liveliness, our thirst for life, depends directly on the patterns in the world, and the extent to which they have this quality themselves.

Patterns which live, release this quality in us.

But they release this quality in us, essentially because they have it in themselves.

CHAPTER 7

THE MULTIPLICITY OF
LIVING PATTERNS

*The more living patterns there are in a
thing—a room, a building, or a
town—the more it comes to life as an
entirety, the more it glows, the more it
has this self-maintaining fire, which is
the quality without a name.*

When one pattern is alive, it resolves its own forces, it is self-sustaining, self-creating, and its internal forces continuously support themselves.

Now we shall see that this is just a special case of a more general effect by which the patterns in a town or building help to sustain each other, in which each pattern which is alive, itself spreads out its life.

Consider the "architecture" of a system in which many patterns co-exist.

Assume, for instance, that a certain building is made up from fifty patterns.

These patterns define the building in its totality. They define its large scale organization, the layout of rooms, the way the ceilings work, the typical positions of the windows, the way the building stands up, its foundations, its roof, its windows, and its ornament.

To all intents and purposes, these fifty patterns define the physical structure of the building, and they are responsible for the events which happen in the building over and again—both the human events, and the non-human physical events.

Each one of these fifty patterns can itself be alive, or dead.

Or, to be more precise, each one of them is relatively more alive, or more dead—of course it is a matter of degree. But anyway, each of these fifty patterns, is relatively stable, and self-sustaining—or it is relatively unstable and self-destroying.

Consider what happens when several of these fifty patterns are more "dead."

Each of these "dead" patterns is incapable of containing its own forces, and keeping them in balance. What happens then, is that these forces leak out, beyond the confines of the pattern where they occur, and start to infect the other patterns.

Consider, for example, the pattern of a column and beam structure without a brace or capital where the column meets the beam.

In every structure, for any given pattern of loading, there are varying stress concentrations throughout the structure. Certain points, because of their configuration, tend to have very high stress concentrations—right-angle connections between columns and beams are one example. In such a configuration, as the stress concentration goes beyond the bounds of the material, small cracks develop. The cracks ripple outward from this point and weaken the structure at other surrounding points. So far the self-destroying nature of the system is still entirely in terms of mechanical forces. But now a new kind of effect begins. The small cracks attract water by capillary action: the water enters into the material, and damages its load-bearing capacities still further. When the ice comes, the water freezes, expands, and does still further damage. Next time the loads create a concentration of stress in that damaged area, they do still further damage, and the structure ruptures further.

Or consider the pattern of a courtyard which is too enclosed.

In the living courtyard, we are nourished; we go out when we feel like going out, the courtyard gets looked after, we still feel like being there; we are relaxed and free whether we go out there or stay inside.

In the dead courtyard none of this is true. We try to go out, but are frustrated, because the courtyard itself pushes us away. We still need, somehow, to go out; the forces remain within us, but can find no resolution here. We have no way of resolving the situation for ourselves. The unresolved conflict remains underground; it contributes the stress which is building up. First, it reduces our capacity to resolve other conflicts for ourselves, and makes it even more likely that unresolved forces will spill over in another situation. Second, if the force does spill over, it may create even greater tension, in another situation, where there is no proper outlet for it.

Suppose, for example, the people who want to be outside go out instead and sit on the road, where trucks are going by. It is OK. But then perhaps a child gets hurt. Or, even if a child does not actually get hurt, the mother fears for it, and shouts, and conveys a continuous sense of unease to the child, so that his play is spoiled. . . . In one fashion or another, the effects always ripple out.

You may say—well, people can adapt. But in the process of adapting, they destroy some other part of themselves. We are very adaptive, it is true. But we can also adapt to such an extent that we do ourselves harm. The process of adaptation has its costs. It may be, for example, that the child adapts, by turning to books. The desire to play in the street conforms now to the dangers, and the mother's cries. But now the person has lost some of the exuberant desire to run about. He has adapted, but he has made his own life less rich, less whole, by being forced to do so.

The "bad" patterns are unable to contain the forces which occur in them.

As a result, these forces spill over into other nearby systems. The cracks in the column-beam connection, in time, cause water damage in the wall. And the courtyard which fails makes children want to play outside and causes stress and danger in the street.

But these forces make other nearby patterns fail as well. The pattern of the street may not be conceived as a place for children to play. So, suddenly, a pattern of the street, which might be in balance without this force, itself becomes unstable and inadequate.

And the pattern of the wall-to-beam connection—which was originally not conceived as having to cope with a leaking flow of water from above, within the beam—is suddenly unstable and inadequate also, because the context and the forces which it tries to put in balance, have changed.

In the end, the whole system must collapse.

The slight stress caused by the overflow of forces from these first unstable patterns spreads first to nearby patterns—and then spreads still further, since these nearby patterns become unstable and destructive too.

The delicate configuration which is self-creating, and in balance with its forces, is for some reason interrupted— prevented from occurring, placed in a position in which its configuration can no longer recreate itself.

What then happens to the forces in this system?

So long as the self-creating balanced configuration existed, the forces were in balance.

But once the configuration is put out of balance, these forces remain in the system, unresolved, wild, out of balance, until in the end, the whole system must collapse.

By contrast, assume now that each one of the fifty patterns out of which the building is made is alive and self-resolving.

In this case just the opposite occurs. Each pattern encompasses, and contains, the forces which it has to deal with; and there are no other forces in the system. Under these circumstances, each event which happens is resolved. The forces come into play, and resolve themselves, within the patterns as they are.

Each pattern helps to sustain other patterns.

The quality without a name occurs, not when an isolated pattern occurs, but when an entire system of patterns, interdependent, at many levels, is all stable and alive.

We may see the sand ripples anywhere where we choose to put loose sand under the wind.

But when the wind blows across the sea, over the inland marshes, and the sand ripples support the dunes between the two, and the sandpiper walks out, the sand fleas hop, the shifting of the dunes is held in check by grasses which maintain themselves and the sandpiper—then we have a portion of the world, alive at many levels at once, beginning to have the quality without a name.

The individual configuration of any one pattern re-
quires other patterns to keep itself alive.

For instance, a WINDOW PLACE is stable, and alive, only if many other patterns which go with it, and are needed to support it, are alive themselves: for instance, LOW WINDOWSILL, to solve the problem of the view and the relation to the ground; CASEMENT WINDOW to solve the problem of the way the air comes in, to allow people to lean out and breathe the outside air; SMALL PANES to let the window generate a strong connection between the inside and the outside.

If these smaller patterns, which resolve smaller systems of forces in the window place, are missing from the window place itself, then the pattern doesn't work. Imagine for instance a so-called window place, with high windowsills, fixed windows, and huge sheets of plate glass. There are so many subsidiary forces, still in conflict, that the window place still cannot work, because it still fails to resolve the special system of forces it is supposed to solve. To be in balance, each pattern must be supported by a situation in which both the larger patterns it belongs to, and the smaller patterns it is made of, are themselves alive.

In an entrance which is whole, many patterns must cooperate.

Try to imagine an entrance which is whole. I have in mind an entry way, perhaps to a larger building: and for it to be whole, it must contain at least these elements: the arch, or beam, which brings the loads down from above; a certain heaviness perhaps, in the members which bring these forces down, and mark the edges of the entrance way; a certain depth, or penetration, which takes the entrance a distance in, deep enough, so that the light is changing on the way through the entry way; some ornament, around the archway, or the opening, which marks the entrance as distinct, and gives it lightness; and, in some form, things that I would somehow see as

"feet"—things sticking out, at the bases of the sides—
they might be seats, the feet of columns, something anyway which connects the sides to the ground, and makes
them one. Now this entrance might be whole. I doubt
though, if it could be whole with any less than that.

So, somehow, this system of patterns, which I have
loosely sketched, forms the basis for what is needed in the
entrance of a larger building: and these patterns are a
system; they are interdependent. It is true that each one
can be explained, in its own terms, as an isolated thing,
which is needed to resolve certain forces. But, also, these
few patterns form a whole, they work as a system. . . .

The same in a neighborhood.

Again there are certain rough patterns, more rooted in
human events, in this case, which must be there together,
in order for us to experience the neighborhood as
whole. . . .

A boundary, certainly, more or less clearly marked; and
gateways, not emphatic, but gently present, where the
paths that pass in and out cross the boundaries: inside, a
piece of common land, with children playing, animals
grazing maybe; seats where old people sit and watch
what is happening; a focus to the whole; the families
themselves, grouped in some kind of clusters, so that
there are a visible number of them, not too many, for
the neighborhood as a whole; water somewhere; workshops and work, perhaps towards the boundary; houses
of course, too, but clustered; trees, somewhere—and sun-

light somewhere too, intense in at least one place. Now, the neighborhood begins to form a whole.

Now we begin to see what happens when the patterns in the world collaborate.

Each living pattern resolves some system of forces, or allows them to resolve themselves. Each pattern creates an organization which maintains that portion of the world in balance.

And a building in which all the patterns are alive has no disturbing forces in it. The people are relaxed; the plants are comfortable; the animals pursue their natural paths; the forces of erosion are in balance with the natural process of repair which the configuration of the building encourages; the forces of gravity are in balance with the configuration of the beams and vaults, and columns, and the blowing of the wind; the rainwater flows naturally, in such a way that it helps just those plants to grow which, for other reasons, are themselves in balance with the cracks in the paving stones, the beauty of the entrance, the smell of roses in the evening outdoor room . . . .

The more life-giving patterns there are in a building the more beautiful it seems.

It shows, in a thousand small ways, that it is made, with care and with attention to the small things we might need.

A seat, an armrest, a door handle which is comfortable to hold, a terrace shaded from the heat, a flower growing just along the entrance where I can bend down and smell it as I pass into the garden, light falling on the top of the stair, where it is dark, so that I can walk toward it, color on the door, ornament around the door, so that I know, with a small leap of the heart, that I am back again, a cellar half down into the ground, where milk and wine can be kept cool.

Just so in a town.

The town which is alive, and beautiful, for me, shows, in a thousand ways, how all its institutions work together to make people comfortable, and deep seated in respect for themselves.

Places outdoors where people eat, and dance; old people sitting in the street, watching the world go by; places where teenage boys and girls hang out, within the neighborhood, free enough of their parents that they feel themselves alive, and stay there; car places where cars are kept, shielded, if there are many of them, so that they don't oppress us by their presence; work going on among the families, children playing where work is going on, and learning from it.

And finally the quality without a name appears, not when an isolated pattern lives, but when an entire system of patterns, interdependent at many levels, is all stable and alive.

A building or a town becomes alive when every pattern in it is alive: when it allows each person in it, and each plant and animal, and every stream, and bridge, and wall and roof, and every human group and every road, to become alive in its own terms.

And as that happens, the whole town reaches the state that individual people sometimes reach at their best and happiest moments, when they are most free.

Remember the warm peach tree, flattened against the wall, and facing south.

At this stage, the whole town will have this quality, simmering and baking in the sun of its own processes.

CHAPTER 8

THE QUALITY ITSELF

And when a building has this fire, then it becomes a part of nature. Like ocean waves, or blades of grass, its parts are governed by the endless play of repetition and variety, created in the presence of the fact that all things pass. This is the quality itself.

Finally, in this last chapter of part 1, we shall see what happens geometrically, when a building or a town is made entirely of patterns which are living.

For when a town or building lives, we can always recognize its life—not only in the obvious happiness which happens there, not only in its freedom and re-laxedness—but in its purely physical appearance too.

It always has a certain geometric character.

What happens in a world—a building or a town—in which the patterns have the quality without a name, and are alive?

The most important thing which happens is that every part of it, at every level, becomes unique. The patterns which control a portion of the world, are themselves fairly simple. But when they interact, they create slightly different overall configurations at every place. This happens because no two places on earth are perfectly alike in their conditions. And each small difference, itself contributes to the difference in conditions which the other patterns face.

This is the character of nature.

"The character of nature" is no mere poetic metaphor. It is a specific morphological character, a geometric char-acter, which happens to be common to all those things in the world which are not man-made.

To make this character of nature clear, let me contrast it with the character of the buildings being built today. One of the most pervasive features of these buildings is the fact that they are "modular." They are full of identical concrete blocks, identical rooms, identical houses, identical apartments in identical apartment buildings. The idea that a building can—and ought—to be made of modular units is one of the most pervasive assumptions of twentieth-century architecture.

Nature is never modular. Nature is full of almost similar units (waves, raindrops, blades of grass)—but though the units of one kind are all alike in their broad structure, no two are ever alike in detail.

1. The same broad features keep recurring over and over again.
2. In their detailed appearance these broad features are never twice the same.

On the one hand all oak trees have the same overall shape, the same thickened twisted trunk, the same crinkled bark, the same shaped leaves, the same proportion of limbs to branches to twigs. On the other hand, no two trees are quite the same. The exact combination of height and width and curvature never repeats itself; we cannot even find two leaves which are the same.

The ocean waves all have this character.

The patterns out of which the wave is made are always the same: the curl of the wave; the drops of spray; the spacing of the waves; the fact that roughly every seventh wave is larger than the others . . . There are not many of these patterns.

Yet at the same time, the actual concrete waves themselves are always different. This happens because the patterns interact differently at every spot. They interact differently with one another. And they interact differently with the details of their surroundings. So every actual wave is different, at the same time that all its patterns are the same precisely as the patterns in the other waves.

So do the drops within the waves.

The distinction between the "global" patterns and the concrete details is not a matter of size. What is true for the waves is also true for the individual droplets. Each drop of a given size has more or less the same shape—yet, again, under a finer microscope, each one is slightly different from the next. At each scale there are global invariants, and detailed variations. In such a system, there is endless variety; and yet at the same time there is endless sameness. No wonder we can watch the waves for hours; no wonder that a blade of grass is still fascinating, even after we have seen a million of them. In all this sameness, we never feel oppressed by sameness. In all this variety, we never feel lost, as we do in the presence of variety we cannot understand.

Even the atoms have this character.

It may surprise you to realize that the same rule even holds for atoms. No two atoms are the same. Each atom is slightly different, according to its immediate environment.

It is particularly crucial to discuss this fact about atoms, because so many people take "modular" construction for granted. If you challenge the builder of a modular environment, and say that such an environment cannot be alive, he will very likely say that nature itself is built from modular components—namely atoms—and that what is good for nature is good enough for him. In this sense, atoms have become the archetypal images of modular construction.

But atoms are all unique, just like raindrops and blades of grass. Because we use the symbol C for every atom of carbon, and because we know that every atom of carbon has the same number of protons and electrons in it, we assume that all atoms of carbon are identical. We think of a crystal as an array of identical parts. Yet the fact is that the orbits of the electrons are influenced by the orbits of electrons in nearby atoms, and are therefore different in each atom, according to its position in the crystal. If we could examine every atom in very great detail indeed, we would find that no two atoms are exactly alike: each is subtly different, according to its position in the larger whole.

There is always repetition of the patterns.

The patterns repeat themselves because, under a given set of circumstances, there are always certain fields of relationships which are most nearly well adapted to the forces which exist.

The shape of the wave is generated by the dynamics of the water, and it repeats itself wherever these dynamics occur. The shape of the drops is generated by the balance between gravity and surface tension in the falling drop, and it repeats itself under all circumstances where these are the dominating forces. And the shape of the atoms is created by the inner forces among particles, which once again repeats itself, approximately, everywhere these particles and forces coincide.

But there is always variation and uniqueness in the way the patterns manifest themselves.

Each pattern is a generic solution to some system of forces in the world. But the forces are never quite the same. Since the exact configuration of the surroundings at any one place and time is always unique, the configuration of the forces which the system is subject to is also unique—no other system of forces is ever subject to exactly the same configuration of forces. If the system is responsible to the forces it is subject to, it follows that the system too, must be unique; it cannot be exactly like any other, even though it is roughly similar. This is not an accidental consequence of the uniqueness of each system: it is an essential aspect of the life and wholeness of each part.

In short, there is a character in natural things which is created by the fact that they are reconciled, exactly, to their inner forces.

For from the play of repetition and variety at every level, it follows that the overall geometry is always loose and fluid. There is an indefinable roughness, a looseness,

147

a relaxedness, which nature always has: and this relaxed geometry comes directly from the balance of the repetition and variety.

In a forest which is alive, it would be impossible for all the trees to be identical; and it would be impossible for one tree itself to be alive, if its leaves were all the same. No system whose component parts are so unresponsive to the forces they are subject to, could maintain itself successfully; it could not be alive or whole. It is a crucial fact about the wholeness of the tree that every leaf be slightly different from the next. And of course, since the same argument applies at every level, it means that the component parts of nature are unique at every level.

This character will happen anywhere, where a part of the world is so well reconciled to its own inner forces that it is true to its own nature.

All those things which we loosely call *nature*—the grass, the trees, the winter wind, deep blue water, yellow crocuses, foxes, and the rain—in short the things which man has not made—are just those things which are *true* to their *own* nature. They are just those things which are perfectly reconciled with their own inner forces. And the things which are not "nature" are just those things which are at odds with their own inner forces.

And any system which is whole must have this character of nature. The morphology of nature, the softness of its lines, the almost infinite variety and the lack of gaps—all this follows directly from the fact that nature is whole. Mountains, rivers, forests, animals, rocks, flowers all have this character. But they do not have it simply by accident. They have it because they are whole, and because all their parts are whole. Any system which is whole must have this character.

It follows that a building which is whole must always have the character of nature, too.

This does not mean that a building or a town which is alive will look like a tree, or like a forest. But, it will have the same balance of repetition and variety that nature does.

On the one hand, patterns will repeat themselves, just as they do in nature.

If the patterns out of which a thing is made are alive, then we shall see them over and over again, just because they make sense. If the way a window looks onto a tree makes sense, then we shall see it over and again; if the relationship between the doors make sense, we shall see it for almost every door; if the way that the tiles are hung makes sense, we shall see almost all the tiles hung in this way; if the arrangement of the kitchen in the house makes sense, it will be repeated in the neighborhood.

In short, we shall find the same elements, repeating over and over again—and we shall see the rhythms of their repetition. The boards in the siding of the house, the

balusters in the railing of a balustrade, the windows in
the buildings, panes within the windows, the same ap-
proximate roof shape repeated over and again, the similar
columns, similar rooms, similar ceilings, ornaments repeated, trees and the boles of trees repeated in their
pattern, seats repeated, whitewash repeated, colors repeated, avenues, gardens, fountains, roadside places, trellises, arcades, paving stones, blue tiles . . . all repeated,
whichever of them are appropriate in any given place.

*On the other hand, of course, we shall find the physi-
cal parts in which the patterns manifest themselves
unique and slightly different each time that they
occur.*

Because the patterns interact, and because the conditions
are slightly different around each individual occurrence,
the columns in an arcade will all be slightly different,
the boards in the siding of the house will be slightly
different, the windows will vary slightly, the house will
vary, trees' positions will vary, seats will be different
even at the same time that they recur . . .

*The repetition of patterns is quite a different thing
from the repetition of parts.*

When two physical windows are identical the relationships which they have to their surroundings are different,
because their surroundings are different.

    But when the relationships to their surroundings—their

patterns—are the same, the windows themselves will all be different, because the sameness of the patterns, interacting with the difference of the contexts, makes the windows different.

Indeed, the different parts will be unique because *the patterns are the same.*

Consider, for example, the pattern SUNNY PLACE, which creates a spot in the sun, along the south side of a building, just where the outdoor space gets used, and where the building opens out to it. This pattern may create a series of similar spots, along the southern edge of a long row of houses—but then, just where the houses turn a corner, it generates a special place, which sticks out half into the street, low walls to protect its sides, perhaps a canvas canopy—a place which everyone in the neighborhood remembers and looks for.

This unique place is not created by some arbitrary searching for uniqueness. It is created by the repetition of the pattern which calls for a spot in the sun, and by the interaction of this pattern with the world.

And we shall find the same at every scale. Where there are many houses, the houses will be similar in form, but each will be unique, according to the nature of the people who live in it, and because each has a slightly different combination of relationships to the land, the sun, the streets, the community.

The windows of a given house will all be broadly similar, according to their patterns, but again no two will be the same in detail—each will be different according to its exact position, the direction of the light, the size of room, the plants outside the room.

And from the repetition of the patterns, and unique-ness of the parts, it follows, as it does in nature, that buildings which are alive are fluid and relaxed in their geometry.

Again, this doesn't mean that buildings ought to look like animals, or plants. The vertical, the horizontal, and the right angle are too central to the nature of human space to make that possible. But in a place which is alive, these right angles are rarely exact; the spacing of parts is hardly ever perfectly even. One column is a little thicker than another, one angle is a little larger than a right angle, one doorway is just a little smaller than the next, each roof line departs just an inch or two from the horizontal.

A building in which angles are all perfectly right angles, in which all windows are exactly the same size, and in which all columns are perfectly vertical, and all floors perfectly horizontal, can only reach its false perfection by ignoring its surroundings utterly. The apparent imperfec-tions of a place which is alive are not imperfections at all. They follow from the process which allows each part to be fitted carefully to its position.

This is the character of nature. But its fluidity, its roughness, its irregularity, will not be true, unless it is made in the knowledge that it is going to die.

No matter how much the person who makes a building is able to understand the rhythm of regularity and irregularity, it will mean nothing so long as he creates it with the idea that it must be preserved because it is so precious.

If you want to preserve a building, you will try to make it in materials which last and last forever. You will try to make sure that this creation can be preserved intact, in just its present state, forever. Canvas must be ruled out because it has to be replaced; tiles must be so hard that they will not crack, and set in concrete, so that they cannot move, and so that weeds will not grow up to split the paving; chairs must be made perfect, of materials which never wear or fade; trees must be nice to look at, but may not bear fruit, because the dropped fruit might offend someone.

But to reach the quality without a name, a building must be made, at least in part, of those materials which age and crumble. Soft tile and brick, soft plaster, fading coats of paint, canvas which has been bleached a little and torn by the wind, . . . fruit, dropping on the paths, and being crushed by people walking over it, grass growing in the cracks between the stones, an old chair, patched, and painted, to increase its comfort . . .

None of this can happen in a world which lasts forever.

The character of nature can't arise without the presence and the consciousness of death.

So long as human images distort the character of nature, it is because there is no wholehearted acceptance of the

153

nature of things. So long as there is not wholehearted acceptance of the nature of things, people will distort nature, by exaggerating differences, or by exaggerating similarities. They do this, ultimately, in order to stave off the thought and fact of death.

So finally the fact is, that to come to this, to make a thing which has the character of nature, and to be true to all the forces in it, to remove yourself, to let it be, without interference from your image-making self—all this requires that we become aware that all of it is transitory; that all of it is going to pass.

Of course nature itself is also always transitory. The trees, the river, the humming insects—they are all short-lived; they will all pass. Yet we never feel sad in the presence of these things. No matter how transitory they are, they make us feel happy, joyful.

But when we make our own attempt to create nature in the world around us, and succeed, we cannot escape the fact that we are going to die. This quality, when it is reached, in human things, is always sad; it makes us sad; and we can even say that any place where a man tries to make the quality, and be like nature, cannot be true, unless we can feel the slight presence of this haunting sadness there, because we know at the same time we enjoy it, that it is going to pass.

THE GATE

To reach the quality without a name
we must then build a living pattern
language as a gate.

CHAPTER 9

THE FLOWER AND THE SEED

*This quality in buildings and in towns
cannot be made, but only generated,
indirectly, by the ordinary actions of the
people, just as a flower cannot be made,
but only generated from the seed.*

We are now in a position to recognize, at least in hazy outline, the character of towns and buildings with the quality without a name in them.

Next we shall see that there is a specific concrete process by which this quality comes into being.

Indeed the main thing we shall deal with in these next nine chapters, is the fact that the quality without a name cannot be made, but only generated by a process.

It can flow from your actions; it can flow with the greatest ease; but it cannot be made. It cannot be contrived, thought out, designed. It happens when it flows out from the process of creation of its own accord.

But we must give up altogether the idea that it is something we can capture, consciously, by working over drawings at the drawing board.

Consider the process by which the Samoans make a canoe, from a tree.

They cut the tree down; scrape the branches from the trunk; take off the bark; hollow the inside out; carve the outside shape of the hull; form the prow and the stern; carve decorations on the prow . . . .

Each canoe made by this process is different; each one is beautiful in its own way, because the process is so ordinary, so simple, so direct. There is no time lost wondering what kind of canoe ought we to build, what shape to make the hull, should we put seats in it—all those decisions are made before you start—so that all the energy and feeling which its makers have goes into the specific character of this particular canoe. . . .

The quality of life is just like that: it cannot be made, but only generated.

When a thing is made, it has the will of the maker in it. But when it is generated, it is generated, freely, by the operation of egoless rules, acting on the reality of the situation, and giving birth, of their own accord. . . .

The brush stroke becomes beautiful, when it is visible only as the end product of a process—when the force of the process takes over the cramped will of the maker. The maker lets go of his will, and lets the process take over.

And just so, any thing which lives can only be achieved as the end product of a process, whose force takes over and replaces the willful act of creation.

In our time we have come to think of works of art as "creations," conceived in the minds of their creators.

And we have come to think of buildings, even towns, also as "creations"—again thought out, conceived entire, designed.

To give birth to such a whole seems like a monumental task: it requires that the creator think, from nothing, and give birth to something whole: it is a vast task, forbidding, huge; it commands respect; we understand how hard it is; we shrink from it, perhaps, unless we are very certain of our power; we are afraid of it.

All this has defined the task of creation, or design, as a huge task, in which something gigantic is brought to birth, suddenly, in a single act, whose inner workings cannot be explained, whose substance relies ultimately on the ego of the creator.

The quality without a name cannot be made like this.

Imagine, by contrast, a system of simple rules, not complicated, patiently applied, until they gradually form a thing. The thing may be formed gradually and built all at once, or built gradually over time—but it is formed, essentially, by a process no more complicated than the process by which the Samoans shape their canoe.

Here there is no mastery of unnameable creative processes: only the patience of a craftsman, chipping away slowly; the mastery of what is made does not lie in the depths of some impenetrable ego; it lies, instead, in the simple mastery of the steps in the process, and in the definition of these steps.

The same thing, exactly, is true of a living organism.

An organism cannot be made. It cannot be conceived, by a willful act of creation, and then built, according to the blueprint of the creator. It is far too complex, far too subtle, to be born from a bolt of lightning in the creator's mind. It has a thousand billion cells, each one adapted perfectly to its conditions—and this can only happen because the organism is not "made" but generated by a process which allows the gradual adaptation of these cells to happen hour by hour. . . .

It is the process which creates the organism—and it must be so. No thing which lives can possibly be made in any other way.

If you want to make a living flower, you don't build it physically, with tweezers, cell by cell. You grow it from the seed.

Suppose you are trying to create a flower—a new kind of flower. How will you do it? Of course you will not try to build it cell by cell, with tweezers. You know that any attempt to build such a complex and delicate thing directly would lead to nothing. The only flowers which men have built directly, piece by piece, are plastic flowers. If you want to make a living flower, there is only one way to do it—you will have to build a seed for the flower and then let *it*, this seed, generate the flower.

This hinges on a simple scientific proposition: the great complexity of an organic system, which is essential to its life, cannot be created from above directly; it can only be generated indirectly.

The sheer amount of differentiation makes this certain. For instance, in a flower there are more than a billion cells—each one different. Obviously, no process of construction can ever create this kind of complexity directly. Only those indirect growth processes, in which order multiplies itself, only these kinds of processes can generate this biological complexity.

This cannot happen unless each part is at least partly autonomous, so that it can adapt to the local conditions in the whole.

The quality without a name, like all forms of organic wholeness, depends essentially on the degree of adaptation of the parts within the whole.

In a system which approaches the character of nature, the parts must be adapted with an almost infinite degree of subtlety: and this requires that the process of adaptation be going on through the system, constantly.

It requires that each part at every level, no matter how small, has the power to adapt itself to its own processes.

This cannot happen unless each part is autonomous.

A building which is natural requires the same.

In the building, every windowsill and every column must be shaped by an autonomous process which allows it to adapt correctly to the whole.

Each bench, each windowsill, each tile, needs to be made by a person, or a process, in tune with the subtle minute forces there, making it a little different at each point along its length and different from all the others.

And the same in the town.

In the town, each building and each garden must also by shaped by an autonomous process, which allows it to adapt to its unique particulars.

This vast variety can only be created by the people. Every house along a road must be shaped by a different person familiar with the different forces peculiar to that place. And within the house, the windows must be shaped by people who are looking out, and seeing what the boundaries of the window need to be.

This does not mean that every person has to design the place he lives in. It simply means that the love, and care, and patience needed to bring every part into adjustment with the forces acting on it, can only exist when each detailed part is cared for, and shaped, by someone who has the time and patience and knowledge to understand the forces acting on it. It is not essential that each person design or shape the place where he is going to live or work. Obviously people move, are happy in old houses, and so on.

It is essential only that the people of a society, together, all the millions of them, not just professional architects, design all the millions of places. There is no other way that human variety, and the reality of specific human lives, can find their way into the structure of the places.

But of course, autonomous creation of the parts, if taken by itself, will produce chaos.

The parts will not form any larger whole, unless the individual adaptation of the parts is under some sort of deeper regulation, which guarantees that the local process of adaptation will not only make the local part truly adapted to its own processes, but that it will also be shaped to form a larger whole.

What makes a flower whole, at the same time that all its cells are more or less autonomous, is the genetic code, which guides the process of the individual parts, and makes a whole of them.

The different cells are able to act in harmony because each one of them contains the same genetic code.

Each part (cell) is free to adapt locally to its own processes, and is helped in this process by the genetic code which guides its growth.

Yet at the same time, this same code contains features which guarantee that the slow adaptation of the individual parts is not merely anarchic, and individual, but that each part simultaneously helps to create those larger parts, systems, and patterns which are needed for the whole.

And, just as the flower needs a genetic code to keep the wholeness of its parts, so do the building and the town.

The individual building needs a code, which guarantees that all the columns and the windows, as they get individually shaped, will form a whole. It must provide the individual builder with a sequence of instructions so clear, and so fluid, that he can freely make each portion of the building perfectly, according to its place.

And the town needs a code, which makes the many actions of the great variety of people whole. It must provide the people of the town with instructions so clear that all of them can take part in the shaping of the town: just like the genetic process which creates the flower, this process must allow each person to shape his own corner of the world, so that each building, each room, each doorstep, is unique according to its place within the whole—but with the built-in guarantee that the town which emerges from these independent acts, will also be alive and whole.

So I began to wonder if there was a code, like the genetic code, for human acts of building?

Is there a fluid code, which generates the quality without a name in buildings, and makes things live? Is there some process which takes place inside a person's mind, when he allows himself to generate a building or a place which is alive? And is there indeed a process which is so simple too, that all the people of society can use it, and so generate not only individual buildings, but whole neighborhoods and towns?

It turns out that there is. It takes the form of language.

CHAPTER 10

OUR PATTERN LANGUAGES

The people can shape buildings for themselves, and have done it for centuries, by using languages which I call pattern languages. A pattern language gives each person who uses it, the power to create an infinite variety of new and unique buildings, just as his ordinary language gives him the power to create an infinite variety of sentences.

We know, from chapter 9, in very vague and general terms, that life cannot be made, but only generated by a process.

In the case of buildings and of towns, this process must be one which lets the people of a town shape rooms, and houses, streets, and churches, for themselves.

Now we shall begin to see what kind of processes can make this possible.

In traditional cultures these processes were commonplace.

Each person knew how to make a house, a window, or a bench, just right.

Each building was a member of a family, and yet unique.

Even though there are a hundred farmhouses, in a valley of the alps, all similar, yet still each one is beautiful, and special to the place where it occurs, and filled with the same elements, but in unique combinations, so that it is alive and wonderful.

Each room is a little different according to the view.

Each garden is different according to its relation to the sun; each path differently placed according to the best route from the street; each stair has a slightly different slope, with different steps, to fit just nicely in between the rooms without a waste of space. . . .

Each tile is set a little differently in the ground, according to the settling of the earth.

Each windowpane is slightly different according to the shrinkage of the wood; each window different according to the view it looks upon; each shelf different according to what it will carry, and how it is placed; each ornament a different color, according to the ornaments and colors round about it; each column with a different capital, according to the moment in the life of the carver who made it; each step worn differently, according to the way that feet move over it; each door a slightly different height and shape according to its position in the frame; each plant a different one according to the angle of the sun, and the position of the wind; each flower box with different flowers in it according to the likes and dislikes of the people inside; each stove made differently, according to the number of the people in the room, and the size of the room; each board cut to fit its position; each nail driven according to the give and shrinkage of the wood.

How was this possible?

How was it possible that any simple farmer could make a house, a thousand times more beautiful than all the struggling architects of the last fifty years could do?

Or—still simpler—how, for instance, could he make

a barn? What is it that an individual farmer did, when he decided to build a barn, that made his barn a member of this family of barns, similar to hundreds of other barns, yet nevertheless unique?

At first sight, we might imagine that each farmer made his barn beautiful, simply by paying attention to its function.

Every barn must have a double door, so that the farmer can drive his hay-wagon right into the barn for unloading; every barn must provide enough hay storage to feed the cows throughout the winter; it must allow the cows to stand in a way that makes it easy to feed them, and easy to move the hay from the place where it is stored to the place where the cows eat; it must provide an easy way of washing down the cow dung and urine which accumulate; it must provide a way of supporting the roof and walls against wind loads. . . .

According to this theory, the farmer is able to make his barn beautiful, because he is so deeply in touch with it function.

But this does not explain the similarity of different barns.

If every new barn were created from scratch, purely from the functional nature of the problem, we should expect to see a much greater variety of forms than actually exists. Why are there no circular barns? Why do some barns not have a double nave, to provide even more storage, or a double pitched roof? It may be true that these kinds of barns would not work as well as the ones which are built; but how could the builders know that, without trying it?

The fact is that they don't try it. They are simply copying the other barns which they already know.

And, indeed, everyone who has ever built anything knows that he goes about it in this way. When you put floor joists at 16″ centers, you don't work out the structural calculations every time you do it; once you are persuaded that this is a good way to build floors, you go on doing it that way, until you have some reason to rethink it.

We might imagine then, that the farmer got his power to build a barn by copying the other barns around him.

Imagine for a moment that the farmer actually had a detailed picture of another barn, or several other barns in his mind, complete down to the last details, and that when he starts to make his own barn, he simply modifies this ideal barn in his mind.

This would certainly explain why one barn looks like other barns in the valley, even where purely functional considerations don't require it.

But this does not explain the great variety of barns.

And it does not explain the enormous variations which the farmer is able to make, in his own barn, without going wrong.

For example, among the old barns in California, I know two which are radically different from the "standard" type. One of them has the same cross section as usual—but it is very very long, about 240 feet—and its main doors, instead of being at the ends, run through it, at right angles to the main axis. The other one is nestled into the slope of a hill, and it has three stories. The two lower stories are just like the normal floors of a barn, but one above the other, and approached from opposite directions.

You can say that these barns are copies too. But, obviously in these cases, the total arrangement of the "typical" barns has not been copied at all. The patterns which are typical of other barns are still present in these two barns; but the way in which the patterns are combined is utterly different.

The proper answer to the question, "How is a farmer able to make a new barn?" lies in the fact that every barn is made of patterns.

It is not the idea of copying which is at fault; only the conception of "what is copied." Obviously the farmer does have some sort of image of a barn in his mind, when he starts to make a new barn. But this image of the barn, which he has in his mind, is not an image like a drawing or a blueprint or a photograph. It is a system of patterns which functions like a language.

178

And the farmer is able to make a new barn, unlike the ones which he has seen before, by taking all the patterns which he knows, for barns, and combining them in a new way.

These patterns are expressed as rules of thumb, which any farmer can combine and re-combine to make an infinite variety of unique barns.

Here are some of the patterns for traditional California barns.

Make a barn in the shape of a rectangle, 30–55 feet wide, 40–250 feet long, the length at least $3x$ feet, where x is the number of cows the barn has to hold. Orient the barn so that its ends connect easily with the paths where cows come in from the fields, and with the local road.

Divide the inside of the barn into three parallel aisles: two cow milking aisles down the outer sides, and a central hay-storage aisle.

Make the central aisle 16–38 feet wide, and the outer aisles 10–16 feet wide. In certain cases, one of the side aisles can be shorter than the central aisle, thus taking a notch out of the rectangle.

Between the outer edge of the central aisle and the two outer aisles, place two rows of columns. The columns are equally spaced, and the distance between the last column and the end wall is equal to the distances between columns. Choose a column spacing between 7 and 17 feet.

If the column spacing is 7–10 feet, make the columns

4 x 4's. If the column spacing is 10–14 feet, make the columns 6 x 6's. If the column spacing is 14–17 feet, make the columns 8 x 8's. The columns are tied together, along the length of the barn, by the main purlins sitting on top of the columns.

Make the roof of the barn a symmetrical pitched roof, and make the pitch over the outer aisles flatter, or equal to, the pitch over the central aisle—so that the pitch will usually break over the main columns along the purlins. Both pitches are between 20 and 40 degrees to the horizontal.

If the length of the barn is less than 150 feet, place the main doors at the ends, roughly on the center line of the central aisle. If the barn is more than 150 feet long, place the main doors in the side walls, roughly halfway along, and let the side aisles be interrupted by the doors.

If the two rows of columns which define the central aisle are more than 18 feet apart, tie them together by horizontal tie beams, all at the same height, and within 3 feet of the tops of the columns.

Make the side walls 7–10 feet high, and the peak of the roof 15–25 feet high.

Frame the side walls by a system of vertical studs, connected by horizontal sill (bottom) and plate (top), and, if you wish, by a middle horizontal member—all these members 2 x 4's.

Place the studs in the side walls to line up with the columns of the central aisle, and place the main rafters in the same planes as the studs and columns, sitting on the plates and purlins which run over these members.

Place rafters from opposite sides of the roof, meeting the main ridge beam.

Brace every corner in the framing of the side walls with a diagonal 2 x 4, about 3 feet long.

Connect the tie beams running across the central aisle to the main columns, by diagonal braces.

Connect the main purlins to the main columns, with diagonal braces 3–4 feet long. If the column spacing is more than about 21 feet also use double braces, the outer ones about 6 feet long.

To understand, in detail, how these patterns work we must extend our definition of "a pattern."

In chapters 4 and 5 we learned to see a pattern as something "in the world"—a unitary pattern of activity and space, which repeats itself over and over again, in any given place, always appearing each time in a slightly different manifestation.

When we ask, now, just where these patterns come from, and also where the variation comes from, which allows each pattern to take on a slightly different form each time that it occurs, we have been led to the idea that these patterns "in the world" are created by us, because we have other, similar patterns in our minds from which we imagine, conceive, create, build, and live these actual patterns in the world.

These patterns in our minds are, more or less, mental images of the patterns in the world: they are abstract representations of the very morphological rules which define the patterns in the world.

However, in one respect they are very different. The patterns in the world merely exist. But the same patterns in our minds are dynamic. They have force. They are generative. They tell us what to do; they tell us how we shall, or may, generate them; and they tell us too, that under certain circumstances, we *must* create them.

Each pattern is a rule which describes what you have to do to generate the entity which it defines.

Consider, for example, the pattern of hillside terracing, used in hilly countries, to make usable farmland on hilly slopes. As a "fact," this pattern merely has certain characteristics. For example: the terraces follow the contour lines; the terraces are spaced vertically at roughly equal intervals; the terrace is formed by a wall, along its outer edge, which keeps the earth from sliding; each of these outer walls rises slightly above the level of the terrace which it retains, so that it also keeps water there, evens out the rainfall, and prevents erosion. All this defines the pattern. These are the relationships which define the pattern "in the world."

Now consider the same pattern "in the farmer's mind." It contains the same information: more detailed probably, less superficial. But it contains, in addition, two other aspects. First, it includes the knowledge which is required to build a system of terraces like this. The fact that the walls are built before the terraces are filled in and leveled; the fact that there are small drain holes in the outer walls; in short, the terracing is described now as a rule. It is a rule which tells the farmer what to do on an existing hillside to transform it into the state which has this pattern in it—in short, to generate the pattern itself, in the world.

And there is an imperative aspect to the pattern. The pattern solves a problem. It is not merely "a" pattern, which one might or might not use on a hillside. It is a *desirable* pattern; and for a person who wants to farm a hillside, and prevent it from erosion, he *must* create this pattern, in order to maintain a stable and healthy world. In this sense, the pattern not only tells him how to create the pattern of terracing, if he wants to; it also tells him that it is essential for him to do so, in certain particular contexts, and that he must create this pattern there.

It is in this sense that the system of patterns forms a language.

When the barn builder applies the patterns for a barn to one another in the proper order, he is able to create a barn. This barn will always have the particular relationships required by the patterns; however, all other sizes, angles, and relationships depend on the needs of the situation, and the whim of the builder. The family of barns produced by this system all share the morphological features specified by the rules (these are the morphological laws we have observed), but beyond that there is literally endless variety.

From a mathematical point of view, the simplest kind of language is a system which contains two sets:

1. A set of elements, or symbols.

2. A set of rules for combining these symbols.

The logical languages are an example. In a logical language, the symbols are completely abstract, the rules are the rules of logical syntax, and the sentences are called well-formed formulas. For instance, such a language might be defined by the set of symbols $*, +, =, x$ and by the rule "The same symbol must never appear twice in a row." In this language, $*+*+*+*+*$ and $*x=*=+=*x$ would be sentences (or well-formed formulas), but $x=x=+**+=$ would not be, because $*$ appears twice in a row.

A natural language like English is a more complex system.

Again, there is a set of elements, in this case the set of words. And again there are rules which describe the possible arrangement of the words. But, there is, in addition, a structure on the words—the complex network of semantic connections, which defines each word in terms of other words, and shows how words are connected to other words.

Take for instance, a very simple sentence like "The tree is standing on the hill." The words here are elements: "The," "tree," "hill" . . . and so on. The elements are combined according to certain rules, which create a sentence. The simplest of these rules are the rules of grammar, which make it clear that the word "to be" must be transformed into "is" in this context; that the word "the" comes before the nouns to which it refers, and so on.

Further, the meaning of the sentence comes from the network of connections among the words which tells us, for example, that a "tree" grows in the "ground" and that a "hill" is a kind of "ground," and that a tree can therefore stand on a hill.

A pattern language is a still more complex system of this kind.

The elements are patterns. There is a structure on the patterns, which describes how each pattern is itself a pattern of other smaller patterns. And there are also rules, embedded in the patterns, which describe the way that they can be created, and the way that they must be arranged with respect to other patterns.

However, in this case, the patterns are both elements and rules, so rules and elements are indistinguishable. The patterns are elements. And each pattern is also a rule, which describes the possible arrangements of the elements —themselves again other patterns.

An ordinary language like English is a system which allows us to create an infinite variety of one-dimensional combinations of words, called sentences.

First of all, it tells us which arrangements of words are legitimate sentences, in a given situation, and which are not. And, furthermore, which arrangements of words make sense in any given situation, and which ones don't. It narrows down the total possible arrangements of words which would make sense in any given situation.

Second, it actually gives us a system which allows us to produce these sentences which make sense. So, it not only defines the sentences which make sense in a given situation; it also gives us the apparatus we need to create these sentences. It is, in other words, a generative system, which allows us to generate sentences that are appropriate to any given situation.

A pattern language is a system which allows its users to create an infinite variety of those three dimensional combinations of patterns which we call buildings, gardens, towns.

First, it defines the limited number of arrangements of spaces that make sense in any given culture. This is a far smaller collection than the total number of arrangements of jumbled nonsense, the piles of bricks and space and air and windows, kitchens on top of freeway interchanges, trees growing upside down inside a railway station—that could be put together, but would make no sense at all.

And second, a pattern language actually gives us the power to generate these coherent arrangements of space. Thus, as in the case of natural languages, the pattern language is *generative*. It not only tells us the rules of arrangement, but shows us how to construct arrangements —as many as we want—which satisfy the rules.

186

In summary: both ordinary languages and pattern languages are finite combinatory systems which allow us to create an infinite variety of unique combinations, appropriate to different circumstances, at will.

Natural Language	*Pattern Language*
Words	Patterns
Rules of grammar and meaning which give connections	Patterns which specify connections between patterns
Sentences	Buildings and places

Here is the outline of a pattern language for a farmhouse in the Bernese Oberland.

NORTH SOUTH AXIS

WEST FACING ENTRANCE DOWN THE SLOPE

TWO FLOORS

HAY LOFT AT THE BACK

BEDROOMS IN FRONT

GARDEN TO THE SOUTH

PITCHED ROOF

HALF-HIPPED END

BALCONY TOWARD THE GARDEN

CARVED ORNAMENTS

Each of these patterns is a field of relationships which can take an infinite variety of specific forms. And, in addition, each one is expressed in the form of a rule, which tells the farmer who is making his house just what to do.

You can see that the variety of possible houses which such a simple system of patterns can create is almost infinite. For instance, here are some houses which it generates.

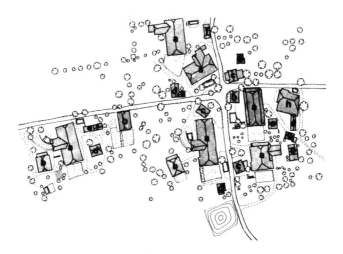

Here is the outline of another simple pattern language for stone houses in the South of Italy.

SQUARE MAIN ROOM, ABOUT 3 METERS

TWO STEP MAIN ENTRANCE

SMALL ROOMS OFF THE MAIN ROOM

ARCH BETWEEN ROOMS

MAIN CONICAL VAULT

SMALL VAULTS WITHIN THE CONE

WHITEWASHED TOP TO THE CONE

FRONT SEAT, WHITEWASHED

This language generates the very simple houses in this drawing:

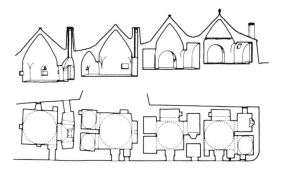

And the more complicated, and less similar houses, in this second drawing:

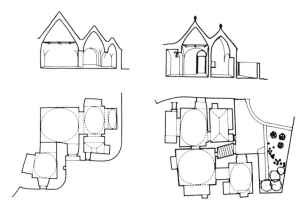

In this case, the pattern language not only helps the people shape their houses, but also helps them shape their streets and town collectively.

For instance, there are further patterns in the language which include:

> NARROW STREETS
>
> STREET BRANCHING

FRONT DOOR TERRACES
CONNECTED BUILDINGS
PUBLIC WELLS AT INTERSECTIONS
STEPS IN THE STREET

These larger patterns create the structure of the town. If every person who makes an individual house, at the same time follows these larger patterns, step by step, and does whatever he can with the layout and placing of his house to help create these larger patterns too, then the town slowly gets its structure from the incremental aggregation of their individual acts.

Each person uses the language a little differently. Each person uses the language to make a building which reflects his dreams, to meet the special needs of his own family, the way they live, the animals they keep, the site, and its relation to the street . . . But overall, throughout the differences, there is a constancy, a harmony, created by the repetition of the underlying patterns.

At this stage, we have defined the concept of a pattern language clearly. We know that it is a finite system of rules which a person can use to generate an infinite variety of different buildings—all members of a family—and that the use of language will allow the people of a village or a town to generate exactly that balance of uniformity and variety which brings a place to life.

In this sense, then, we have found an example of the kind of code which does, at certain times play just the role in buildings and in towns that the genetic code plays in a living organism.

What we do not know yet, is that these kinds of languages are ultimately responsible for every single act of building in the world.

CHAPTER 11

OUR PATTERN LANGUAGES:
CONTINUED

*These pattern languages are not confined
to villages and farm society. All acts of
building are governed by a pattern
language of some sort, and the patterns
in the world are there, entirely because
they are created by the languages which
people use.*

We have seen, so far, that pattern languages were the secret of the farmer's power to build in simple villages.

But languages are more widespread, and more profound than that. The fact is that every work of building, large or small, humble or magnificent, modern or ancient, is made in this same way.

For the use of pattern languages is not merely something that happens in traditional societies. It is a fundamental fact about our human nature, as fundamental as the fact of speech.

For example, our own towns and buildings, just like any others, are all made of patterns, too.

Look around our world. Our world is made of freeways, gas stations, houses, sidewalks, kitchens, buildings, bare concrete walls, flat roofs, front doors, television, parking garages, skyscrapers, elevators, high schools, hospitals, parks, parking places, gutters, trees in concrete boxes, tubs of artificial flowers, neon signs, telephone wires, picture windows, front gardens, back gardens, gilt plastic-framed pictures, motels, supermarkets, hamburger joints, sandwich machines.

The patterns of our time, like all other patterns in the built environment, come from the pattern languages which people use.

For instance, the freeways are built from handbooks, which contain, more or less exactly in the form of patterns, rules which prescribe the optimum spacing of exits, at different densities, the best configurations for the exits under different conditions, the proper curvature and inclination of the petals of a cloverleaf . . . .

And the gas stations built by any one company are often built from a little book, which describes the essential features of, for instance, a "Shell" gas station—and describes how these essential features may be combined differently, in different situations, to provide a gas station which is still one of the family of Shell gas stations, but adapted to a local site.

Indeed, as we shall see now, these patterns always come from languages. They come into the man-made world, because we always put them there—and we put them there by using languages.

Each window, room, house, street and neighborhood, gets those patterns which identify it, which give it its structure, from a language: and each entity within the world is governed, and guided in its development, by an internal pattern language which functions for it, just as the genetic code works for an organism.

Of course, these patterns do not come only from the work of architects or planners.

Architects are responsible for no more than perhaps 5 percent of all the buildings in the world.

Most buildings, streets, shops, offices, rooms, kitchens, cafes, factories, gas stations, freeways, bridges . . .

which give the world its form, come from an entirely different source.

They come from the work of thousands of different people.

They come from the decisions of administrators, hardware storeowners, housewives, the officials in the building department, local bankers, carpenters, public works departments, gardeners, painters, city councils, families . . . .

Each of them builds by following some rules of thumb.

Example: The British government makes the decision to build Stevenage New Town, a town of 50,000 people, 30 miles outside of London. The pattern governing this decision was created by Ebenezer Howard in 1890, and was known to the British Government for 50 years before they used it to build Stevenage.

Example: A group of highway engineers, from the California State Highway Department, locate, and design, a freeway interchange, on Interstate 80, east of San Francisco. They are following patterns which are explicitly laid down in the form of rules, in the AASHO manual: these rules define the optimum spacing of freeway interchanges, most efficient ramp configurations, minimum radii and super-elevations for different design speeds, etc.

Example: A New York architect defines the outer shape

of an office building on Park Avenue. He is confined by law, to make the building envelope conform to the daylight requirements of the building code, and knows before he starts that he will have to create a more or less pyramidal envelope.

Example: A housewife asks her husband to build shelves across the kitchen windows, the way she saw in last month's *House and Garden*. Again, the pattern, which says that shelves across a kitchen window are a good idea in general, is in her mind before her decision to try it in her own kitchen.

Everybody follows rules of thumb.

Example: A man who is fixing the bathroom goes to the local hardware store, and buys an expanding shower curtain rail, which can be force-fitted between the bathroom walls above the bathtub. The fact that this fixture is available on the market, and is the easiest to fix, is the controlling force behind the pattern in his mind which tells him how to place the shower curtain rod.

Example: A small town decides to close off the central street in town, to form a pedestrian precinct. It is probably acting under guidance from architects: and the architects base their advice on a pattern that has been emerging in architectural thought for more than twenty years.

Example: The landscape architect who is called in to do the detailing of the pedestrian precinct, uses brick walks, planters, and benches—all part of the current vernacular for pedestrian precincts, and all in his mind long before he started this particular job.

Example: A bank decides to lend money to one developer, and not to another. The bank bases its decisions on rules of thumb about the density of land coverage which will bring a reasonable financial return. Their patterns tell them not to lend money to people who want to put small buildings on large pieces of land, in central cities.

Example: The Parks Department is thinning the trees in the park. If they are pine trees, they are left spaced at about 15 foot centers; any extra trees are taken out, so that the trees won't stop each other from growing. This spacing for pine trees is a widely known pattern taught in forestry school and used all over the world.

And all these rules of thumb—or patterns—are part of larger systems which are languages.

For, of course, these rules of thumb, which I have given as examples, do not exist, independently, isolated, free-floating.

Each one is part of a system of other rules of thumb, organized, so that the rules of thumb, or patterns, can be used, not only to make isolated decisions, but to create complete things—complete parks, buildings, park benches, freeway interchanges . . . and so on.

Every person has a pattern language in his mind.

Your pattern language is the sum total of *your* knowledge of how to build. The pattern language in your mind is slightly different from the language in the next person's mind; no two are exactly alike; yet many patterns, and fragments of pattern languages, are also shared.

When a person is faced with an act of design, what he does is governed entirely by the pattern language which he has in his mind at that moment. Of course, the pattern languages in each mind are evolving all the time, as each person's experience grows. But at the particular moment he has to make a design, he relies entirely on the pattern language he happens to have accumulated up until that moment. His act of design, whether humble, or gigantically complex, is governed entirely by the patterns he has in his mind at that moment, and his ability to combine these patterns to form a new design.

This is as true of any great creative artist, as of the humblest builder.

Palladio used a pattern language to make his designs. And Frank Lloyd Wright too used a pattern language to make his designs. Palladio happened to record his patterns in books, with the idea that other people could use them too. Wright tried to keep his patterns secret, like a master chef who keeps his recipes secret. But this difference is inessential. What matters is that both of them, and all the other great architects who have ever lived, have had their own pattern languages, the condensation of their own experience, in the form of private rules of thumb, which they could use whenever they began to make a building.

And you yourself make your designs by using a pattern language.

Imagine for a moment that I ask you to lay out a simple cottage for yourself.

Now, let me ask you this: Are the rooms in your cottage circular? Almost certainly not. Most likely you have a rule in your mind which tells you that the rooms in your building should be more or less rough rectangles.

I do not say, for the moment, that this rule is good or bad. I only ask you to recognize that you do have a rule of some kind, which tells you roughly what kind of shape to make the rooms. . . .

And you have many, many rules like this.

Indeed it is the system of these rules that is your present language.

And your creative power is entirely given by the power of these patterns. Your power to create a building is limited entirely by the rules you happen to have in your language now.

At the moment when a person is faced with an act of design, he does not have time to think about it from scratch.

He is faced with the need to act, he has to act fast; and the only way of acting fast is to rely on the various rules of thumb which he has accumulated in his mind. In short, each one of us, no matter how humble, or how elevated, has a vast fabric of rules of thumb, in our minds, which tell us what to do when it comes time to act. At the time of any act of design, all we can hope to do is to use the rules of thumb we have collected, in the best way we know how.

Even when a person seems to "go back to the basic problem," he is still always combining patterns that are already in his mind.

Although he may manage to transform these patterns, slightly, according to a new analysis of the problem, it is still the pattern language in his mind which forms the groundwork of what he does.

You may think: Well, I do not have any kind of pattern language in my mind at present.

There are people who may deny the existence of patterns in their own minds. To such a person I ask a simple question: If you know anything about how to make buildings, what is it that you know?

Your answer may be that you rely on the depths of your emotion and intuition to respond, in a unique fashion, to each new problem that presents itself to you. But even this emotion and intuition is guided by some principles—however deep. Even if you have never tried to make these principles explicit for yourself, and even if you cannot do so, still, somewhere in your mind there are these principles, couched in who knows what form—and it is these principles which come into action, through intuition and emotion, when you make a design.

It is only because a person has a pattern language in his mind, that he can be creative when he builds.

You may be unwilling to admit that your creative power comes from a language in your mind, because you are afraid that the rules of a language in your mind may prevent you from being free and creative. The very opposite is true. A pattern language is the very source of creative power in the individuals who use it, and without a language they could create nothing. It is the language they could create nothing. It is the language which *makes* them creative.

Remember English. It would be ridiculous to say that the rules of English in your head restrict your freedom. When you say something, you say it *in* English; and even though you may sometimes be frustrated by what cannot be said, still, when you speak you have no wish to be free of the rules. In fact, a vast part of what you know is captured in the fabric of these rules—every concept which you understood because you can express it in terms of other concepts is part of the English in your mind.

The rules of English make you creative because they save you from having to bother with meaningless combinations of words.

Most possible combinations of words are mere jumbles

("cat work house tea is," and so on). There are far more of these nonsensical combinations than of the combinations which make sense.

Suppose you had to search in your mind, among all the possible combinations of words every time you wanted to say something—you would never even get to the things you want to say: and you certainly would be unable to say anything that expressed deep feeling or meaning.

The rules of English steer you away from the vast number of nonsensical sentences, and towards the smaller —though still vast—number of sentences which make sense; so that you can pour all your effort into the finer shades of meaning. If it were not for the rules of English, you would spend all your time struggling to say anything at all.

A pattern language does the same.

A pattern language is really nothing more than a precise way of describing someone's experience of building. If a man has a great deal of experience of building houses, his language for houses is rich and complex; if he is a greenhorn, his language is naïve and simple. A poet of houses, a master builder, couldn't possibly work without his language—it would be as if he were a greenhorn.

Again, if you think of all the possible combinations of columns, and studs, and walls, and windows, most of them are meaningless jumbles. The number of meaningless combinations is vastly larger than the number of combinations which make sense as buildings. A man without a language would have to comb his mind to find even one meaningful design among all these meaningless combinations, and he would never even get to the subtleties which make a building work.

So the use of language is not merely something that happens in traditional societies. It is a fundamental fact about our human nature, as fundamental as the fact of speech.

Every creative act relies on language. It is not only those creative acts which are part of a traditional society which rely on language: all creative acts rely on pattern languages: the fumbling inexperienced constructions of a novice are made within the language which he has. The works of idiosyncratic genius are also created within some part of language too. And the most ordinary roads and bridges are all built within a language too.

And now at last it becomes clear just where the patterns in the world come from.

In chapter 5, we saw that every part of the world is given its character, essentially, by a small number of patterns which repeat themselves over and over again. Patterns which repeat to create the floorboards in the floor; patterns which repeat to create the rooftops of a town; patterns which create the overall arrangement of the town which gives one place the character of Paris, and another place the character of London . . .

Where does all this repetition come from? Where does

the order come from? Where does the coherence come from? Where, above all, do the patterns come from, and why are just a few of them repeated over and over again?

We now know the answer to this question.

The patterns, which repeat themselves, come simply from the fact that all the people have a common language, and that each one of them uses this common language when he makes a thing.

Each person has his own version of this common language, no doubt; but, broadly speaking, each person knows the same patterns, and the same patterns therefore keep repeating and repeating and repeating, always with infinite variety, simply because these are the patterns in the language which people use.

Every single part of the environment is governed by some portion of a pattern language.

There are languages for the layout of fields, for the arrangement of the streets, for public squares, for building public buildings, churches, temples, languages for laying out the way that buildings group, for mending walls, for making stairs, for the arrangement of the shops and cafés along the street, and for the way the inside of the shops are going to be made and used. . . .

And the enormous repetition of patterns, which makes up the world, comes about because the languages

*which people use to make the world are widely
shared.*

The millionfold repetition of patterns comes into the
world because a million people share the languages which
have these patterns in them.

All the places that man has ever built, traditional or
newly invented, built a thousand years ago or built today,
designed by architects or laymen, under the influence of
laws or not, by many people or by one person, all of
them get their shape directly from the languages their
builders use.

*At all times, in every human culture, the entities of
which the world is made are always governed by the
pattern languages which people use.*

*Every window, every door, each room, each house,
each garden, every street, each neighborhood, and
every town: it always gets its shape directly from
these languages.*

*They are the origin of all the structure in the man-
made world.*

CHAPTER 12

THE CREATIVE POWER
OF LANGUAGE

*And, beyond that, it is not just the shape
of towns and buildings which comes to
them from pattern languages, it is
their quality as well. Even the life and
beauty of the most awe-inspiring great
religious buildings came from the languages their builders used.*

From chapter 11, we see that pattern languages are responsible for all the ordinary structure of the world.

But pattern languages are still more basic, even than that. It is not just the form of buildings, but their life as well, their beauty as created things, which comes from pattern languages. The patterns are responsible not only for the specific shape a building has, but also for the extent to which the building comes to life.

The life and beauty of the great cathedrals comes from their pattern languages. So does the beauty of the smallest place which comes to life. And the degree to which a building comes to life, and moves us, always hinges on the power of the pattern language which its builders used.

Let us start by seeing how the great cathedrals, Chartres and Notre Dame, were made within a pattern language too.

In one sense, this is obvious. Of course, the rules which formed the great cathedrals were, to some extent, common rules of thumb, which defined the general form of "a" cathedral. Nave, aisles, transepts, east end, west end, tower . . . .

And it was not only the obvious large scale organization which was composed of common patterns. At a smaller scale, there were patterns too. The clustering of columns, the form of the arch, the great rose window in the west, the chapels round the east end, the spacing of the columns, the buttresses and flying buttresses.

Indeed, even the most beautiful details were patterns too. The column capitals, the window tracery, the way the stones within the vaults were cut, the hammer beam roof, the gargoyles on the flying buttresses, the carvings round the doorways, stained glass in the windows, polished stones which made the floor, the carved and inlaid tombs . . . .

Of course, these buildings were not built by lay people.

There were hundreds of people, each making his part within the whole, working, often for generations. At any given moment there was usually one master builder, who directed the overall layout . . . but each person in the whole had, in his mind, the same overall language. Each person executed each detail in the same general way, but with minor differences. The master builder did not need to force the design of the details down the builders' throats, because the builders themselves knew enough of the shared pattern language to make the details correctly, with their own individual flair.

But still the power and beauty of the great cathedrals came mainly from the language which the master builder and his builders shared.

The language was so coherent that anyone who understood this language well and devoted his whole life to the building of a single building, working at it slowly, piecemeal, shaping all the parts within the common language, would be able to make a great work of art.

The building grew slowly, magnificently, from the impact of the common pattern language from which it was made, guiding its individual parts, and the acts which created them, just as the genes inside the flower's seed guide and then generate the flower. . . .

All the great buildings in history have been built like this, by languages.

Chartres, The Alhambra, the mosque at Kairouan, Japanese houses, Brunelleschi's dome . . .

We imagine, because of the distorted view of architecture we have learnt, that some great architect created these buildings, with a few marks of the pencil, worked out laboriously at the drawing board.

The fact is that Chartres, no less than the simple farmhouse, was built by a group of men, acting within a common pattern language, deeply steeped in it of course. It was not made by "design" at the drawing board.

The same process which the simple farmer used to make his house, the same process exactly, was the process which allowed people to generate these greater buildings.

The builders who built the great cathedrals, the great mosques, the palaces, and the Alhambra, used the same language as ordinary people.

The people had a passing knowledge of their language, they built no more than a house or two, and helped to build a public building—they were occupied essentially with something else.

But the builders were those men who spent their whole lives with that same language, deepening it, understanding more about its patterns, practicing, building over and again, until they knew exactly how to realize these patterns best.

You may have a fundamental doubt about the possibility of capturing the deepest architectural knowledge in any "language."

It is, after all, common to say that a great creator has talent which lesser persons do not have, and to assume that the power to create a wonderful building which is full of life, depends simply on this talent.

However, many people will agree that a great architect's creative power, his capacity to make something beautiful, lies in his capacity to observe correctly, and deeply. A painter's talent lies in his capacity to see—he sees more acutely, more precisely, what it is that really matters in a thing, and where its qualities come from. And an architect's power also comes from his capacity to observe the relationships which really matter—the ones which are deep, profound, the ones which do the work.

In this sense, then, a pattern language which is deep is a collection of patterns which correspond to profound observations about what makes a building beautiful.

We have a habit of thinking that the deepest insights, the most mystical, and spiritual insights, are somehow less ordinary than most things—that they are extraordinary.

This is only the shallow refuge of the person who does not yet know what he is doing.

In fact, the opposite is true: the most mystical, most religious, most wonderful—these are not less ordinary than most things—they are more ordinary than most things.

It is because they are so ordinary, indeed, that they strike to the core.

And this is connected to the fact that these things can, indeed, be expressed clearly, discovered, talked about. These deep things which really matter, they are not fragile—they are so solid that they can be talked about, expressed quite clearly. What makes them hard to find is not that they are unusual, strange, hard to express—but on the contrary that they are so ordinary, so utterly basic in the ordinary bread and butter sense—that we never think of looking for them. Let me give two examples: one from the beauty of old prayer rugs, the other from the art of building.

The old Turkish prayer rugs, made two hundred years ago, have the most wonderful colors.

All of the good ones follow this rule: wherever there are two areas of color, side by side, there is a hairline of a different third color, between them. This rule is so simple to state. And yet the rugs which follow this rule have a brilliance, a dance of color. And the ones which do not follow it are somehow flat.

Of course this is not the only rule which makes a rug great—but this one rule, simple, banal, almost as it seems, will triple the brilliance and the beauty of a rug. A person who knows this rule may be able to make a beautiful rug. A person who does not will almost certainly not be able to.

And all the other features of the great old rugs also depend on other rather simple rules. But now most of these rules have been forgotten—and now they can no longer make the great rugs, with their glorious colors.

The depth, and spirituality, of the rug is not made less by the fact that this rule can be expressed, nor that it is so simple. What matters, simply, is that this rule is extremely deep, extremely powerful.

And the light in many glorious rooms is also governed by a simple rule.

Consider the simple rule that every room must have daylight on at least two sides (unless the room is less than 8 feet deep). This has the same character, exactly, as the rule about the colors. Rooms which follow this rule are pleasant to be in; rooms which do not follow it, with a few exceptions, are unpleasant to be in.

Or consider one of the most beautiful small buildings in the world: the shrine at Ise, in Japan.

What is it that makes it beautiful? It is the steepness of the roof, the way the roof beams cut the sky, the walk around the building, the height of the railing, the perfectly smoothed and rounded wooden columns, the brass covers, which protect the open grain at the end of every beam, the brass bolts let into the smoothly polished planks, the spacing of the columns in the walls, the fact that there are columns at the corners, marking space, the gravel path which leads around the building, the position of the steps, which form the entrance, and provide a place to stop . . . .

Again it is the particular patterns there, and the repetition of the patterns, which creates the magic of the building.

For each of these facts about the building is not just a chance event. It is a rule which is repeated over and again; it is followed exactly, and the building varies only in the way permitted by these rules; the rules adapt to different places in the building and create a slightly different version there; but it is above all their repetition, over and again, and the fact that there is almost nothing else which makes the building come to life, and sit, inspiring, and inviting for us. . . .

You may wonder—if the rules are so simple to express—what is there that makes a builder great?

And indeed, there is an answer. Even though the rules are simple, by the time you have twenty, perhaps fifty rules like this in your mind, it takes almost inhuman singleness of purpose to insist on them—not to let go of them.

It is so easy to say—oh well, it is too hard to have light on two sides of this room, and that room—at the same time as all other things we are trying to do. It will be alright if we allow this room to have light on just one side. The fact is that it will not be alright. But to insist, to keep all the rules which matter, freely in your mind, and not to let go of them—that does perhaps require unusual character of purpose.

But of course, the fact that these rules are simple does not mean that they are easy to observe, or easy to invent.

Just as a great artist is one who observes very carefully the things which make the difference—so it does, indeed, take great powers of observation—great depth, great concentration, to formulate these simple rules.

A man who knows how to build has observed hundreds of rooms, and has finally understood the "secret" of making a room with beautiful proportions say. . . . This knowledge exists, in his mind, in the form of a rudimentary pattern, which tells him, under such and such circumstances, create the following field of relationships . . . for such and such reasons. It may have taken years of observation for him finally to understand this rule.

It may be hard to believe that one might make a work of art by simply combining patterns.

It sounds almost as though there was a box of "magic" parts, so powerful, that anyone can make a beautiful thing, simply by combining them.

This is absurd, because, of course, it is not possible to make something beautiful, merely by combining fixed components.

But once again, the difficulty of believing it may have to do with the fact that we tend to think of patterns as "things," and keep forgetting that they are complex, and potent fields.

Each pattern is a field—not fixed, but a bundle of relationships, capable of being different each time that it occurs, yet deep enough to bestow life wherever it occurs.

A collection of these deep patterns, each one a fluid field, capable of being combined, and overlapping in entirely unpredictable ways, and capable of generating an entirely unpredictable system of new and unforeseen relationships.

When we remember this, it may be easier to recognize how powerful they are—and that we do indeed, have our creative power as a result of the system of patterns which we have.

The source of life which you create lies in the power of the language which you have.

If your language is empty, your buildings cannot be full. If your language is poor, you cannot make good buildings until you enrich your language. If your language is rigid, your buildings must be rigid. If your language is florid, your buildings will be florid. Your language generates the buildings which you make, and the buildings live or not, according to the life your language has.

Pattern languages are the source of beauty and of ugliness. They are the source of all creative power: nothing is made without a pattern language in the maker's mind; and what that thing becomes, its depth, or its banality, comes also from the pattern language in the builder's mind.

And now we realize the truly immense power which pattern languages have.

For it is not only true that every building gets its structure from the languages which people use.

It is also true that the spirit which the buildings have, their power, their life, comes from the pattern languages their builders use as well. The beauty of the great cathedrals, the fire in the windows, the touching grace of ornaments, the carving of the columns and the column capitals, the great silence of the empty space which forms the heart of the cathedral . . . all these come from the pattern languages their builders use as well.

CHAPTER 13

THE BREAKDOWN OF LANGUAGE

But in our time the languages have broken down. Since they are no longer shared, the processes which keep them deep have broken down: and it is therefore virtually impossible for anybody, in our time, to make a building live.

We know now that language has the power to bring things to life. The most beautiful houses and villages—the most touching paths and valleys—the most awe inspiring mosques and churches—attained the life they have in them because the languages their builders used were powerful and deep.

But, so far, we have not dealt at all with the conditions under which a language is itself alive; or the conditions under which a language dies.

For all the ugliest and most deadening places in the world are made from patterns as well.

Consider, for example, the language which generated my office at school.

It is an ugly place, terrible, dark and dead. It is one of many similar offices, in the same building: and these offices are generated by the following language:

LONG AND NARROW

DAYLIGHT AT ONE END ONLY

WINDOW THE FULL WIDTH OF THE WALL

CONCRETE WAFFLE CEILING, 5' GRID

FLUORESCENT LIGHTS AT 10' CENTERS

FLAT CONCRETE WALL

UNPAINTED CONCRETE CEILING SURFACE

STEEL WINDOW

PLYWOOD WALL SURFACE

This terrible language has generated hundreds of offices. But the person who has this language in his mind can never make an office live until he abandons this language altogether. There is not a single pattern in this list, except perhaps the fourth, which is not derelict and at odds with the forces actually at work in such a context.

It is therefore obvious that the mere use of pattern languages alone does not ensure that people can make places live.

Some towns and buildings live, and others don't. If all of them are made by pattern languages, there must be some distinction in the content of these languages, and in the way that they are used.

And, indeed, there is a fundamental difference between those societies in which people are able to make their environment alive, and those in which the towns and buildings become dead.

Pattern languages are used in both. But the pattern languages in the two kinds of societies are different. In one case, the pattern languages themselves are somehow alive and help people give life to their surroundings. In the other case, the languages themselves are dead: and with these languages it is only possible for people to make towns and buildings which are dead.

In a town with a living language, the pattern language is so widely shared that everyone can use it.

In agricultural societies everyone knows how to build; everyone builds for himself, and helps his neighbor build.

And in later traditional societies there are bricklayers, carpenters, plumbers—but everyone still knows how to design. For example, in Japan, even fifty years ago, every child learned how to lay out a house, just as children learn football or tennis today. People laid out their houses for themselves, and then asked the local carpenter to build it for them.

When the language is shared, the individual patterns in the language are profound. The patterns are always simple. Nothing which is not simple and direct can survive the slow transmission from person to person. There is nothing in these languages so complex that someone cannot understand it.

Cornerstones for a stone building; a shelf by the window; a seat by the front door; dormer windows; care for a tree; light and shade where we sit; running water in the neighborhood; a brick edge to the water . . .

Just because every detail has to make sense to every man and woman, the patterns are heartfelt, and profound.

The language covers the whole of life.

Every facet of human experience is covered, in one way or another, by the patterns in the language.

The seven ages of man are all covered, and the variety of all possible acts is covered. The entire culture, and the environment which supports it, forms a single unbroken fabric.

The connection between the users and the act of building is direct.

Either the people build for themselves, with their own hands, or else they talk directly to the craftsmen who build for them, with almost the same degree of control over the small details which are built.

The whole emerges by itself and is continually repaired. Each person in a town knows that his own small acts help to create and to maintain the whole. Each person feels tied into society, and proud because of it.

The adaptation between people and buildings is profound.

Each detail has meaning. Each detail is understood. Each detail is based on some person's experience, and gets shaped right, because it is slowly thought out, and deeply felt.

Because the adaptation is detailed and profound, each place takes on a unique character. Slowly, the variety of places and buildings begins to reflect the variety of human situations in the town. This is what makes the town alive. The patterns stay alive, because the people who are using them are also testing them.

But, by contrast, in the early phases of industrial society which we have experienced recently, the pattern languages die.

Instead of being widely shared, the pattern languages

231

which determine how a town gets made become specialized and private. Roads are built by highway engineers; buildings by architects; parks by planners; hospitals by hospital consultants; schools by educational specialists; gardens by gardeners; tract housing by developers.

The people of the town themselves know hardly any of the languages which these specialists use. And if they want to find out what these languages contain, they can't, because it is considered professional expertise. The professionals guard their language jealously to make themselves indispensable.

Even within any one profession, professional jealousy keeps people from sharing their pattern languages. Architects, like chefs, jealously guard their recipes, so that they can maintain a unique style to sell.

The languages start out by being specialized, and hidden from the people; and then within the specialities, the languages become more private still, and hidden from one another, and fragmented.

Most people believe themselves incompetent to design anything and believe that it can only be done properly by architects and planners.

This has gone so far that most people shrink, in fear, from the task of designing their surroundings. They are afraid that they will make foolish mistakes, afraid that people will laugh at them, afraid that they will do something "in bad taste." And the fear is justified. Once people withdraw from the normal everyday experience of

building, and lose their pattern languages, they are literally no longer able to make good decisions about their
surroundings, because they no longer know what really
matters, and what doesn't.

*People lose touch with their most elementary intui-
tions.*

If they read somewhere that large plate glass picture
windows are a good idea, they accept this as wisdom from
a source wiser than themselves—even though they feel
more comfortable sitting in a room with small windowpanes, and say how much they like it. But the fashionable
taste of architects is so persuasive that people will believe, against the evidence of their own inner feelings,
that the plate glass window is better. They have lost confidence in their own judgment. They have handed over
the right to design, and lost their own pattern languages
so utterly that they will do anything which architects tell
them.

Yet, architects themselves, have lost their intuitions too.
Since they no longer have a widely shared language which
roots them in the ordinary feelings people have, they are
also prisoners of the absurd and special languages which
they have made in private.

*Even the buildings built by architects start to be full
of obvious "mistakes."*

The recently built College of Environmental Design at the University of California, Berkeley, was designed by three well-known architects. In a certain part of this building, at the end of each floor, there are two seminar rooms. These seminar rooms are long and narrow; one of the short walls is filled by a window; the blackboard is mounted along one of the long walls; each room is filled by a long narrow table. These rooms are functionally defective in a number of obvious ways. First of all, a long narrow table, and the long narrow group of people which form around it, are not suitable for intense discussion; this is a seminar room—it should be more nearly square. Second, the position of the blackboard with respect to the window means that half of the people in the room see the window reflected on the blackboard, and can't read what is written there—the blackboard should be opposite the window. Third, because the window is so large, and so low, the people who sit near it appear silhouetted to those who are sitting further away. It is extremely difficult to talk properly with someone seen in silhouette—too many of the subtle expressions of the face get lost. Seminar communication suffers. The window should be above the height of a sitting person's head.

Specific patterns, like, for instance, the LIGHT ON TWO SIDES *pattern, vanish from people's knowledge about building.*

At one time it would have been unthinkable to build any

room, except a stable or a workshed, without windows on two sides. In our own time, all knowledge of this pattern is forgotten. Most rooms, in most buildings, have light from one side only. And even a "great" architect like Le Corbusier, builds whole apartments, long and narrow, with windows only at the narrow end—as he did in the Marseilles apartments block—with terrible glare and discomfort as results.

There is not a single building built in recent times, nor a single part of a city laid out by planners, in which such trivial mistakes—caused by the loss of patterns—cannot be described a hundredfold. This is as true of the greatest works of so-called modern masters, as of the most mundane works built by tract developers.

And those few patterns which do remain within our languages becomes degenerate and stupid.

This follows naturally from the fact that the languages are so highly specialized. The users, whose direct experience once formed the languages, no longer have enough contact to influence them. This is almost bound to happen, as soon as the task of building passes out of the hands of the people who are most directly concerned, and into the hands of people who are not doing it for themselves, but instead for others.

So long as I build for myself, the patterns I use will be simple, and human, and full of feeling, because I understand my situation. But as soon as a few people begin to build for "the many," their patterns about what is needed become abstract; no matter how well meaning they are,

235

their ideas gradually get out of touch with reality, because they are not faced daily with the living examples of what the patterns say.

If I build a fireplace for myself, it is natural for me to make a place to put the wood, a corner to sit in, a mantel wide enough to put things on, an opening which lets the fire draw.

But, if I design fireplaces for other people—not for myself—then I never have to build a fire in the fireplaces I design. Gradually my ideas become more and more influenced by style, and shape, and crazy notions—my feeling for the simple business of making fire leaves the fireplace altogether.

So, it is inevitable that as the work of building passes into the hands of specialists, the patterns which they use become more and more banal, more willful, and less anchored in reality.

Of course, even now a town still gets its shape from pattern languages of a sort.

The architects and planners and bankers have pattern languages which tell them to build gigantic steel and concrete buildings. The users have a few shattered patterns left in their vocabulary: a sheet of plastic to make a kitchen counter; huge plate glass windows for the living room; wall-to-wall carpet in the bathroom—and they enthusiastically piece these patches together, whenever they have a free weekend.

But these remnants of our former languages are dead and empty.

They are based mainly on the by-products of industry. People use plate glass windows, formica counters, wall-to-wall carpet, because industry makes them available, not because these patterns contain anything essential about life, or how to live it.

The time when a pattern language was a song, in which people could sing the whole of life, is gone. The pattern languages in society are dead. They are ashes and fragments in the people's hands.

As the pattern languages die, everyone can see the chaos which emerges in our towns and buildings.

But the people do not know that it is the pattern languages which cause it. They know that buildings are less human than they used to be. They are willing to pay great prices for old buildings which were made at a time when people still knew how to make them human. They complain bitterly about the lack of life, the danger, the merciless inhuman quality of their environment. But they do not know what to do about it.

In panic, people try to replace the lost order of the organic process, by artificial forms of order based on control.

Since the natural processes of building towns no longer work, in panic, people look for ways of "controlling" the design of towns and buildings. Those architects and planners who have become concerned by the insignificance of their influence on the environment make three kinds of efforts to gain "total design" control of the environment:

1. They try to control larger pieces of the environment (this is called urban design).
2. They try to control more pieces of the environment (this is called mass production or system-building).
3. They try to control the environment more firmly, by passing laws (this is called planning control).

But this makes things still worse.

These totalitarian efforts, although they do control more of the environment, have exactly the wrong effect. They cannot create a whole environment, because they are not sufficiently responsive to the real needs, forces, demands, problems, of the people involved. Instead of making the environment more whole, they make it less whole.

At this stage, the pattern languages become still more fragmented, and more dead. They are controlled by even fewer people; they have even less of the living connection with the people which they need.

The variety, once created by organic and natural processes, disappears altogether.

238

Experts try to make towns and buildings which are adapted to people's needs, but they are always trivial. They can only deal with general forces, which are common to all men, and never with the particular forces that make one particular man unique and human.

Adaptation of buildings to people becomes impossible.

Even when experts make buildings which are "adaptable," to solve this problem, the result is still trivial, because the unique particulars are still subservient to the common generalities. Huge machine-like buildings which allow people to move the walls around, so that they can express themselves, still make them subject to the "system."

And, finally, people lose their ability to make life altogether.

Once the common language has been broken down, the individual languages which, in a living culture, are always private versions of the common language, are also broken down.

And not only that. It even becomes impossible for people to create, or re-create, new private languages, because the absence of a common language means that they lack the core of fundamental stuff they need to form a living language for themselves.

At this stage, people can no longer even make a window or a door which is beautiful.

It must be obvious from all of this, that a town cannot become alive without a living language in it.

It is impossible, utterly impossible, to make a building or a town which is alive by control from above. And it is impossible for the people to make the town for themselves with the ashes of the dead language which they now have.

The fact is, that the creation of a town, and the creation of the individual buildings in a town, is fundamentally a genetic process.

No amount of planning or design can replace this genetic process.

And no amount of personal genius can replace it either.

Our emphasis on objects, has blinded us to the essential fact that it is above all the genetic process which creates our buildings and our towns, that it is above all this genetic process which must be in good order . . . and that this genetic process can only be in good order, when the language which controls it, is widely used, and widely shared.

People need a living language, in order to make buildings for themselves. But the language needs the people too . . . so that its constant use, and feedback, keeps its patterns in good order.

And this conclusion, simple though it is, calls for a shattering revision of our attitude to architecture and planning.

In the past, each act of planning or design was thought of as a self-contained, and original, response to the demands of a local situation. Architects and planners assumed, implicitly, that the structure of the town is generated by the accumulation of these self-contained acts.

The picture which our arguments have led us to is radically different. According to this view, there are underlying languages which already contain most of the structure that will appear in the environment. The acts of design which have been thought of as central are acts which *use* the structure already present in these underlying languages to generate the structure of specific buildings.

In this view, it is the structure of the underlying language which is doing most of the hard work. If you want to influence the structure of your town, you must help to change the underlying languages. It is useless to be innovative in an individual building, or an individual plan, if this innovation does not become part of a living pattern language which everyone can use.

And we may conclude, even more strongly, that the central task of "architecture" is the creation of a single, shared, evolving, pattern language, which everyone contributes to, and everyone can use.

So long as the people of society are separated from the language which is being used to shape their buildings, the buildings cannot be alive.

If we want a language which is deep and powerful, we can only have it under conditions where thousands of people are using the same language, exploring it, making it deeper all the time.

And this can only happen when the languages are shared.

In the next four chapters, we shall see how it is possible to share our language, and to make it living once again.

CHAPTER 14

PATTERNS WHICH CAN BE SHARED

*To work our way toward a shared and
living language once again, we must first
learn how to discover patterns which are
deep, and capable of generating life.*

If we hope to bring our towns and buildings back to life, we must begin to re-create our languages, in such a way that all of us can use them: with the patterns in them so intense, so full of life again, that what we make within these languages will, almost of its own accord, begin to sing.

To start with this requires simply that we find a way of talking about patterns, in a way that can be shared.

How can this be done? In a traditional culture, these patterns exist as independent entities within your mind, but it is not necessary for you to recognize them as separate atomic units, nor to know them by name, nor to be able to speak about them. It is no more necessary than it is for you to be able to describe the rules of grammar in the language which you speak.

However, in a period when languages are no longer widely shared, when people have been robbed of their intuitions by specialists, when they no longer even know the simplest patterns that were once implicit in their habits, it becomes necessary to make patterns explicit, precisely and scientifically, so that they can be shared in a new way— explicitly, instead of implicitly—and discussed in public.

In order to make patterns explicit, so that they can be shared in this new way, we must first of all review the very complex structure of a pattern.

Throughout this book we have had a gradual awakening,

a growing understanding of what a pattern is. This awakening began, in chapters 4 and 5, where the concept was first defined; the concept was then extended and refined, in chapter 6 and then again in chapters 10, 11 and 12.

I shall now describe the structure of a single pattern precisely, in a way that includes all the properties which living patterns have to have, as they have been discussed in all these chapters.

Each pattern is a three-part rule, which expresses a relation between a certain context, a problem, and a solution.

As an element in the world, each pattern is a relationship between a certain context, a certain system of forces which occurs repeatedly in that context, and a certain spatial configuration which allows these forces to resolve themselves.

As an element of language, a pattern is an instruction, which shows how this spatial configuration can be used, over and over again, to resolve the given system of forces, wherever the context makes it relevant.

The pattern is, in short, at the same time a thing, which happens in the world, and the rule which tells us how to create that thing, and when we must create it. It is both a process and a thing; both a description of a thing which is alive, and a description of the process which will generate that thing.

Patterns can exist at all scales.

247

Patterns can be stated equally well for the human details of buildings, the overall layout of a building, ecology, large-scale social aspects of urban planning, regional economics, structural engineering, details of building construction.

For example, the distribution of subcultures in a region, the layout of major roads, the organization of work groups in an industry, the arrangement of trees at the edge of a forest, the design of a window, the planting of flowers in a garden, the layout of a sitting room, might all be specified by patterns.

And a pattern may deal with almost any kind of forces. (All the following patterns are defined in Volume 2 of this series).

ENTRANCE TRANSITION resolves a conflict among inner psychic forces.

MOSAIC OF SUBCULTURES resolves a conflict among social and psychological forces.

WEB OF SHOPPING resolves a conflict among economic forces.

EFFICIENT STRUCTURE resolves a conflict among structural forces.

GARDEN GROWING WILD resolves the conflict between forces of nature, the natural growing process in plants, and people's natural actions in a garden.

WEB OF TRANSPORTATION resolves forces which lie partly in the field of human need, and partly in the politics of public agencies.

STILL WATER resolves conflicts among forces which are

partly ecological, and partly in the realm of human fear and danger.

COLUMNS AT THE CORNERS resolves conflicts among forces which arise within the process of construction.

WINDOW PLACE resolves forces which are purely psychological.

To make a pattern explicit, we merely have to make the inner structure of the pattern clear.

Let us start with a very simple commonsense example. Suppose that we are in a place. We have a general sense that something is "right" there; something is working; something feels good; and we want to identify this "something" concretely so that we can share it with someone else, and use it over and over again.

What do we have to do? As we shall now see, there are always three essential things we must identify.

What, exactly, is this something?

Why, exactly, is this something helping to make the place alive?

And *when*, or *where*, exactly, will this pattern work?

We must first define some physical feature of the place, which seems worth abstracting.

Take, for the sake of an example, Ostenfeldgaarden—a beautiful old Danish house built in 1685, now in the Copenhagen Open Air Museum. As soon as I went there, I knew that it had special qualities which would be useful even today, if I could only pin them down. How

is it possible to pin them down—in a way that is precise
enough to use over and over again?

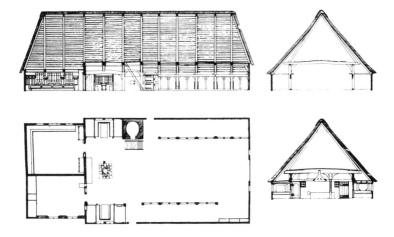

Suppose for the sake of argument, I start with features
like "coziness" or "spaciousness." These features are
no doubt there. But they are not directly usable. Even if
I try to pin down the idea of coziness further, by saying
that the form of the house somehow ties the family together, and that this is what makes it cozy, this is still not
clear enough to copy in another house. Until I have
identified particular spatial relationships which help to
create this quality at Ostenfeldgaarden, I have still not
managed to identify anything which I can use directly in
another house.

Suppose, then, in an effort to be more concrete, I seize
on a particular spatial relation: the fact that there are
alcoves round the edge of the main room, that the al-

coves have seats in them, that each one is big enough to hold one or two members of the family, and that they both open into the common living room. It is complex, but fairly well defined. It identifies certain parts (living room, alcoves, seats) and specifies a spatial relation between these parts.

This pattern is well defined. If you were designing a house, you could incorporate this pattern in the design directly. You could explain the idea to a third person and he could decide, by looking at any house plan, whether or not it had this feature. So far so good. But even so this pattern still wouldn't be sharable. For it to be sharable, we have to be able to criticize it. And to criticize it, we have to know its functional purpose.

Next, we must define the problem, or the field of forces which this pattern brings into balance.

Why is it a good idea? What is the problem which is solved by putting alcoves around a room? In answer to this question, I might propose something like: Living rooms *without* alcoves don't work, for the following reasons: the members of a family like to be together; but, in the evenings and on weekends, when they could be, each one follows up his personal hobbies—sewing, homework . . . . Because these things are messy, and often need to be left standing, people cannot do them in the living room—the living room is a place which mustn't get too messy, since visitors might come at any moment, and it must be a suitable place to receive them. Instead the various members of the family go off to their own private areas to do these things—the kitchen, the bedroom, the basement—and the family cannot be together.

There are three forces at work here:

1. Each person in the family has his own private hobbies—sewing, carpentry, model-building, homework. These activities being what they are, things often need to be left lying about. People therefore tend to do them somewhere where things can be left lying safely.

2. Communal places in the house have to be kept tidy, partly on account of visitors, and partly also so that no one person or thing encroaches too heavily on the comfort and convenience of the whole family.

3. The people in the family would like to be together while they are doing these different things.

In an ordinary house, with an ordinary living room, these three forces are mutually incompatible. The alcove brings them into resolution.

Finally, we must define the range of contexts where this system of forces exists and where this pattern of physical relationships will indeed actually bring it into balance.

By now the pattern is clear and sharable. But one question is still open. Where exactly does this pattern make sense? Does it make sense in an igloo? Hardly. Does it make sense in the living room of a cottage where a single person lives alone? Obviously not. When exactly does it make sense?

To make the pattern really useful, we must define the exact range of contexts where the stated problem occurs, and where this particular solution to the problem is appropriate.

In this case, we should have to define the fact that the pattern applies to the living rooms of all dwellings for large families in the United States and Western Europe (perhaps in other cultures, too—depending on specific local habits and life styles). Further, if a dwelling has more than one "living room" in it—like some English houses which have a front parlor and a back parlor— then the alcove idea would not apply to both these living rooms—only to the one where the family spends most of its time.

We see, in summary, that every pattern we define must be formulated in the form of a rule which establishes a relationship between a context, a system of forces which arises in that context, and a configuration which allows these forces to resolve themselves in that context.

It has the following generic form:

Context → System of forces → Configuration.
And, in the previous case, the following specific content:

Communal → Conflicts between → Alcove opening
    rooms   privacy and   off communal
                 community   room.

Every living pattern is a rule of just this kind.

And because it includes the context, each pattern is a self-contained logical system which makes a double statement of fact, not merely a declaration of value, and is therefore capable of being true or not. It says, first, that the given problem (the stated conflict among forces) exists within the stated range of contexts. This is an empirical statement, which can be true or false. And it says, second, that in the given context, the given solution solves this given problem —again an empirical statement, which can again be true or false.

The statement that the pattern is alive, is thus not a matter of taste, or culture, or point of view. It establishes, instead, a definite empirical relationship between a limited context, a set of forces which occurs there, and the pattern which resolves those forces.

In order to discover patterns which are alive we must always start with observation.

The discovery of a pattern which lives is not different from the discovery of any profound thing. It is a slow, deliberate process, tentative, in which we seek to discover something profound, and where we recognize that we shall usually be wrong to start with, and that we may only approach a proper formulation slowly.

Let us take the case of entrances, as an example.

Start by walking around, looking at house entrances,

paying attention to whether they feel right to you or not, whether they feel comfortable, alive . . . .

Put the entrances in two classes: those in which the process of entering feels good, and those in which it doesn't.

Now try to discover some property which is common to all the ones which feel good, and missing from all the ones which don't feel good.

Of course, you won't be able to do this perfectly. One entrance may not feel good, but be beautiful in some entirely different way; however, with all the imperfections of experiment, come as near as you can to defining some property which all the good ones have, and which all the bad ones lack: in short, look for the criterial property which makes the difference.

This property will be a highly complex relationship.

It will not be simple, like "all the good ones are blue, all the bad ones are not blue." In the case of the entrance, for instance, it turns out, in my experience, that all the good ones have an actual place, between the road and the front door, a place in which there is a change of surface; change of view; perhaps a change of level; perhaps you pass under a branch, or hanging rose, there is often a change of direction, and there is above all this actual place, halfway between the two, so that you pass first from the street to this place, and then again from this

255

place to the front door. Very often, in the best cases, this place has a glimpse of a distant view—of something which you cannot see from the street, nor from the door, but see only for an instant in between the two. Or sometimes it is more mundane than that. In a typical London house, there is just a short platform, raised a couple of steps, marked by its railing, a place to pause. It is rudimentary; perhaps too sparse; but in this very restricted and dense situation, at least it does a little of the work.

Now try to identify the problem which exists in entrances which lack this property.

To do this, we must try to make explicit just which forces are at work; and we must formulate the pattern in terms which make it clear just why it helps resolve some system of forces that cannot be resolved without it.

If we ask ourselves why entrance transitions are important, we recognize that they create some kind of "in between," a breathing space between the outside and the inside—a place of preparation, where a person can change his frame of mind, and adapt to the different conditions: from the loud, noisy, public, vulnerable, exposed feeling of the street, to the private, quiet, intimate, protected feeling of indoors.

If we try to formulate the forces governing this transition precisely, we see that they shed a great deal of light on the invariant which makes transitions function.

For example, there is evidence that this "cleaning" of

the street mask happens when a person passes through a
zone which is different to the senses, and discontinuous,
from the street.

*Knowledge of the problem then helps shed light on
the invariant which solves the problem.*

If, indeed, there are forces like this at work, we can
deduce that the kind of transitions which will work best
are those where many different sensual qualities change
during the passage from outside to inside: a change of
view, a change of surface underfoot, a change of light, a
change of sound, a change of height or level, steps, a
change of smell—a hanging jasmine . . . .

If we then take this, the product of our inferences
which can be built out of the statement of the problem,
and look at some more entrances, with this in mind, our
capacity to distinguish entrances which work from those
which don't gets sharper.

The statement of the problem and the forces helps us
to sharpen the pattern which is responsible for making
the system of forces come to equilibrium.

The process of observation does not proceed in linear
fashion from the problem to the solution, nor from the
solution to the problem . . . it is a global process, in
which, by any means we can, looking at the matter from
all directions at once, we try to identify a solid and
reliable invariant, which relates context, problem, and
solution, in an unchanging way.

Sometimes we find our way to this invariant by starting with a set of positive examples.

That is what we have been doing in the case of the alcoves, and in the case of the entrances. In each of these cases we manage to identify an essential feature of a number of places which make us feel good.

At other times, we may discover the invariant by starting from the negative examples, and resolving them.

For instance: The problem of gloom and shade. I notice, let's say, that the northside of my house is dank and dark, and no one ever seems to go there, or use it for anything.

I wonder what I can do about it.

I look around, and find that those outdoor areas to the immediate north of buildings often seem to be disarrayed, not working, falling apart.

Then I start looking for those places which don't have any land around them like that. I realize that it happens whenever houses, buildings, manage to be to the north of the land they sit on, with the open land left to the south, so that it gets the sun.

I do an experiment to find out if my intuitions are born out by careful observation.

We ask people where they sit outside, around their houses, and where they never sit. In 19 cases out of 20, the place they sit is to the south of the house, and next to it; the places where they never sit are all to the north.

And so we formulate the pattern, SOUTH FACING OUT-DOORS.

The positive and negative approaches to finding patterns are always complementary—not exclusive. The alcove which started as an abstraction from something positive, might just as well have started with an analysis of what is wrong in modern living rooms.

The south facing open space, which started as a solution to something negative—the dark and unused character of northern space—also is inspired, of course, by the wonder and warmth of sunny lawns and terraces which do face south.

And occasionally, we do not start from concrete observation at all, but build up the invariant by purely abstract argument.

For of course, the discovery of patterns is not always historical. Some of the examples I have given might make it seem as though the only way to find patterns is to get them from observation. This would imply that it was impossible to find patterns which do not already exist in the world already: and would therefore imply a claustrophobic conservatism; since no patterns which do not already exist could ever be discovered. The real situation is quite different. A pattern is a discovery in the sense that it is a discovery of a relationship between context, forces, and relationships in space, which holds absolutely. This discovery can be made on a purely theoretical level.

For example, the pattern PARALLEL STREETS was discovered by purely mathematical reasoning, based on the forces which connect high speed vehicular movement to the needs of pedestrians, the problem of accidents, the huge travel time, the very slow average speeds, etc. At the time we discovered it, we were unaware that it actually was an emerging pattern in the world of the 1960s— and only later realized that separated parallel arteries, without cross streets, was emerging as a pattern in several major cities.

In this same sense, it was possible to "discover" uranium, by postulating the existence of a chemical element with certain properties, before it had actually been observed.

In all these cases, no matter what method is used, the pattern is an attempt to discover some invariant feature, which distinguishes good places from bad places with respect to some particular system of forces.

It tries to capture just that essence—that field of relationships—which is common to all possible solutions to the stated problem, in the stated context. It is the invariant behind the huge variety of forms which solve the problem. There are millions of particular solutions to any given problem; but it may be possible to find some one property which will be common to all these solutions. That is what a pattern tries to do.

Many people say they don't like the fact that a pattern gives "one solution" to a problem. This is a serious misunderstanding. Of course, there are thousands, millions, in fact, an infinite number of solutions to any given problem. There is, of course, no way of capturing the details of all these solutions in a single statement. It is always up to the creative imagination of the designer to find a new solution to the problem, which fits his particular situation.

But when it is properly expressed, a pattern defines an invariant field which captures all the possible solutions to the problem given, in the stated range of contexts.

The task of finding, or discovering, such an invariant field is immensely hard. It is at least as hard as anything in theoretical physics.

My experience has shown that many people find it hard to make their design ideas precise. They are willing to express their ideas in loose, general, terms, but are unwilling to express them with the precision needed to make them into patterns. Above all, they are unwilling to express them as abstract spatial relations among well-defined spatial parts. I have also found that people aren't always very good at it; it is hard to do.

It is easy to say that a house entrance should have a sort of mysterious quality, which both hides the house from the public domain, and also exposes it to the public domain.

Argument about the statement is imprecise. Architects have been doing a great deal of woolly thinking of this sort. It is a kind of refuge. If I say, instead, that the front door must be at least 20 feet from the street, that it should be visible, that windows from the house should look onto the area in front of the house, but that it should not be possible to see into these windows from the street, that a change of surface is required during the transition, that the person arriving should enter a domain of a character as different as possible from either of the two domains inside the house or on the street, and that he should have a glimpse of some view which lies entirely hidden from the street—then these statements can be challenged, because they are precise.

But it is very hard to be precise.

Even once you are determined to do it it is terribly hard to make precise statements which really get to the heart of the matter. Every observation, like the one about the mystery of house entrances which I have just made, starts with intuition. The task of identifying just precisely those relations that are at the heart of such an intuition, is no easier in architecture than it is in physics, or biology, or mathematics. Making abstractions which are powerful and deep is an art. It requires tremendous ability to go to the heart of things, and get at the really deep abstraction. No one can tell you how to do it in science. No one can tell you how to do it in design.

And it is especially hard to be precise, because there is never any one formulation of the pattern which is perfectly exact.

It is easy to understand this, when we recognize how limited we are in our mathematical ability even to express simple patterns in precise terms.

Take, for example, the idea of a "rough circle." If I ask you to point to things which are rough circles, you can do it easily. But if I ask you to define precisely, what we mean by a rough circle, it turns out to be very hard to do. The strict mathematical definition of a circle (points exactly equidistant from a point center), is much too narrow. None of the rough circles in nature follow this rule exactly. On the other hand a looser definition (points between nine and ten inches from some given point, for instance), is much too loose. It would include, for instance, a weird zigzagging structure, in which no two points of the "circumference" are near each other. Yet even a rough circle has some kind of continuity along its circumference.

To capture "rough circles" exactly, we must find a formulation which just falls between being too narrow and too loose. But this turns out to be a deep, and difficult mathematical problem.

And if a simple circle, which any child can draw with his finger in the dust, is so hard to pin down, it is easy to see that a complex invariant like "entrance transition," is almost impossibly difficult to pin down precisely.

Instead, to strike the balance between being too narrow and too loose, you must express and visualize a pattern as a kind of fluid image, a morphological feeling, a swirling intuition about form, which captures the invariant field which is the pattern.

The pattern ENTRANCE TRANSITION deals with the fact

that people on the street are in a public frame of mind, and need to pass through a zone where they can take this frame of mind off, before they enter into the kind of personal intimacy or closeness typical in a house.

As we have seen, there is evidence that this "cleaning" of the street mask happens when a person passes through a zone which is different to the senses, and discontinuous, from the street. So at one time the pattern was formulated as: "Make a path between the street and the front door of the house; pass through a transition zone where it changes direction, changes level, changes surface, has a change of view, and a change of light quality."

For some houses (e.g., in a California suburb) this phrasing is perfectly exact. But, at higher densities, when there are no front gardens, and the front door on the street allows people to stand in doorways, in touch with the street, the transition cannot be between the front door and the street.

In a case like this, the transition can be handled perfectly well *inside*. For example, in our Peru houses, we made a court, inside the front door, with the main living areas surrounding this court, and opening off it. To pass into the house, a person first passes through the front door, then under the darkness of the entry way, then into the light of the patio, then into the cool of the veranda which connects the family room and sala. This is the traditional Spanish solution: and, of course, it does contain the ENTRANCE TRANSITION pattern.

But, as you can see, it does not follow the letter of

the pattern, *as stated above:* the transition isn't between the street and the front door—it is inside the front door. To make sense of the design, it was necessary to follow the spirit of the pattern, not the letter.

What is really happening, is that there is a feeling for a certain kind of morphology, which is geometrical in character, but which is a feeling, not a precisely statable mathematically precise relationship.

A pulsating, fluid, but nonetheless definite entity swims in your mind's eye. It is a geometrical image, it is far more than the knowledge of the problem; it is the knowledge of the problem, coupled with the knowledge of the kinds of geometrics which will solve the problem, and coupled with the feeling which is created by that kind of geometry solving that problem. It is above all, a feeling— a morphological feeling. This morphological feeling, which cannot be exactly stated, but can only be crudely hinted at by any one precise formulation, is the heart of every pattern.

Then, once you discover a fluid field of relationships like this, you must redefine it, as an entity, to make it operational.

It is only when you do this that it becomes useful operational instruction—because you can now tell a person to build "one of those."

Remember that our patterns are the building blocks in terms of which we see the world. Kitchen, sidewalk, high-rise office building—these are the patterns of our time—and our world is made of them. New patterns must be the new building blocks with which we wish to build; and the mental building blocks with which we want to see the world.

Again, consider the ENTRANCE TRANSITION. The original discovery shows that it is necessary for a person to experience many different changes of light, surface, direction, view, and sound when he enters a house, so that the house is sufficiently separated from the public quality of the street. This can be expressed as a property of the path from the street to the door. We can say that this path must have certain properties. But at this state the insight is not yet properly formulated as a pattern.

To make it a pattern, I have to ask myself: What new entity do I want to put in the world, to create these properties?

What entity sums up and captures the field of relationships which these properties define? The answer is, an entity which is an actual space, *"the transition,"* where the light and color and view and sound and surface change.

Of course, we know that this "thing" I now call *"the transition"* is really nothing but a fiction: because what seems to be a thing is entirely defined by its field of relations anyway. But there is some quality of the human mind which requires that this field be treated as a thing, in order for it to be understood, and made, and used as part of a language.

We must make each pattern a thing so that the human mind can use it easily and so that it may take its part among the other patterns of our pattern languages.

For the same reason you must be able to draw it.

If you can't draw a diagram of it, it isn't a pattern. If you think you have a pattern, you must be able to draw a diagram of it. This is a crude, but vital rule. A pattern defines a field of spatial relations, and it must therefore always be possible to draw a diagram for every pattern. In the diagram, each part will appear as a labeled or colored zone, and the layout of the parts expresses the relation which the pattern specifies. If you can't draw it, it isn't a pattern.

And finally, for the same reason too, you must give it a name.

The search for a name is a fundamental part of the process of inventing or discovering a pattern. So long as a pattern has a weak name, it means that it is not a clear concept, and you cannot clearly tell me to make "one."

Suppose that I am in the process of discovering the entrance transition pattern. Let us say that I am dimly aware of the need for some kind of change, between street and house: that sensory changes help to create this change of attitude. Perhaps, to begin with, I call the pattern ENTRY PROCESS. I hope that the name entry process will explain this fact to you. But actually, you do not know how to create this change of feeling. Entry process is still too vague.

Now suppose I call the pattern HOUSE STREET RELATIONSHIP. At this stage, I am aware that it is the concrete geometry which will create the transition. I am aware that some kind of relationship is needed. But I still don't know what the relationship is.

Now suppose I change the name to FRONT DOOR INDIRECTLY REACHED FROM STREET. This specifies a particular relationship, which I can actually build into a design. But it is still a relationship. It is still hard for me to be sure that it is present, or missing, from a design.

So finally, I call it ENTRANCE TRANSITION, with the idea that the transition is an actual place, between the street and the house, with certain definite characteristics. Now I can simply ask myself, Have I built an ENTRANCE TRANSITION into my design? I can answer at once. If I tell you to build an ENTRANCE TRANSITION, you know exactly what to do, and you can do it.

It is concrete, and easy to do. And it is more accurate. Finally, I understand fully what the problem is, and know what to do about it.

At this stage, the pattern is clearly sharable.

People can discuss it, reuse it themselves, improve it, check the observations out for themselves, decide for themselves whether they want to use the pattern in a particular building which they are making. . . .

And, perhaps even more important, the pattern is open enough to become empirically vulnerable.

We can ask ourselves: Is it true that this system of forces actually does occur, within the stated context?

Is it true that the actual solution, as formulated, really does resolve this field of forces in all cases?

Is it true that the precise formulation of the solution is actually necessary: that any entrance which lacks this feature must inevitably have unresolvable conflicts in it, which will communicate themselves to people who pass through it?

We can therefore intensify our empirical observations, and begin a second round of observations, which will fine-tune the first observations.

Of course, even now the pattern is still tentative.

It is an *attempt* to define an invariant: but always only an attempt. Just because it is solid, a thing, precisely formulated, does not alter the fact that it is still only a guess at what it is that makes an entrance marvelous.

This guess may be wrong in the formulation of the problem; for instance, the forces may be quite different from the ones which have been described.

And this guess may be wrong in the formulation of the solution; for instance, the actual pattern of relationships required to help resolve the problem may be incorrectly stated.

But it is clear enough, now, so that it can be shared.

Anyone who takes the trouble to consider it carefully can understand it. It has a clearly formulated problem, based on empirical findings that anyone can check for themselves, and check against their own experience. It has a clearly formulated solution that anyone can understand, and check against the entrances which seem to work in their part of the world. It has a clearly formulated context, which allows a person to decide whether the pattern is applicable or not, and lets him see if he agrees with the range of its application. And finally, of course, anyone can use the pattern. It is so concrete, so clearly expressed as a rule, and as a thing, that anyone can make one, or conceive one, in the buildings where he lives, or in a building which is going to be created.

In short, whether this formulation, as it stands, is correct or not, the pattern can be shared, precisely because it is open to debate, and tentative. Indeed, it is the very fact that it is open to debate, that makes it ready to be shared.

To show you finally, how natural it is for anyone to formulate patterns which can be shared, I shall now describe a conversation with an Indian friend, in which I tried to help her define a pattern from her own experience.

Chris: First of all, just tell me a place that you like very much.

Gita: Shall I describe it to you?

C. No, just think of it, and visualize it, and remember what you like about it.

G. It is an Inn.

C.   Now, please try to tell me what it is that makes this Inn a special and wonderful place.

G.   Well, it is the things which happen there—it is a place where people who are on long journeys meet, and spend a little time together, and it is the wonderful atmosphere of all these things which happen there. I like it very much.

C.   Can you try and isolate any feature of its design, which makes it so wonderful? I would like you to try and tell me, as clearly as you can, what I must do to create another place which is as nice as your Inn—please give me an instruction which captures one of the good things about the design.

G.   It is not the building which makes this Inn so wonderful, but it is the things that happen there— it is the people you meet, the things you do there, the stories which people tell before they go to sleep.

C.   Yes, this is exactly what I mean. Of course, it is the atmosphere which makes the Inn so wonderful—not the beauty of the building, or its geometry; but I am asking you if you can define for me, which features of the building it is, that make this atmosphere possible, the people who pass through the Inn to create this atmosphere, all that . . . .

G.   I don't understand what you are saying. I have just told you it really doesn't depend on the buildings, but on the people.

C.   Well, let me put it like this. Imagine an American

motel. Could the atmosphere which you are describing, happen in an American motel?

G.   Oh, now I see what you are saying. No, in these
American motels it does not happen; there are so
many private rooms, and the people who come to
the motel, they just pass through the main lobby,
they talk at the counter for a few minutes, and
then they go to their rooms. The Inn I am talking
about is not like that—but perhaps it is not possible
in America to have an Inn like this—it is a social
problem—here in America people want to be so
private, they do not want to meet and talk—and
they do not like to sleep with their husbands or
wives where everyone can see them—so perhaps
it is very special, this atmosphere that I am describing—it depends on the people who are using
the Inn, and their habits, and way of life.

C.   Yes, that is fine. Every pattern has a context. Of
course, the pattern you are trying to define may
not make sense for the United States—perhaps it
applies only to the context of India. Let's say that
this pattern is true just for India—now try and
tell me what it is all about.

G.   Alright. In India, there are many of these Inns.
There is a courtyard where the people meet, and
a place to one side of the courtyard where they
eat, and also on one side there is the person who
looks after the Inn, and on the other three sides
of the courtyard there are the rooms—in front of
the rooms is an arcade, maybe one step up from

the courtyard, and about ten feet deep, with another step leading into the rooms. During the
evening everyone meets in the courtyard, and they
talk and eat together—it is very special—and then
at night they all sleep in the arcade, so they are
all sleeping together, round the courtyard. I think
it is very important, too, that all the rooms are
similar, so that when they stay here, all the people
feel equal, and free to talk to everyone else.

C. It sounds wonderful. Now, let's talk about the
problem which the pattern solves. Is it necessary?
Do you think that people can manage just as well,
without the pattern as you have described it?

G. I can't see how else it can be done; if you have
the rooms separate, and private, it becomes just
like a motel, and everyone is alone. And if you
don't eat together, what chance is there for talking? I think it must be just as I have described it.
All the Inns I know in the religious towns of
India are like this—I can't even imagine one
which isn't.

C. Let's define the problem like this: "When people
travel, they are a little lonely; and also since they
travel in order to be opened up to the world, they
want a chance to be together with other travelers."
Now, can you tell me when you think this pattern makes sense, and when it doesn't—what is
the right context for the pattern?

G. Well, it must be for a place where people are
traveling very far, and where they are in this

273

mood—in India most of these Inns are at religious places, where people come to make a pilgrimage— I think it is a very special kind of crossroads in a journey, that must be like this.

C. Would it make sense in Greenland?

G. I do not understand.

C. Do you think the climate is a part of the context?

G. Oh yes, it is very important that it is a hot place, so that you do not sleep out under the arcade for social reasons only, but because of the heat also— you find the place where there are breezes, and you put your bed where it is most comfortable.

C. So the pattern makes sense for any Inn where people are on long journeys, in a society where they are open to meet people in a very simple way, and in a climate where it is hot so that people want to sleep outside.

Now, once again, we have the beginnings of a pattern.

We have stated a problem—so far in very intuitive terms—as an atmosphere which plays an important part in the life of an inn where people meet. We have described the field of spatial relationships—the arrangement of the courtyard, the arcade, the eating place, the sleeping, and the innkeeper—which make this atmosphere possible. And we have stated the context in which it seems that this pattern makes sense. Each of these three needs to be refined, and perhaps made more precise—but we have the beginnings of a pattern now. . . .

A great variety of patterns with this format have been discovered.

Ten years ago a group of us began defining patterns, to create a language. 253 of these patterns are now published in volume 2 of this series, *A Pattern Language.*

The 253 patterns range from the very large to the very small. The largest ones deal with the structure of a region, with the distribution of towns, and with the internal structure of a town. . . . middle range patterns cover the shape and activity of buildings, gardens, streets, rooms . . . . and the smallest patterns deal with the actual physical materials and structures out of which the buildings must be made: the form of columns, vaults, windows, walls, windowsills, even the character of ornament.

Each of these patterns is an attempt to capture that essence of some situation which makes it live.

Each one is an invariant field, needed to resolve a conflict among certain forces, expressed as an entity which has a name, with instructions so concrete that anyone can make one (or help to make one), and with its functional basis so clearly stated that everyone can decide for himself whether it is true, and when, and when not, to include it in his world.

Gradually, by hard work, it is possible to discover many patterns which are deep, and which can help to bring a building or a town to life.

They vary from culture to culture; sometimes they are very different, sometimes there are versions of the same pattern, slightly different, in different cultures.

But it is possible to discover them, and to write them down so that they can be shared.

CHAPTER 15

THE REALITY OF PATTERNS

*We may then gradually improve these
patterns which we share, by testing them
against experience: we can determine,
very simply, whether these patterns
make our surroundings live, or not, by
recognizing how they make us feel.*

We have seen in the last chapter that there is a process by which a person can formulate a pattern; and make it explicit, so that other people can use it. Many such patterns have been written down, in volume 2.

But so far, there is no guarantee at all that any one of these patterns will actually work. Each one is intended to be a source of life, a generative, self-sustaining pattern. But is it actually? How can we distinguish patterns which work, which are deep and worth copying, from those which are simply pipe dreams, mad imaginings . . .

Suppose that we are trying to agree about a pattern.

How can we agree whether it lives or not?

Or, suppose that you are reading a pattern which someone has written down.

How can you decide whether to make it part of your language or not?

One test says that a pattern is alive if its individual statements are empirically true.

We know that every pattern is an instruction of the general form:

context $\rightarrow$ conflicting forces $\rightarrow$ configuration

So we say that a pattern is good, whenever we can show that it meets the following two empirical conditions:

1. *The problem is real.* This means that we can express the problem as a conflict among forces which really do occur within the stated context, and cannot normally be resolved within that context. This is an empirical question.

2. *The configuration solves the problem.* This means that when the stated arrangement of parts is present in the stated context, the conflict can be resolved, without any side effects. This is an empirical question.

But a pattern is not alive just because its component statements are true, one by one.

One of the funniest examples of a pattern I have ever heard of is the "madhouse balcony."

This is a pattern which a student once invented. It says that the balcony of any mental patient's room should have a chest-high railing on it. The argument is this: on the one hand, people want to be able to enjoy the view—and this applies as much to mental patients as anyone else. On the other hand, mental patients "have a tendency to jump off buildings." In order to resolve this conflict between forces, the railing on the balcony must be high enough to prevent a patient from jumping over, but low enough so that he can enjoy the view.

We laughed for hours when we first saw this. And yet, absurd as it is, it seems to follow the format of a pattern. It has a context, problem and solution: and the problem is expressed as a system of conflicting forces.

What is it that makes it absurd?

The fact is that even though its individual component statements are true, the pattern has no empirical reality as a whole.

A balcony of this kind will not allow a mad person to heal himself: it will not help to make the world more whole.

It is absurd because we can feel in our bones that it would make no difference at all whether such a balcony was built into the world or not. We know that the problem cannot really be solved in this or any related way.

Even the fact that a pattern seems sensible, and has clear reasoning behind it, does not mean at all that the pattern is necessarily capable of generating life.

For example, the famous radiant city pattern of high towers, freestanding in the landscape, was "invented" by Le Corbusier with great devotion and seriousness. He believed that it would be possible to give every family light, and air, and access to green, within this pattern: and he spent many years developing this pattern, in theory and practice.

However, he forgot, or did not realize, that there was one additional essential force at work in the system—the human instinct for protection and territoriality. The huge, abstractly beautiful green spaces around his high buildings are not used, because they are too public, they belong to too many people at the same time, and they are under the eyes of too many hundreds of apartments

hovering above them. Under these circumstances, this
one force—a kind of animal territorial instinct—destroys
this patttern's capacity to generate life. . . .

*A pattern only works, fully, when it deals with all
the forces that are actually present in the situation.*

On the face of it this is a simple intellectual concept.
When we find a pattern which does bring forces into
balance, then this pattern will of course begin to generate
the quality without a name which is described in chapter 2—because it will contribute to that process in which
the forces of the world run free. On the other hand, a
pattern always lacks this quality if it resolves some forces
at the expense of others which it leaves unresolved.

It should be reasonably easy to identify these patterns
which are alive, in these terms, and to distinguish them
from those patterns which aren't alive.

In practice, though, it turns out to be very difficult.

*The difficulty is that we have no reliable way of
knowing just exactly what the forces in a situation
are.*

The pattern is merely a mental image, which can help
to predict those situations where forces will be in harmony, and those in which they won't.

But the actual forces which will occur in a real situation, although objectively present there, are, in the end
unpredictable, because each situation is so complex, and

forces may grow, or die, according to subtle variations of circumstance.

If we formulate a pattern in terms of some system of forces, which we think describes a situation, and our description of the system happens to be incomplete, then the pattern can easily become absurd.

Yet we have no analytical way of being sure just what the forces are.

What we need is a way of understanding the forces which cuts through this intellectual difficulty and goes closer to the empirical core.

We need a way of knowing which patterns will really help to bring the world to life and which ones won't.

And we need a way of doing it which is more reliable than analytical formulation. Above all, we need a way of doing it, which is anchored in the empirical reality of what will actually happen, without necessarily requiring complex and extensive experiments which are too expensive to do.

To do this, we must rely on feelings more than intellect.

For although the system of forces in a situation is very hard to define analytically, it is possible to tell, in a holistic way, whether the pattern is alive or not.

The fact is that we feel good in the presence of a pattern which resolves its forces.

And we feel ill at ease, uncomfortable, when a pattern leaves its forces unresolved.

The pattern ALCOVE *feels good to us, because we feel the wholeness of the system there.*

There is an intellectual formulation of the forces which alcoves resolve. For instance, they allow us to be private at the edge of a communal gathering, and, at the same time, remain in touch with whatever is communal there. But what clinches it, what makes us certain that this formulation has some substance to it, is the fact that alcoves make us feel good. The conflict is real, because the alcove makes us feel alive; and we know the pattern is complete, because we can feel no residual tension there.

The pattern T-JUNCTIONS *makes us feel good, because we feel the wholeness of the system there.*

There is an intellectual formulation of the forces which T-junctions resolve. A T-junction creates less crossing movements, and less conflicts for the drivers, and this puts the pattern on a firm empirical foundation. But what clinches it, and makes us certain that the problem is a real one, and complete, is that we feel more comfortable, more relaxed, when we are driving in a street whose junctions are all T-junctions. We know, then, that there are no hidden crossing movements which we don't expect; there is no possibility of unexpected cars shooting across our path—in short we feel good there; and we feel good be-

287

cause the system of conflicting forces which T-junctions resolves is real, and complete.

And MOSAIC OF SUBCULTURES *makes us feel good, because, again, we feel the wholeness of the system there.*

Again there is an intellectual argument, which shows that when subcultures are separated from one another by communal land, each one can grow in its own way. In this case the system of forces is immensely intricate, and we must wonder, indeed, if we have managed to identify a complete balanced system of forces in this pattern. Again, the certainty comes from the fact that we feel good in places where this pattern does exist. In places like the Chinatown of San Francisco, or in Sausalito, which are vivid with their own life because they are a little separate from the nearby communities, we feel good. We feel good because we can feel, in our bones, the lack of inhibition, the spontaneous growth, which follows its own course in these communities, because they are uninhibited by pressure from surrounding communities which have a different way of life.

By contrast, patterns made from thought, without feeling, lack empirical reality entirely.

The madhouse balcony makes us feel nothing. Certainly, we know at once, when we first hear it, that a balcony like this will not make us feel wonderful. There is no

288

feeling in it: and this lack of feeling is the way our knowledge of its emptiness presents itself to us.

And Le Corbusier's radiant city makes us feel worse: it actively makes us feel bad. It may excite our intellect, or our imagination; but when we ask ourselves how we shall feel in a place which is really built like this, we know again, that it will not make us feel wonderful. Again, our feeling is the way our knowledge of its functional emptiness presents itself to us.

We see then, that there is a fundamental inner connection between the balance of a system of forces, and our feelings about the pattern which resolves these forces.

It comes about because our feelings always deal with the totality of any system. If there are hidden forces, hidden conflicts, lurking in a pattern, we can feel them there. And when a pattern feels good to us, it is because it is a genuinely wholesome thing, and we know that there are no hidden forces lurking there.

This makes it easier to test any given pattern.

When you first see a pattern, you will be able to tell almost at once, by intuition, whether it makes you feel good or not: whether, you want to live in a world which has that pattern in it, because it helps you to feel more alive.

If a pattern does make you feel good, there is a very good chance that it is a good pattern. If a pattern does not help you to feel good, there is very little chance that it is a good pattern.

We can always ask ourselves just how a pattern makes us feel. And we can always ask the same of someone else.

Imagine someone who proposes that modular aluminum wall panels are of great importance in the construction of houses.

Simply ask him how he *feels* in rooms built out of them.

He will be able to do dozens of critical experiments which "prove" that they are better, and that they make the environment better, cleaner, healthier . . . . But the one thing he will not be able to do, if he is honest with himself, is to claim that the presence of modular panels is a distinguishing feature of the places in which he feels good.

His feeling is direct, and unequivocal.

It is not the same, at all, as asking someone his opinion.

If I ask someone whether he approves of "parking garages" say—he may give a variety of answers. He may say, "Well it all depends what you mean." Or he may say, "There is no avoiding them"; or he may say, "It is the best available solution to a difficult problem" . . . on and on.

None of this has anything to do with his feelings.

It is also not the same as asking for a person's taste.

If I ask a person whether he likes hexagonal buildings, say, or buildings in which apartments made like shoe boxes are piled on top of one another, he may treat the question as a question about his taste. In this case he may say, "It is very inventive," or, wishing to prove that he has good taste, "Yes, this modern architecture is fascinating, isn't it?"

Still, none of this has anything to do with his feelings.

And it is also not the same as asking what a person thinks of an idea.

Again, suppose I formulate a certain pattern, and it describes, in the problem statement, a variety of problems which a person can connect up with his philosophical leanings, his attitudes, his intellect, his ideas about the world—then he may again give me a variety of confusing answers.

He may say, "Well, I don't agree with your formulation of this or this fact"; or he may say, "The evidence you cited on such and such a point has been debated by the best authorities"; or again, "Well, I can't take this seriously, because if you consider its long term implications you can see that it would never do" . . .

All this again, has nothing to do with his feelings.

It simply asks for feelings, and for nothing else.

Go to places where the pattern exists, and see how you feel there.

Compare this with the way you feel in places where the pattern is missing.

If you feel better in the places where the pattern exists, then the pattern is a good one.

If you feel better in the places where the pattern does not exist, or you can honestly detect no difference, between the two groups of cases, then the pattern is no good.

The success of this test hinges on a fact which I have not said enough about so far—the extraordinary degree of agreement in people's feelings about patterns.

I have found that whereas people can get into the most amazing and complex kinds of disagreement about the "ideas" in a pattern, or about the philosophy expressed in the pattern, or about the "taste" or "style" which seems to be implied in a pattern, people who come from the same culture do to a remarkable extent agree about the way that different patterns make them feel.

Take, for instance, the need that children have for water. A few years ago I was at a meeting in San Francisco where two hundred people met, for an afternoon, to try to identify things that they wanted in their city. They met in groups of eight, around small tables, and spent the afternoon discussing what they wanted. At the end of the afternoon, a spokesman from each group summarized the things they wanted most.

Several different groups, quite independently, mentioned the fact that they wanted an opportunity for their children to play in, and with, mud and water—especially water—instead of the hard asphalt playing grounds which parks and schools provide.

This fascinated me. It happened that one of the patterns in the language we had been developing, POOLS AND STREAMS, goes into great detail about the fact that children especially, and all of us, need the opportunity to play with water—because it liberates essential subconscious processes. And here, unasked for, was tenfold spontaneous confirmation of the pattern, born directly out of people's feelings.

Or take the question of the size of hospitals. Officials in Sao Paulo have recently begun construction of the largest hospital in the world—a hospital with 10,000 beds. Now 9 out of ten people—probably 95 out of 100—will agree that a 10,000 bed hospital fills them with fear and apprehension.

Contemplate that simply as an empirical fact. It is an empirical fact of an order of magnitude far vaster than any piddling experiments and surveys which the experts can muster.

There are few experiments, in science, where a phenomenon is capable of generating this extraordinary level of agreement.

And, yet, for some strange reason we are not yet willing to recognize the depth, and power and centered-

293

ness of just these feelings. If the fact that Brazilian people do not feel good when they think about this hospital were mentioned in the legislature as a means of shedding doubt on the experts' opinions, the legislators would smile politely; it would even be embarrassing to mention feelings in this situation. And yet this ocean of shared feeling is the place where we become one with one another—this is the source, in the end, of our agreement about pattern languages.

It is easy to dismiss feelings as "subjective" and "unreliable," and therefore not a reasonable basis for any form of scientific agreement. And of course, in private matters, where people's feelings vary greatly from one person to the next, their feelings cannot be used as a basis for agreement.

However, in the domain of patterns, where people seem to agree 90, 95, even 99 percent of the time, we may treat this agreement as an extraordinary, almost shattering, discovery, about the solidity of human feelings, and we may certainly use it as scientific.

But for fear of repeating myself, I must say once again that the agreement lies only in peoples' actual feelings, not in their opinions.

For example, if I take people to window places (window seats, glazed alcoves, a chair by a low windowsill looking out onto some flowers, a bay window . . .) and ask them to compare these window places with those windows in rooms where the windows are flat inserts into the wall, almost no one will say that the flat windows actually *feel* more comfortable than the window places—so we shall have as much as 95 percent agreement.

And if I take the same group of people to a variety of places which have modular wall panels in them, and compare these places with places where walls are built up from brick, and plaster, wood, paper, stone . . . almost none of them will say that the modular panels make them *feel* better, so long as I insist that I only want to know how they feel. Again, 95 percent agreement.

But the moment I allow people to express their opinions, or mix their ideas and opinions with their feelings, then the agreement vanishes. Suddenly the staunch adherents of modular components, and the industries which produce them, will find all kinds of arguments to explain why modular panels are better, why they are economically necessary. And in the same way, once opinion takes over, the window places will be dismissed as impractical, the need for prefabricated windows discussed as so important . . . all these arguments in fact fallacious, but nevertheless presented in a way which makes them seem compelling.

In short, the scientific accuracy of the patterns can only come from direct assessment of people's feelings, not from arguments or discussions.

These feelings which are in touch with reality are sometimes very hard to reach.

Suppose, for instance, that a person proposes a pattern in

which water flows in four directions from a fountain.

If I say to this person—does that make you feel good, he says yes, of course, that is exactly why I do it—it makes me feel good.

It needs enormous discipline, to say, no, no, wait a minute, I am not interested in that kind of glib stuff. If you compare the situation where the water comes out in one substantial flow from the pool, and can irrigate an orchard, with the situation where the water trickles out in four directions—and ask yourself, honestly now, *honestly*—which of the two makes you feel better—then you know that it makes you feel better when the flow is more substantial—it makes more sense, the world becomes more whole.

But it is hard to admit this, because it takes so much hard work to concentrate attention on the feelings.

It is not hard because the feeling is not there, or because the feeling is unreliable.

It is hard, because it takes an enormous and unusual amount of attention, to pay attention for long enough to find out which does actually feel better.

Yet it is only this true feeling, this feeling that requires attention, this feeling that requires effort, which is reliable enough to generate agreement.

And it is only this much deeper feeling, which is connected directly to the balance of forces, and to the emergence of reality.

Once a person is willing to take his feelings as seriously

as this, and pay attention to them—and exclude opinions and ideas—then his perception of a pattern can approach the quality without a name.

We see then that the concept of a balanced pattern is deeply rooted in the concept of feeling.

And that our feelings, when they are real feelings, provide us with a powerful way of finding out just which patterns are balanced and which ones are not.

But even so, feelings themselves are not the essence of the matter.

For what is at stake, in a pattern which lives, is not merely the fact that it makes us feel good, but, much more than that, the fact that it does actually liberate a portion of the world, allow the forces to run free: and liberate the world from the imprisoning effect of concepts and opinions.

In short, what is at stake at last, is nothing but the quality without a name itself.

Some patterns have this quality; and others don't. Those which do make us feel good, because they help to make us whole, and we feel more at one with ourselves in their presence: but still it is the quality itself which matters most; not the effect which it has on us.

297

It is, in the end, the presence of this quality in a pattern which makes the difference between one which lives and one which doesn't. . . .

Take as an example the relationship between pedestrians and cars.

Conventional wisdom has it that pedestrians ought to be separated from cars because it is quiet, and safe for them.

But nagging reality shows us that even in towns where they are kept completely separate, the children still run out to play in parking lots, and people still walk casually along the roads reserved for cars. The fact is that people take the shortest paths, and that cars are where the action is.

There is no doubt that pedestrians do need some measure of protection from cars, for peace and quiet, and for safety. But also, paths need to pass where the action is, where pedestrians can meet the cars.

It is possible to deal with both of these forces at the same time. If we put pedestrian paths at right angles to roads, crossing them, but not entirely separate from them, we create peace and safety, but also create places where people on foot and cars can meet, hubs where the action is, where the two systems cross.

And this pattern, which does in fact resolve the conflict in the forces, also corresponds, of course, to just the places where we feel most comfortable about the relation between cars and people. Isn't it true that in the busy part of a city, a system of paths which is entirely separate from cars is too quiet, artificial, almost unreal? Isn't it, instead, those paths which are quiet, beautiful, pedestrian paths but which do lead up to a road, which make us feel perfectly in balance with these forces? Ask yourself, if you don't know a path like this in a city, where the road with cars on it is in sight, crossing the path, but at one end—and ask yourself, when you are there, if you don't feel just right.

To this extent, this pattern, NETWORK OF PATHS AND CARS, is based on reality. So long as the context remains in which we have cars in the world, this is the pattern which takes the forces as they are and resolves them, without bias, by treating them exactly as they really are.

It is reality itself which makes the difference.

Take another example: In the houses we built in Peru, we based our patterns on the underlying forces we could detect in people's lives. Since many of these forces are ages old, we were led to create houses which have many features in common with the ancient and colonial Peruvian traditions. For example, we gave each house a "Sala"—a special formal living room, right inside the front door, for receiving formal guests, and a family room, where the family themselves might live, further back into the house (see the pattern INTIMACY GRA-DIENT). And we gave the houses leaning niches, outside the front doors, where people could stand, half in, half outside the house, watching the street (see the pattern FRONT DOOR RECESSES). These patterns are both common in traditional Peru. People criticized us strongly for trying to go back to the past, when they said, the Peruvian families themselves were struggling to catch up with the future, and wanted houses just like American houses, so they could have a modern way of life.

The issue here is not one of past or present or future. It is a simple fact, that a Peruvian family with a single living room, will experience conflict whenever a stranger visits them—they try to keep their family around the dinner table, talking and watching TV; yet, at the same time, they try to present the visitor with a formal way of entering the house, not mixed up with the family. And again, if it is not possible to stand in the front door, watching the street, many of the women will experience a conflict between the fact that, being women, they are expected to retire, not to be too forward, or to sit openly on the street—and yet, being shut inside the house, they want to experience some connection with the street and the street life.

I do not judge these facts. They are simply facts about the dynamics of being Peruvian in 1969. So long as these forces exist, people will experience unresolvable conflicts, unless the patterns are present and will, to this extent, be less able to become whole.

And it is in the end only when our feelings are perfectly in touch with the reality of forces, that we begin to see the patterns which are capable of generating life.

That is what is hard—because so often people choose to put their own opinions forward, in place of reality.

In many cases, people react to the description of these forces by saying "it should be otherwise." For instance, ENTRANCE TRANSITION is based, in part, on the fact that in a city street, people have a mask of street behavior, which needs to be wiped off by a transition, before a person can relax in a private or secluded place.

One person's comment on this pattern was: This fact is bad; people should learn to be the same in the street as they are in private places, so that we can all love one another.

The comment is nice in its intent. But human beings are not so malleable. The street mask is created by us, in spite of our own volition: the fact that it comes into being is a fundamental fact about human nature in urban situations.

There is little purpose, then, in saying: It would be better if this force did not exist. For if it does exist anyway, designs based on such wishful thinking will fail.

The beauty of an ENTRANCE TRANSITION, and the fact that it is capable of making us feel at one with ourselves, is based on thoroughgoing acceptance of these forces as they really are.

Yet it is hard to give up preconceptions of what things "ought to be," and recognize things as they really are.

For instance, the other day a radio advertisement for the

boy scouts said: "When your boy is sitting on the street corner with other boys, this is unhealthy—give him the chance to do what all boys are yearning to do—going on long hikes, fishing, and swimming." This statement was presented with religious fervor—and is, of course, a deliberate attempt, by believers in the puritan ethic, to impose their conception of what a boy ought to be like, on what a boy is actually like. Of course, a real boy sometimes wants to go swimming—but sometimes he wants to hang out on the street corner with his friends, and sometimes he wants to look for girls. A person who believes that these pursuits are "unhealthy" will never be able to see the forces which are actually at work in the boy's life—and will never be able to use a pattern language with any sense of reality.

How could such a person recognize the reality of the pattern TEENAGE COTTAGE which says that a teenager needs a cottage slightly remote from his parents, so as to nurture the beginnings of his independence; or how could he recognize the reality of PUBLIC OUTDOOR ROOM, which specifically pays attention to the needs which teenagers have to gather, in urban public places, away from their houses.

A person who believes in slum clearance will be blind to the real facts about the lives of people living in slums. A person who is convinced that skid row ought to be cleaned up will be oblivious to the real forces at work in a hobo's life, because he can't accept the existence of a hobo. A person who is convinced that offices ought to be "flexible" will be oblivious to the real forces at work in groups of people who are trying to work.

Any preconception about the way things "ought to be" always interferes with your sense of reality; it prevents you from seeing what is actually going on—and this will always prevent you from making the environment alive. It will prevent you from inventing or discovering new patterns when you see them—and, most of all—it will prevent you from using such patterns properly, to create a whole environment.

In this respect attention to reality goes far beyond the realm of values.

Usually people say that the choice of patterns depends on your opinions about what is important. One person thinks high buildings are best; another person likes low ones; one person likes plenty of space for cars, because he likes driving fast; another one likes the emphasis to be given to pedestrians, because he doesn't like driving.

When we try to resolve disagreements like this, we are led back to people's fundamental aims in life: to their fundamental goals, or values. But people do not agree about their values. So this kind of discussion still leaves us in a position where patterns seem only to depend on opinions—the best you can say, according to this view, is that a certain pattern does or doesn't help to satisfy a certain goal or value. Or that some "forces" are "good" and others "bad."

But a pattern which is real makes no judgments about the legitimacy of the forces in the situation.

By seeming to be unethical, by making no judgments about individual opinions, or goals, or values, the pattern rises to another level of morality.

Its result is to allow things to be alive—and this is a higher good than the victory of any one artificial system of values. The attempt to have a victory for a one-sided view of the world cannot work anyway, even for the people who seem to win their point of view. The forces which are ignored do not go away just because they are ignored. They lurk, frustrated, underground. Sooner or later they erupt in violence: and the system which seems to win is then exposed to far more catastrophic dangers.

The only way that a pattern can actually help to make a situation genuinely more alive is by recognizing all the forces which actually exist, and then finding a world in which these forces can slide past each other.

Then it becomes a piece of nature.

When we see the pattern of the ripples in a pond, we know that this pattern is simply in equilibrium with the forces which exist: without any mental interference which is clouding them.

And, when we succeed, finally, in seeing so deep into a man-made pattern, that it is no longer clouded by opinions or by images, then we have discovered a piece of nature as valid, as eternal, as the ripples in the surface of a pond.

304

CHAPTER 16

THE STRUCTURE OF A LANGUAGE

Once we have understood how to discover individual patterns which are alive, we may then make a language for ourselves, for any building task we face. The structure of the language is created by the network of connections among individual patterns: and the language lives, or not, as a totality, to the degree these patterns form a whole.

It is clear, then, that we can discover living patterns, and share them, and reach some reasonable degree of confidence in their reality.

The patterns cover every range of scale in our surroundings: the largest patterns cover aspects of regional structure, middle range patterns cover the shape and activity of buildings, and the smallest patterns deal with the actual physical materials and structures out of which the buildings must be made.

So far, though, we have said little about language. In this chapter we shall see how it is possible to put these patterns together to form coherent languages.

As we shall see, the possibility of language is latent in the fact that patterns are not isolated. But it comes out, in its full force, when we experience the desire to make something. As soon as we want to make something—any-thing—a small thing like a garden seat, a large thing like a neighborhood—and want to see it whole, then we experience the desire which puts a structure on the patterns, and makes language out of them.

Imagine that I am going to build a garden.

From chapters 10, 11, and 12, we know now that the garden will not live, nor be a beautiful and stirring place, unless we have a powerful, and deep and living language for the garden—before we start to lay it out.

Somehow, then, I must try to find, or create for myself, a pattern language for a garden.

THE GATE

One way to start a language for a garden is to get some patterns from the pattern language we have published in volume 2.

If you go through the patterns in that language, choosing the patterns for a garden which seem relevant for you, you might, for instance, choose the following list of patterns:

> HALF-HIDDEN GARDEN
> TERRACED SLOPE
> FRUIT TREES
> TREE PLACES
> GARDEN GROWING WILD
> ENTRANCE TRANSITION
> COURTYARDS WHICH LIVE
> ROOF GARDEN
> BUILDING EDGE
> SUNNY PLACE
> OUTDOOR ROOM
> SIX-FOOT BALCONY
> CONNECTION TO THE EARTH
> GREENHOUSE
> GARDEN SEAT

But what is it, now, which makes these patterns form a language?

I can get these patterns from the published language, simply ticking off the ones I like, and writing them down in the order of the larger language.

And, of course, I might also include patterns which I have invented myself, or which my friends have told me about—mixed in with the others.

But what makes a language of them; and what makes this language whole?

The structure of a pattern language is created by the fact that individual patterns are not isolated.

To understand this idea, fully, think about the pattern "garage," and concentrate, in particular, on the garage of a single-family house. How do you know that a particular building that you see is a garage?

Of course, you recognize it partly by the smaller patterns it contains: by the fact that it is the size of a car, by the fact that it has small windows or none at all, by the fact that it has a large, full-height door in front, etc. These facts are defined by the pattern which we call "garage."

But the pattern of the garage and the smaller patterns it contains are not enough to define the garage fully. If a building with these patterns in this arrangement were floating on a boat, you might call it a houseboat, but certainly not a garage; if it were standing in the middle of a field, with no road leading to it, it might be a tool-shed, or a storehouse, but certainly not a garage.

For a building to be a garage, it has to have a drive-way leading to it, from the street; and it will probably be to one side of a house, not directly in front or directly behind; and it will probably be fairly near the house—with a direct path to the house. These larger patterns are part of the garage pattern too.

Each pattern then, depends both on the smaller patterns it contains, and on the larger patterns within which it is contained.

Exactly the same is true of all the patterns in the language for a garden. Each one is incomplete, and needs the context of the others, to make sense.

For example, a GARDEN WALL taken out of context is merely a pile of bricks. It becomes a garden wall only when it surrounds a garden; that is, for instance when it helps to complete HALF-HIDDEN GARDEN or GARDEN GROWING WILD.

ENTRANCE TRANSITION, taken by itself, is merely a place in the open air. What makes it an entrance transition is its position in between the front door and the street, and its view into the more distant garden; in short, the fact that it helps to complete the language pattern MAIN ENTRANCE, and is itself completed by the smaller pattern ZEN VIEW.

And perhaps most extreme of all, COURTYARDS WHICH LIVE. Of course a courtyard is not a courtyard at all, unless it is surrounded by the buildings which create it: so it is only when this pattern helps to complete the pattern BUILDING COMPLEX, and is itself completed by the patterns BUILDING EDGE and GALLERY SURROUND, that it becomes a courtyard at all.

Each pattern sits at the center of a network of connections which connect it to certain other patterns that help to complete it.

Suppose we use a dot to stand for each pattern, and use an arrow to stand for each connection between two patterns. Then

means that the pattern A needs the pattern B as part of it, in order for A to be complete; *and* that the pattern B needs to be part of the pattern A, in order for B to be complete.

If we make a picture of *all* the patterns which are connected to the pattern A, we see then that the pattern A sits at the center of a whole network of patterns, some above it, some below it.

Each pattern sits at the center of a similar network.

And it is the network of these connections between patterns which creates the language.

313

Thus a language for a garden might have the structure illustrated here, in which each pattern has its place, connected to the other patterns:

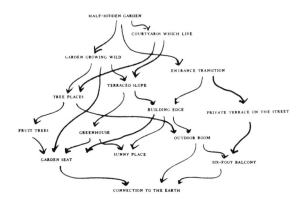

In this network, the links between the patterns are almost as much a part of the language as the patterns themselves.

Consider, for example, PRIVATE TERRACE ON THE STREET and ENTRANCE TRANSITION.

So long as I imagine these two patterns as free-floating entities, I can imagine an enormous variety of possible houses, or gardens, which contain these patterns: and I can imagine an enormous number of different possible relationships between these patterns.

But suppose, now, that they are connected in the language, and that PRIVATE TERRACE ON THE STREET is a part of ENTRANCE TRANSITION. Suddenly I imagine people sipping drinks on the terrace, while arriving guests pass the terrace, pass through the people who are sitting there.

Or suppose, on the contrary, that I imagine PRIVATE TERRACE ON THE STREET to be a part of the back of INTIMACY GRADIENT instead. Now I have quite the opposite picture: people passing through a more somber, more peaceful entrance transition, passing through the house, and then coming out on another side, to the terrace, also on the street, but much more private, more secluded.

Each time, my image of the individual patterns is changed. And each time it intensifies them.

It is, indeed, the structure of the network which makes sense of individual patterns, because it anchors them, and helps make them complete.

Each pattern is modified by its position in the language as a whole: according to the links which form the language.

And in virtue of its position in the whole, each pattern becomes especially intense, vivid, easy to visualize, and more richly visualized. The language not only connects the patterns to each other, but helps them to come to life, by giving each one a realistic context, and encouraging imagination to give life to the combinations which the connected patterns generate.

But even when I have the patterns connected to one another, in a network, so that they form a language, how do I know if the language is a good one?

315

Is it complete? Should I add other patterns to it? Should I take certain patterns out? Does it hang together? And, above all: Will it help me to generate a garden which comes alive? We may assume that the patterns are individually alive if they follow the precepts of chapters 13 and 14. But what about the garden as a whole?

Will the language allow me to create a wonderful, live garden as a whole? And how can I be sure of this?

The language is a good one, capable of making something whole, when it is morphologically and functionally complete.

It is morphologically complete, when the patterns together form a complete structure, filled out in all its details, with no gaps.

And it is functionally complete when the system of patterns has that peculiar self-consistency in which the patterns, as a system, generate only those forces which they themselves resolve—so that the system as a whole, can live, without the action of self-destroying inner conflicts.

The language is morphologically complete when I can visualize the kind of buildings which it generates very concretely.

It means that the general "species" of buildings which this language specifies can be visualized, completely—not as a vague shadowy creature, full of gaps, but as a solid

316

entity, whose only lack of clarity lies in the particulars.

Suppose, for instance, that I have the pattern for HALF-HIDDEN GARDEN: but that I have no patterns which tell me what the major components of the garden are. Concretely: I have no idea how to form its edge; I do not know what its main components are; I do not know where there are any special focal points; I do not know what happens where the garden meets the house. Under these circumstances, I cannot really visualize the garden at all: because I do not know enough about it.

This is quite different from not knowing how to connect a particular garden with a particular house. It means that there is a fundamental gap in my understanding of how to put this kind of garden together: and it means that when I get to this stage in a real case, I shall have to scratch my head, and start to think it out from the beginning.

On the contrary, the language for a garden is morphologically complete when I can visualize the garden clearly, as a global structure, even if I don't yet have any specific garden in mind.

And the language is functionally complete, when the system of patterns it defines is fully capable of allowing all its inner forces to resolve themselves.

Again, consider the garden. We know from chapters 6 and 7 that it is very possible that inconsistent systems of conflicting forces can exist, and that these forces, when not resolved internally, can gradually destroy the system.

317

For instance, suppose that the garden makes no provision for the ecological interaction of trees, foundation systems, and shade. The shade falls in bad places, systems of roots start to undermine foundations—and the entire relation between building and trees is unstable, because it causes progressive problems, which will, in the end, force drastic changes on the garden, which may themselves then lead to other instabilities.

It is functionally complete only when all these internal systems of forces are completely covered—in short, when there are enough patterns to bring all these forces into equilibrium.

In both cases, the language is complete only when every individual pattern in the language is complete.

For obviously, the language cannot be complete as a whole, so long as any individual pattern is itself incomplete. Every pattern must have enough patterns "under" it, to fill it out completely, morphologically. And every pattern must also have enough patterns under it, to solve the problems which it generates.

Thus the pattern BUILDING EDGE is morphologically complete only when the patterns under it are enough to create a full, developed, solid picture of the major global structure of a building edge.

And it is functionally complete only when the patterns under it, together, solve all the major problems, or systems of unresolved conflicting forces, which the existence of a building edge creates.

318

We must therefore invent new patterns, whenever necessary, to fill out each pattern which is not complete.

Take BUILDING EDGE again, as an example. The patterns in the present language which lie directly below BUILDING EDGE are SUNNY PLACE, GALLERY SURROUND, OUTDOOR ROOM, GARDEN SEAT, and ENTRANCE TRANSITION.

Are there any unresolved problems along the building edge, in the presence of these five patterns? This is the question of functional completeness. And, are there any parts of the building edge which are geometrically unclear, and not adequately delineated by these five patterns? This is the question of morphological completeness.

It happens that the answer to both questions is "yes." There *is* an unresolved problem. And there *is* an unclear geometric zone. There is one part of a building edge— the place where a long blank wall simply runs along a stretch of garden—which is still problematical, because it has no pattern covering it. The blank wall is unfriendly, it will create a part of the garden, which is uncomfortable, not easy to use. The pattern BUILDING EDGE itself, says, in very general terms, that the edge should be a definite place, and that it should look both ways, both towards the inside of the house, and towards the outside. But, in detail, this question of the long blank wall remains unsolved. To solve it, it will be necessary to invent some new pattern, which is part of BUILDING EDGE, and below it in the language, and which somehow succeeds in showing how to handle this long, blank, unfriendly wall.

319

I do not know, just now, exactly what this pattern is. But the example helps to show clearly, that the functional intuition which tells me there is a "problem" there, cannot be separated from the morphological intuition which tells me that there is a gap in the geometry.

We keep working at every pattern until we have a collection of patterns below it which completely resolve both functional and morphological problems.

And I complete the language by creating patterns, and eliminating patterns, until each pattern is complete.

But I must also make sure that the patterns below a given pattern are its principal components.

There must not be too many patterns underneath a given pattern. Consider HALF-HIDDEN GARDEN this time. There is one corner of the garden which will be the SUNNY PLACE; another place will be an OUTDOOR ROOM perhaps; there is a need for trees, forming a place; there is the character of the garden as a whole; GARDEN GROWING WILD; there is the relation between the garden and the street, in detail; PRIVATE TERRACE ON THE STREET. There is the possibility of the relation between the house and the garden: covered perhaps by GREENHOUSE . . . . There is the character of flowers in the garden: perhaps RAISED FLOWERS, and the need for vegetables and fruit: VEGETABLE GARDEN and FRUIT TREES . . . .

But not all of these need to be directly underneath HALF-HIDDEN GARDEN. The reason is that some of them embellish *each other*. For example, GARDEN GROWING

WILD, which gives the gardens global character, is itself filled out and completed by RAISED FLOWERS and VEGE-TABLE GARDEN; and TREE PLACES is itself filled out by FRUIT TREES. These patterns which can be "reached" through another pattern, do not need to appear directly below the pattern HALF-HIDDEN GARDEN.

It is essential to distinguish those patterns which are the principal components of any given pattern, from those which lie still further down.

If I have to make a HALF-HIDDEN GARDEN and I can understand it as a thing which has three or four parts, I can visualize it, and begin to create one, for myself, in my own garden.

But if the HALF-HIDDEN GARDEN has twenty or thirty patterns, all equally its parts, I will not be able to imagine it coherently.

It turns out that there are just five patterns which do *have* to appear immediately below HALF-HIDDEN GAR-DEN. They are GARDEN WALL, GARDEN GROWING WILD, PRIVATE TERRACE ON THE STREET, SUNNY PLACE, and TREE PLACES.

So, within this particular language, these are the chief "components" of a HALF-HIDDEN GARDEN.

And this process of defining the principal components of a given pattern is what finally completes it.

Originally we think, perhaps, that the main parts of a "garden" are lawns, and flower beds, and paths.

But now, after careful consideration of the pattern HALF-HIDDEN GARDEN, we begin to see that it has five main components: GARDEN GROWING WILD, PRIVATE TERRACE ON THE STREET, SUNNY PLACE, TREE PLACES, and GARDEN WALL.

Now our whole functional and morphological understanding of the garden has changed. It is not only that we now see the garden as made up of these particular five new entities, which changes our vision of the garden's form. The fact that these five patterns solve five particular problems also changes entirely, our vision of the garden's function.

When every pattern has its principal components given by the smaller patterns which lie immediately below it in the language, then the language is complete.

And you see then what a beautiful structure a pattern language has.

Each pattern is itself a part of some larger pattern—it is born out of these larger patterns through the forces which occur there, and the conditions which allow these forces to be in harmony.

And each pattern itself gives birth to smaller patterns which, once again, through forces which must also be in harmony, gives birth to smaller patterns again created by the conditions which put the lower level forces into harmony.

*Now we can see the full extent to which the design
of the garden lies within the language for the garden.*

If you like the family of gardens which your garden language generates, then the language is fine; but if the language does not conjure up an image of a marvelous place,
then there is something wrong with it; and what is wrong
can't possibly be corrected later when you get to the process of design. At that stage it is much too late.

We tend to imagine that the design of a building or a
garden takes a long time; and that the preparation for the
process of design is short. But in the process where the
language plays its proper part, this gets reversed. The
preparation of the language may take a very long time:
weeks, months, years. But the use of the language, as we
shall see concretely in chapters 21 and 22 and 23, takes
no more than a few hours.

*Essentially, this means that the language which you
have prepared must be judged as if it were itself a
finished garden (or a finished building).*

Since the finished garden (or building) is controlled anyway by just those patterns which appear in it, then you
can tell, even before you use the language, whether you
will like the places which the language will generate.

If the collection of patterns makes a coherent and satisfying whole, and requires no further insights, and no
further beauties, to complete them, then the language is

323

alright. But if you think of the language merely as a convenient tool, and imagine that the garden or the building you create will become beautiful later, because of the finesse with which you handle it, but that the collection of patterns which lie in the language now are not enough to make it beautiful, then there is something deeply wrong with the language; and you must modify it, until you are satisfied.

So, the real work of any process of design lies in this task of making up the language, from which you can later generate the one particular design.

You must make the language first, because it is the structure and the content of the language which determine the design. The individual buildings which you make, will live, or not, according to the depth and wholeness of the language which you use to make them with.

But of course, once you have it, this language is general. If it has the power to make a single building live, it can be used a thousand times, to make a thousand buildings live.

CHAPTER 17

THE EVOLUTION OF A COMMON
LANGUAGE FOR A TOWN

*Then finally, from separate languages
for different building tasks, we can create
a larger structure still, a structure of
structures, evolving constantly, which is
the common language for a town. This
is the gate.*

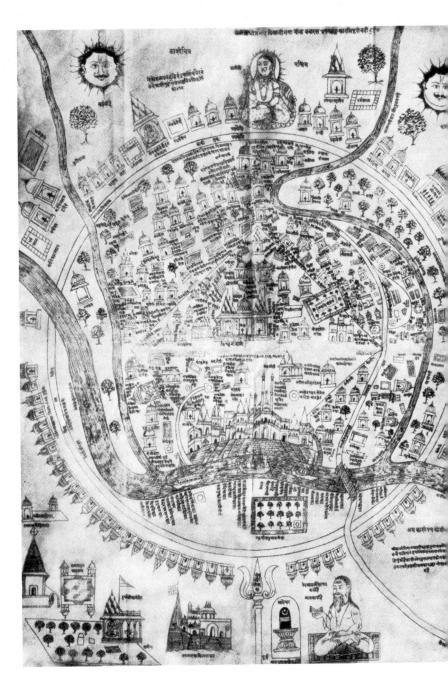

From chapter 16, we know how to construct an individual language, for a specific individual building type.

We shall see now, in this last chapter of part two, how many of these languages can fit together, to become the common language of a town.

Imagine, to begin with, that we have made a dozen languages for different building tasks.

One for a house, one for a garden; one for a street; one for a neighborhood, one for a window, one for an office, a concert hall, one for a building with apartments in it, one for an office building, one for a shop, one for a public holy place, one for a river's edge, one for a busy crossroads in a town.

As we make the different individual languages, we find the patterns overlap.

For example, we find that ENTRANCE TRANSITION is part of the language for the garden, and also part of the language for the house.

ROAD CROSSING is part of the language for the street, and also part of the language for the busy crossroads.

ALCOVE is part of the language for the house, and part of the language for the workshop—and, in some peculiar outdoor version, perhaps also a part of the language for the river's edge.

LIGHT ON TWO SIDES OF EVERY ROOM applies to every habitable room, in every kind of building—so it is in almost all these languages.

And, more subtly, we find also that different patterns in different languages, have underlying similarities, which suggest that they can be reformulated to make them more general, and usable in a greater variety of cases.

For example, in the University of Oregon, we discovered a pattern which we called DEPARTMENT HEARTH. In our work on clinics, we discovered a pattern which we called TANGENT PATHS. In our work on houses in Peru, we discovered a pattern called FAMILY ROOM CIRCULATION.

All these patterns had the same essential bundle of relationships in common. All of them required a common area at the heart of a social group, placed in such a way that people's natural paths passed tangent to this common area, every time that they moved in and out of the place.

So, it seemed natural to formulate a deeper, and more general, pattern which applied to all these different languages, which we called COMMON AREA AT THE HEART.

Gradually it becomes clear that it is possible to construct one much larger language, which contains all the patterns from the individual languages, and unifies them by tying them together in one larger structure.

This larger language is identical in structure to the smaller languages. But in addition, it contains all these smaller languages within it.

A group of us began to construct such a language eight or nine years ago. To do it, we discovered and wrote down many hundreds of patterns. Then we discarded most of these patterns during the years, because we decided that they were absurd; or because we found more subtle formulations of the same ideas; or because we found that they didn't hold water empirically—or we noticed that they didn't account, empirically, for differences between the places where we felt good and the places where we felt bad.

The 253 patterns which remain are just a handful which at this moment still seem valuable to us. They form the explicit language, which is the second volume of this series, called *A Pattern Language*.

Our version of such a language begins with patterns for the region (#1–7):

INDEPENDENT REGIONS, THE DISTRIBUTION OF TOWNS, CITY COUNTRY FINGERS, AGRICULTURAL VALLEYS, LACE OF COUNTRY STREETS, COUNTRY TOWNS, THE COUNTRY-SIDE.

It has patterns for a town (#8–27):

MOSAIC OF SUBCULTURES, SCATTERED WORK, MAGIC OF THE CITY, LOCAL TRANSPORT AREAS, COMMUNITY OF 7000, SUBCULTURE BOUNDARY, IDENTIFIABLE NEIGH-BORHOOD, NEIGHBORHOOD BOUNDARY, WEB OF PUBLIC TRANSPORTATION, RING ROADS, NETWORK OF LEARN-

331

ING, WEB OF SHOPPING, MINI-BUSES, FOUR-STORY LIMIT, NINE PER CENT PARKING, PARALLEL ROADS, SACRED SITES, ACCESS TO WATER, LIFE CYCLE, MEN AND WOMEN.

It has patterns for communities and neighborhoods (#28–48):

ECCENTRIC NUCLEUS, DENSITY RINGS, ACTIVITY NODES, PROMENADE, SHOPPING STREET, NIGHT LIFE, INTER-CHANGE, HOUSEHOLD MIX, DEGREES OF PUBLICNESS, HOUSE CLUSTER, ROW HOUSES, HOUSING HILL, OLD PEOPLE EVERYWHERE, WORK COMMUNITY, INDUSTRIAL RIBBON, UNIVERSITY AS A MARKETPLACE, LOCAL TOWN HALL, NECKLACE OF COMMUNITY PROJECTS, MARKET OF MANY SHOPS, HEALTH CENTER, HOUSING IN BE-TWEEN.

It has patterns for the public land inside a neighbor-hood (#49–74):

LOOPED LOCAL ROADS, T JUNCTIONS, GREEN STREETS, NETWORK OF PATHS AND CARS, MAIN GATEWAYS, ROAD CROSSING, RAISED WALK, BIKE PATHS AND RACKS, CHIL-DREN IN THE CITY, CARNIVAL, QUIET BACKS, ACCESSIBLE GREEN, SMALL PUBLIC SQUARES, HIGH PLACES, DANCING IN THE STREET, POOLS AND STREAMS, BIRTH PLACES, HOLY GROUND, COMMON LAND, CONNECTED PLAY, PUBLIC OUTDOOR ROOM, GRAVE SITES, STILL WATER, LOCAL SPORTS, ADVENTURE PLAYGROUND, ANIMALS.

332

It has patterns for the private land and institutions in the neighborhood (#75–94):

THE FAMILY, HOUSE FOR A SMALL FAMILY, HOUSE FOR A COUPLE, HOUSE FOR ONE PERSON, YOUR OWN HOME, SELF-GOVERNING WORKSHOPS AND OFFICES, SMALL SERVICES WITHOUT RED TAPE, OFFICE CONNECTIONS, MASTER AND APPRENTICES, TEENAGE SOCIETY, SHOP-FRONT SCHOOLS, CHILDREN'S HOME, INDIVIDUALLY OWNED SHOPS, STREET CAFE, CORNER GROCERY, BEER HALL, TRAVELER'S INN, BUS STOP, FOOD STANDS, SLEEP-ING IN PUBLIC.

Patterns for the broad layout of the buildings in a building complex (#95–126):

BUILDING COMPLEX, NUMBER OF STORIES, SHIELDED PARKING, CIRCULATION REALMS, MAIN BUILDING, PEDESTRIAN STREET, BUILDING THOROUGHFARE, FAM-ILY OF ENTRANCES, SMALL PARKING LOTS, SITE REPAIR, SOUTH FACING OUTDOORS, POSITIVE OUTDOOR SPACE, WINGS OF LIGHT, CONNECTED BUILDINGS, LONG THIN HOUSE, MAIN ENTRANCE, HALF-HIDDEN GARDEN, EN-TRANCE TRANSITION, CAR CONNECTION, HIERARCHY OF OPEN SPACE, COURTYARDS WHICH LIVE, CASCADE OF ROOFS, SHELTERING ROOF, ROOF GARDEN, ARCADES, PATHS AND GOALS, PATH SHAPE, BUILDING FRONTS, PEDESTRIAN DENSITY, ACTIVITY POCKETS, STAIR SEATS, SOMETHING ROUGHLY IN THE MIDDLE.

Patterns for the building and its rooms ($\#$127–158):

INTIMACY GRADIENT, INDOOR SUNLIGHT, COMMON AREAS AT THE HEART, ENTRANCE ROOM, THE FLOW THROUGH ROOMS, SHORT PASSAGES, STAIRCASE AS A STAGE, ZEN VIEW, TAPESTRY OF LIGHT AND DARK, COUPLE'S REALM, CHILDREN'S REALM, SLEEPING TO THE EAST, FARM-HOUSE KITCHEN, PRIVATE TERRACE ON THE STREET, A ROOM OF ONE'S OWN, SEQUENCE OF SITTING SPACES, BED CLUSTER, BATHING ROOM, BULK STORAGE, FLEXIBLE OFFICE SPACE, COMMUNAL EATING, SMALL WORK GROUPS, RECEPTION WELCOMES YOU, A PLACE TO WAIT, SMALL MEETING ROOMS, HALF-PRIVATE OFFICE, ROOMS TO RENT, TEENAGER'S COTTAGE, OLD AGE COTTAGE, SET-TLED WORK, HOME WORKSHOP, OPEN STAIRS.

Patterns for the gardens and the paths between the buildings ($\#$159–178):

LIGHT ON TWO SIDES OF EVERY ROOM, BUILDING EDGE, SUNNY PLACE, NORTH FACE, OUTDOOR ROOM, STREET WINDOWS, OPENING TO THE STREET, GALLERY SUR-ROUND, SIX-FOOT BALCONY, CONNECTION TO THE EARTH, TERRACED SLOPE, FRUIT TREES, TREE PLACES, GARDEN GROWING WILD, GARDEN WALL, TRELLISED WALK, GREENHOUSE, GARDEN SEAT, VEGETABLE GAR-DEN, COMPOST.

Patterns for the smallest rooms and closets within the rooms ($\#$179–204):

ALCOVES, WINDOW PLACE, THE FIRE, EATING ATMO-
SPHERE, WORKSPACE ENCLOSURE, COOKING LAYOUT,
SITTING CIRCLE, COMMUNAL SLEEPING, MARRIAGE BED,
BED ALCOVE, DRESSING ROOM, CEILING HEIGHT VARIETY,
THE SHAPE OF INDOOR SPACE, WINDOWS OVERLOOKING
LIFE, HALF-OPEN WALL, INTERIOR WINDOWS, STAIR-
CASE BAY, CORNER DOORS, THICK WALLS, CLOSETS BE-
TWEEN ROOMS, SUNNY COUNTER, OPEN SHELVES, WAIST-
HIGH SHELF, BUILT-IN SEATS, CHILD CAVES, SECRET
PLACE.

*Patterns for the overall configuration of construction
and materials ($\#205$–213):*

STRUCTURE FOLLOWS SOCIAL SPACES, EFFICIENT STRUC-
TURE, GOOD MATERIALS, GRADUAL STIFFENING, ROOF
LAYOUT, FLOOR AND CEILING LAYOUT, THICKENING THE
OUTER WALLS, COLUMNS AT THE CORNERS, FINAL
COLUMN DISTRIBUTION.

Patterns for the details of construction ($\#214$–232):

ROOT FOUNDATIONS, GROUND FLOOR SLAB, BOX COL-
UMNS, PERIMETER BEAMS, WALL MEMBRANES, FLOOR-
CEILING VAULTS, ROOF VAULTS, NATURAL DOORS AND
WINDOWS, LOW SILL, DEEP REVEALS, LOW DOORWAY,
FRAMES AS THICKENED EDGES, COLUMN PLACE, COL-
UMN CONNECTION, STAIR VAULT, DUCT SPACE, RADIANT
HEAT, DORMER WINDOWS, ROOF CAPS.

*And the language finishes with patterns for details
and color and ornament (#233-253):*

FLOOR SURFACE, LAPPED OUTSIDE WALLS, SOFT INSIDE
WALLS, WINDOWS WHICH OPEN WIDE, SOLID DOORS WITH
GLASS, FILTERED LIGHT, SMALL PANES, HALF-INCH
TRIM, SEAT SPOTS, FRONT DOOR BENCH, SITTING WALL,
CANVAS ROOFS, RAISED FLOWERS, CLIMBING PLANTS,
PAVING WITH CRACKS BETWEEN THE STONES, SOFT TILE
AND BRICK, ORNAMENT, WARM COLORS, DIFFERENT
CHAIRS, POOLS OF LIGHT, THINGS FROM YOUR LIFE.

*Such a language is, in principle, complex enough and
rich enough to be the language for a town.*

It covers all scales, all kinds of social institutions, all the
major kinds of buildings, all the major kinds of outdoor
space; and ways of building which are deep enough to be
used for the full variety of buildings in the town.

But it is not yet fully living as a language.

First, to be living as a language, it must be the shared
vision of a group of people, very specific to their culture,
able to capture their hopes and dreams, containing many
childhood memories, and special local ways of doing
things.

The language we have constructed, and written down,
is built on our own cultural knowledge, of course: but it is
more abstract, more diffuse, and needs to be made con-

crete in a particular time and place, by local customs, local climate, local ways of cooking food, local materials.

To be the common language of a people, and alive, it has to contain much deeper stuff—a vision of a way of life, personal, able to make concrete people's feelings for their parents and the past, able to connect them to a vision of their future as a people, concrete in all their individual particulars, the flowers which grow there in that place, the winds which blow there, the kinds of factories there are . . . .

And further, a living language must be personal.

A language is a living language only when each person in society, or in the town, has his own version of this language.

For it is then not only an intellectual thing which expresses patterns as invariants, as rules to follow, as knowledge about what makes a building or a town work right.

It is, a deeper thing, a felt thing, a thing lived through, which expresses people's innermost attitudes about their way of life, their hopes and fears about the ways in which they live and work together—a communal knowledge of a way of life that will be good for them.

To reach this deeper state, in which each person has a pattern language in his mind as an expression of his attitude to life, we cannot expect people just to copy patterns from a book.

337

I can tell you that ENTRANCE TRANSITION is a good pattern. I can explain the problem to you; and define, in great detail, the physical relationships which make this pattern. But you will not have the pattern in your own mind, as part of your own pattern language, until you have yourself seen several entrances which have this property, seen how wonderful they are, compared them with other entrances which lack this property, and have then, for yourself, invented your own abstraction which pinpoints the difference between the entrances you like and those you don't.

A living language must constantly be re-created in each person's mind.

Even the ordinary language in a person's mind (English, French, whatever) is *created* by him—it is not learned.

When a baby "learns" language from his parents, or from the people around him, he does not learn the rules which they have in their languages—because he cannot see or hear the rules. He only hears the sentences which they produce. What he does then, is to invent systems of rules, for himself, rules which are entirely invented, for the first time, by him. He keeps changing these rules, until with them, he can produce a language similar to the language he hears. And at that stage, we say that he has "learned" the language.

Of course, his rules are similar to his parents' rules, because they have to generate approximately the same kinds of sentences. But in fact, the language he has "learned" is a system of rules, entirely created by him, in his own

338

mind. And as he modifies his language, and improves it, deepens it, throughout his life—he does it, always, by creating, and improving rules, which he invents.

Just so with pattern languages.

Your mind has the innate capacity to create a pattern language. But its exact contents—the specific nature of the patterns in your language—is up to you. You must create them for yourself.

Since your experience is never exactly the same as anyone else's, the versions of the patterns which you create are necessarily a little different from the versions that each other person finds out for himself.

This does not in any way deny the fact that there are objective, deep, invariant truths.

It merely means that each person will, when he finds out this truth for himself, wrest a slightly different version of this truth out for himself.

Then, as each person makes up his own language for himself, the language begins to be a living one.

And just as there will be variations from person to person, so too there will be even more noticeable variation from culture to culture.

The variation from person to person happens because different people actually do have, to some extent, different forces in themselves, and in their lives, and they will therefore experience different configurations of forces as life-giving, or life-destroying.

339

In two different cultures, the forces which exist are even more different, and there is even more opportunity for people to experience different systems of forces as life-creating or life-destroying.

Two neighborhoods with different cultures will have different collections of patterns in their languages.

Obviously, for instance, a Latin neighborhood will be more likely to include the PROMENADE, in the language for their neighborhood, because they have the habit of the evening stroll. A culture which values privacy will be more likely to have COURTYARDS WHICH LIVE in their houses, because they are secluded, than PRIVATE TERRACE ON THE STREET, which is more open to the street.

Different neighborhoods, just like different people, will quite often have different versions of the patterns.

Suppose that many people have the pattern INTIMACY GRADIENT in their languages. In its pure Peruvian form, the family has the most public room in front, the family rooms further back, and the kitchen and bedrooms furthest from the street, in strict order.

In an English neighborhood, the people may have some version of this pattern in their languages: but modified, so that the kitchen comes closer to the front.

In a neighborhood of workshops, this pattern makes little sense in its original form. But even there, it may be that there is some version of it, which implies that the workshops themselves have a front and a back, and that the front part is more public, and the back more private.

And, in different neighborhoods, the people may have systematically different connections in their languages.

For instance, in one neighborhood, people may have a connection between COMMON AREAS AT THE HEART and FARMHOUSE KITCHEN. This means that for them, the farmhouse kitchen *is* the center of the house, the place where everybody comes and goes, the heart of social life.

But, in another neighborhood, nearby, they have these two patterns in their language too—but *not* connected. For these people, their houses have a COMMON AREA AT THE HEART, which is a kind of general comfortable milling space, near the front of the house: and the FARMHOUSE KITCHEN is a small, private area, towards the back, where only close friends of the family meet.

We see then, that a language which is shared within a town is a vast structure, far more complex than an individual language.

Not merely a network, but a network of networks, a structure of structures, a vast pool of changing, varying, languages which people create for themselves as they take on their different building tasks.

341

*And once this kind of structure exists, we have a
living language in a town, in just the same sense that
our common speech is living.*

Think about ordinary language. All of us who speak
English have a common language, yet it is also true that
each of us has created his own language for himself, in
his own brain—and that each of us has a language which
is to some extent idiosyncratic. That is why we can recognize each person's favorite words, his style, his funny and
special ways of putting things. Yet even though each of
us has his own language, the overlap between our languages is enormous—and it is this which gives us a common language.

The same thing happens in genetics.

Each individual member of a given species has a slightly
different set of genes on his chromosomes. If two individuals are closely related, there is enormous overlap in
the genes—only a few are different. As the overlap decreases, we say that the two individuals are members of
different subspecies within the species. And when the
overlap decreases below a certain threshold, we say that
they are members of altogether different species.

*The genetic character of a species is defined by its
gene pool.*

This gene pool is the collection of all the genes currently

possessed by all the individuals in the species. Some of these genes are much more common than others. The genes which are most common define the shared character of the species—the ones which are less common, define individual families and strains.

Since every new individual in the species gets a combination of genes taken from the gene pool (except for very occasional mutations), the overall statistical distribution of genes in the gene pool stays roughly constant, but drifts as evolution makes some genes die out and others multiply.

Just so, a common pattern language is defined by a pool of patterns.

Suppose that every person in society has his own personal pattern language. Now imagine the collection of all the patterns which anyone has in his language. Call this collection of patterns the pattern pool. Some of the patterns will occur much more often in the pattern pool than others. The ones which occur most often are the ones which are shared by everyone. The ones which occur less often are shared by fewer people—these will probably be peculiar to some subculture within society. And the ones which occur least often of all, these are the purely personal patterns, which represent individual people's idiosyncracies.

The common pattern language is not any one language which any one person has in his mind—it is defined by the overall distribution of patterns in the pattern pool.

343

And, once people share a language in this way, the language will begin evolving of its own accord.

Once there is a pool of patterns, and thousands of people are taking patterns from this pool, and using them, exchanging them, replacing them, it is certain that, simply by itself, this language will evolve.

As good patterns get shared more widely, and bad patterns die out, the pattern pool will gradually contain more and more good patterns—and in this sense we may say that a common language is evolving, and becoming better, even at the same time that we recognize that each person will always have his own personal language, which is just one version—a unique version—of this common language.

In this sense, even though any one person's pattern language will always be unique, the overall collection of languages in society will gradually drift towards a common language, represented by the overall character of the pool of patterns.

The language will evolve, because it can evolve piecemeal, one pattern at a time.

Genetic evolution can happen only because the genes can mutate independently. The genes are independent enough, so that a new species can evolve by a process in which one gene changes at a time. If it were not for this, the evolution of a complex organism would never have been possible.

The key to the improvement of patterns is also in the fact that it can be piecemeal. Suppose the language you have now has 100 patterns. Since the patterns are independent, then you can change one at a time, and they can always get better, because you can always improve each pattern, individually. (If the patterns were linked, so that as you improved one pattern, you would also have to change 50 others, the system would be unstable, and you could never improve it cumulatively.)

This means that we can define, discuss, criticize, and improve one pattern at a time: so that we never have to throw away all the other patterns in a language just because one of them is faulty. And any pattern, created by anyone, can fit into any pattern language. In short, as soon as someone defines a really good pattern, it can spread and become part of all the pattern languages in the world, without regard for the other patterns which these millions of different languages contain.

It is this one simple fact, which guarantees that the evolution of pattern languages will be cumulative.

As people exchange ideas about the environment, and exchange patterns, the overall inventory of patterns in the pattern pool keeps changing.

Some patterns drop out altogether, some become rare, some patterns multiply, some new patterns enter the pool. Since there are criteria for deciding which patterns are good, and which ones are bad, people will copy good patterns when they see them, and won't copy bad ones.

345

This means that good patterns will multiply and become more common, while bad patterns will become rarer, and will gradually drop out altogether.

Gradually, as people modify these published languages, add to them, erase from them, a pool of common languages, unique to different places, unique to individuals, and yet broadly shared, will evolve of its own accord.

First, the good patterns will persist; the bad ones will drop out.

Second, since better patterns will persist, and worse ones will drop out, the languages will become more common. In each area, a common language will evolve.

And third, a natural differentiation will occur, in which each town, each region, each culture, adopts a different set of patterns—so that the great stock of pattern languages across the earth will gradually get differentiated.

Of course, this evolution will never end.

Although the process of evolution will always move towards greater depth and greater wholeness, there is no end to it—there is no static perfect language, which, once defined, will stay defined forever. No language is ever finished.

The reason is this. Each language specifies a certain structure for some environment. Once realized, in practice, the very existence of that structure will create new forces, which are born for the first time, out of that structure—and these new forces will, of course, create new problems, new conflicts, that need to be resolved by new patterns—which, when added to our languages, will create still newer forces once again.

This is the eternal cycle of development. There is no hope of stilling it, and no need either. We must simply accept the fact that in the process of evolution, there is no final equilibrium. There are passing phases which approach equilibrium—but that is all. The search for equilibrium, the brush in the dark with a moment of stability, the wave which hesitates a moment before it crashes into the sea again—that is the closest constancy will ever come to being satisfied.

Yet, changing as it is, each language is a living picture of a culture, and a way of life.

The patterns it contains, widely shared, reflect a common understanding about attitudes to life, about the ways that people want to live, the way they want to rear their children, the way they want to eat their meals, the way they want to live in families, the way they want to move from place to place, the way they work, the way they make their buildings look towards the light, their feelings about water, above all, their attitudes towards themselves.

It is a tapestry of life, which shows, in the relationships among the patterns, how the various parts of

347

life can fit together, and how they can make sense, concretely in space.

And, above all, it is not just a passive picture. It has power in it. It is a language, active, powerful, which has the power to let men transform themselves, and their surroundings.

Imagine that one day millions of people are using pattern languages, and making them again. Won't it impress itself then, as extraordinary, that these poems which they exchange, this giant tapestry of images, which they create, is coming alive before their eyes. Will it be possible then, for people to say stonily, that poems are not real, and that patterns are nothing but images: when, in fact, the world of images controls the world of matter.

In early times the city itself was intended as an image of the universe—its form a guarantee of the connection between the heavens and the earth, a picture of a whole and coherent way of life.

A living pattern language is even more. It shows each person his connection to the world in terms so powerful that he can re-affirm it daily by using it to create new life in all the places round about him.

And in this sense, finally, as we shall see, the living language is a gate.

THE WAY

Once we have built the gate, we can
pass through it to the practice of the
timeless way.

CHAPTER 18

THE GENETIC POWER OF LANGUAGE

*Now we shall begin to see in detail how
the rich and complex order of a town can
grow from thousands of creative acts.
For once we have a common pattern
language in our town, we shall all have
the power to make our streets and buildings live, through our most ordinary
acts. The language, like a seed, is the
genetic system which gives our millions
of small acts the power to form a whole.*

Assume, to start with, that some version of the pattern language has been adopted in a town, or in a neighborhood, or by a group of people or a family who adopt it as the basis for the reconstruction of their world.

What is the relation between this common pattern language and the constant process of construction and destruction which gives the town its shape?

Recognize, first of all, that each person in the town has the capacity to shape his own surroundings.

A farmer in a traditional culture "knew" how to make a beautiful house for himself. We envy him, and think that only he was able to do this because his culture made it possible. But this power the primitive farmer had lay in his pattern language.

And if the people of the town now have a pattern language which is whole, they have the same power, exactly. Whatever act of building or repair is contemplated— building a bench, a flower bed, a room, a terrace, a small cottage, a whole house, a group of houses, a remaking of the street, a shop, a café trellis, a complex of public buildings, even the replanning of a neighborhood—they have the power to do it for themselves.

A person with a pattern language can design any part of the environment.

He does not need to be an "expert." The expertise is in the language. He can equally well contribute to the

353

planning of a city, design his own house, or remodel a single room, because in each case he knows the relevant patterns, knows how to combine them, and knows how the particular piece he is working on fits into the larger whole.

And it is essential that the people do shape their surroundings for themselves.

A town is a living thing. Its patterns are both patterns of action and patterns of space. And in the process of making itself, it is the patterns of activity and space, not space alone, which are continuously built, and destroyed, and rebuilt. For this reason, it is essential, once again, that people do it for themselves.

If the town's patterns lay merely in its bricks and mortar, you might argue that these bricks and mortar could be shaped by anyone.

But since the patterns are patterns of action, and the action will not happen unless the patterns are felt, and created, and maintained by the people whose action goes into the patterns, there is no way the living town can be built by professionals, for other people to live in. The living town can only be created by a process in which patterns are created and maintained by the people who are a part of them.

This means, then, that the growth and rebirth of a living town is built up from a myriad of smaller acts.

In a town where the common language has vanished, the acts of construction and design are in few hands, and are large and clumsy.

But once each person in the town can shape a building for himself, or a part of the street, or help to shape a public building, or add a garden or a terrace to a corner of a building—then, at this stage, the growth and rebirth of the town is the concrescence of a million acts.

It is a flux of millions upon millions of these tiny acts, each one in the hands of the person who knows it best, best able to adapt it to the local circumstances.

Within this flux, the people of the town are constantly building, and rebuilding, tearing down, maintaining, modifying, changing, and building again.

A room, a building, or a neighborhood is not made by a single act of building, in a single day. It is the temporary end-result of a thousand different acts, extended over time, and done by unrelated people.

But what guarantee is there that this flux, with all its individual acts, will not create a chaos?

How does the pattern language, which exists behind this flux, steer it, and enter into it?

It hinges on the close relationship between the process of creation and the process of repair.

When an organism grows from a seed, the process of its growth is guided by the genetic materials. Each cell contains the DNA, and every cell is able to take on its part within the whole, by following the growth process which the genetic stuff defines. Somehow, because each cell contains the same material, the cells together, growing independently, create a whole which is complete.

And once the organism is grown the same genetic process guides the process of repair. If I cut myself, the same genetic process which originally created me now takes charge of the smaller process of healing the cut, and guarantees that all the cells around the cut cooperate to form a whole again.

In fact, there is no difference between the way the genes control the process of genetic growth which forms the embryo, and the process of repair which heals the cut. The genes operate continuously, every day, and every moment.

An organism, which seems at first sight like a static thing, is in fact a constant flux of processes.

Cells are born, and die, unceasingly. The organism which exists today is made of different materials from the organism of yesterday. It preserves those broad invariants, which define its character, within the flux. Yet even these are changing slowly, over time. So, what there is, in fact, is a perpetual flux of growth and decay, in which the "organism" is not so much an object, but the character of the invariants behind the flux, which is reborn and reshaped every day.

A town or building also is a constant flux of processes.

If we visit London or New York today, it is a different thing from what it was five years ago. As in an organism there is a process going on which shapes new buildings constantly, destroys the old, replaces and rebuilds and modifies the fabric.

But again, just as in an organism, there is also something which remains the same—there is an invariant continuity behind the flux, a character, a "thing," a "structure," which remains the same.

And it is the pattern language which, like the genes distributed throughout the cells, makes certain that there is this structure, this invariant permanency, in the flux of things, so that the building or the town stays whole.

We know, already, that the common pattern language in a town or a community defines the fundamental situations, the archetypal moments, the components of the way of life which people want to lead.

What we shall now see is the way this pattern language, once it is whole, and widely spread, also maintains the slow pulsating growth and death of situations, buildings, moments, places, in the history of the town.

Imagine the constant process of creation which is happening in a town.

Roads being widened; roads closed; markets being built; new houses; old houses rebuilt; public buildings used for offices; a park made on the corner of a block; people dancing and eating in the streets; street vendors catering to them; a seat is made from which to watch the street; a girl sews cushions for her favorite corner; an orchard blooms; old people take their canvas chairs and sit out underneath the blossoms; a new hotel begins; a farmhouse gets torn down; a corner where a bus stop was becomes a place where people speak in public; the new hotel creates a need for taxis, and the taxi company builds a taxi rank. . . .

All this is guided by the fact that every act which helps to shape the buildings and the town, and their activities, is governed by the pattern language people share—and governed, above all, by just that portion of the language which is especially relevant to that especial act.

In short, that flux in which the town gives birth to new activities, maintains its old ones, modifies them, changes them, is guided by the common pattern language, just as the slow flux of a flower, while it is alive, is governed by the seed within it.

How does the language do it?

Each concrete building problem has a language. The town as an entirety has a language. And each small building task within the town has its own language.

The largest possible pattern language covers the town. It contains, as sublanguages, languages for the different cultures and subcultures in the town. These contain the particular sublanguages for particular climates or local conditions, and these in turn contain the languages for individual neighborhoods. These contain the languages for different kinds of buildings, and for the individual building which is to be built on any individual site—and these once again contain as smaller sublanguages the languages which different families, or individuals, might require for themselves, to build their rooms, and gardens, and the various individual little corners of the greater buildings. . . .

Here is a language for a window seat:

ZEN VIEW

WINDOW PLACE

BUILT-IN SEAT

FRAMES AS THICKENED EDGES

DEEP REVEALS

WINDOWS WHICH OPEN WIDE

SMALL PANES

FILTERED LIGHT

Here is a language for a house:

THE FAMILY

HALF-HIDDEN GARDEN

TREE PLACES

WINGS OF LIGHT

MAIN ENTRANCE

INTIMACY GRADIENT

COMMON AREAS AT THE HEART

SLEEPING TO THE EAST

COURTYARDS WHICH LIVE

INDOOR SUNLIGHT

FARMHOUSE KITCHEN
SEQUENCE OF SITTING SPACES
COUPLE'S REALM
HOME WORKSHOP

Here is a language for repairing common land inside a neighborhood:

ACTIVITY NODES
NETWORK OF PATHS AND CARS
GREEN STREETS
MAIN GATEWAYS
ACCESSIBLE GREEN
SMALL PUBLIC SQUARE
HIGH PLACES
DANCING IN THE STREET
HOLY GROUND
PUBLIC OUTDOOR ROOM
STREET CAFÉ

Here is a language for determining the boundary of a city's growth:

CITY COUNTRY FINGERS
AGRICULTURAL VALLEYS
LACE OF COUNTRY STREETS
LOCAL TRANSPORT AREAS
RING ROADS
SACRED SITES

Every act of building, brings a handful of patterns into existence.

In a town with a common language, this handful is always chosen from the same few hundred patterns which

define the town—so, as different acts of building occur—
even though they may be far apart, or physically unconnected—still, gradually the same few hundred patterns
get created, over and over again—and give the town its
coherence as a fabric.

*And we see, then, how each act of building, because
its pattern language is part of the larger language for
the town, contributes to the larger process which creates the town.*

Just as each gene, or group of genes within a chromo-
some, guide the growth and repair of individual portions
of the organism, so in a town each sublanguage of the
common language also guarantees the complete and
coherent emerging organization of the whole.

As in the organism, there is no sharp difference between the process of construction and the process of
repair. Each process of construction helps repair some
larger whole, of which it is merely a part. No thing is
whole unto itself.

And the larger pattern language which is shared, lies
behind the flux of acts of building and repair, and makes
sure that there is a structure, an invariant permanency in
the flux of things, which makes the town stay whole.

*But the process which integrates the millions of small
acts, and makes them one, is not merely given by
the fact that all these acts are guided by parts of one
great language.*

The common language has an integrative power which goes far beyond this simple coordination. This happens, essentially, because each pattern is connected through the network of the language to every other pattern in the language. And this simple structural fact reflects the more important fact that every act of building can also go beyond its own limits, and help the other patterns in the town to grow.

Each pattern language in the larger language, can, because it is connected to the entire language, help all the other patterns to emerge.

Remember how each pattern in a language is linked to the patterns above it and below it. So, for example, the pattern of PRIVATE TERRACE ON THE STREET helps to complete the larger patterns of the street—GREEN STREETS, HIERARCHY OF OPEN SPACE, and COMMON LAND. And it, in turn, is then completed by the smaller patterns which lie below it in the language: OUTDOOR ROOM, HALF-OPEN WALL, SOFT TILE AND BRICK.

When we use a common language to build a pattern into our world, we automatically build these larger and these smaller patterns too. As we build a PRIVATE TER-RACE on the street, within the framework of a common language, we also try to take care to place it in a way which helps to form the HIERARCHY OF OPEN SPACE out on the street, which helps to form a GREEN STREET; and we also complete it with the shelter of an OUTDOOR ROOM—perhaps a trellis, or a row of columns to enclose it; with a HALF-OPEN WALL which helps to make the half connection to the street; and tiles or bricks or wooden surfaces, which gradually wear, and show the marks of use, and let small plants grow in between.

Each language tugs at the fabric of the larger language, pulls with it other larger patterns, and in this fashion then helps to repair the larger whole.

Thus, within the larger language, it is impossible for any act not to help to repair the larger whole. It is impossible for any act of building to remain an isolated act: it always becomes a portion of the flux of acts which is helping to maintain the whole.

The neighborhood group who take steps to improve their common land and streets will also help to generate the larger patterns for the traffic and the density and shopping areas in the larger town.

A man who builds a house, and has a language for a house, will also help to build the larger street outside his house, generate the patterns which form the street outside his house.

A child who helps to shape his room will also help to generate the larger patterns for the stairway and the common space outside his room.

Even the laying of a brick, to mend a wall, will not only be used to mend that wall, but will be used to help repair the seat, the terrace, or the fireplace which that wall helps to form.

And the pattern language is the instrument by means of which the flux which is the town perpetuates itself, maintains its structure, and keeps itself continuously alive.

It guides the acts of all the individuals there in such a way that every act of building, and each smaller act which seems more modest too, is guided by the patterns in the language which are necessary to it, and gradually generates these patterns, day by day, continuously, so that this place is kept alive, continuously, by the gradual process of creation and destruction. It is not the end product of this process which is alive, but the incessant flux itself. There is no product of this process: the buildings and the town, which live, are that incessant flux, which, guided by its language, constantly creates itself.

We see then the enormous power which a common pattern language has.

The process of life is marked by the continuous creation of wholes from parts. In an organism, cells cooperate to form organs and the body as a whole. In a society the individual actions of the people cooperate to form institutions and larger wholes. . . .

And in a town a pattern language is a source of life, above all, because it helps to generate the wholes, from the cooperation of the individual acts.

CHAPTER 19

DIFFERENTIATING SPACE

Within this process, every individual act of building is a process in which space gets differentiated. It is not a process of addition, in which pre-formed parts are combined to create a whole: but a process of unfolding, like the evolution of an embryo, in which the whole precedes its parts, and actually gives birth to them, by splitting.

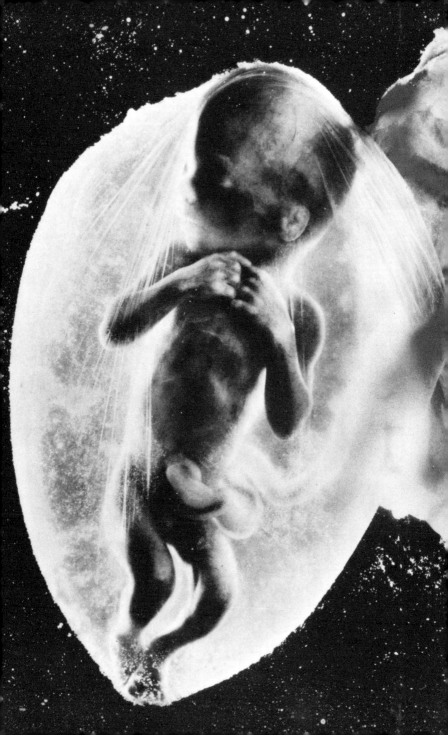

Consider now a single act of building.

As we have seen, there is some language, part of the larger language, which is specific to this act of building, and governs it to give it order.

But how, exactly, does this language work.

In chapters 21 and 22 we shall go through some specific examples, which show exactly how the process works to help a person lay out the plan of a building. And then, in chapter 23 we shall see how the building, once it is laid out, can then be built, in a way which continues the process of development.

However, we shall not understand these examples fully until we first understand two general points about the way a pattern language works. In this chapter we shall learn the importance of the order of the patterns in the language. In the next we shall learn the importance of the intensity of each pattern in the sequence.

Start by remembering the fundamental truth about the parts of any system which is alive.

Each part is slightly different, according to its position in the whole. Each branch of a tree has a slightly different shape, according to its position in the larger tree. Each leaf on the branch is given its detailed form by its position on the branch.

And they must have this character, because, to be alive, they must be patterned properly: and this means that they must contain hundreds of different patterns, overlapped and interwoven at the same time—and this multiple patterning can only be contained in the geometry of nature.

Ask yourself, then, what kind of process can create a building or a place that has this character.

What kind of process will allow us to cram a hundred patterns together, in a limited space?

Or, more concretely—remembering from our discussion in chapter 8 that a geometry which does contain hundreds of interacting patterns will always make every part unique—we may ask, again, what kind of process can create a thing in which every part is slightly different.

Design is often thought of as a process of synthesis, a process of putting together things, a process of combination.

According to this view, a whole is created by putting together parts. The parts come first: and the form of the whole comes second.

But it is impossible to form anything which has the character of nature by adding preformed parts.

When parts are modular and made before the whole, by definition then, they are identical, and it is impossible for every part to be unique, according to its position in the whole.

368

Even more important, it simply is not possible for any combination of modular parts to contain the number of patterns which must be present simultaneously in a place which is alive.

It is only possible to make a place which is alive by a process in which each part is modified by its position in the whole.

Imagine, for the sake of argument, that a certain FARM-HOUSE KITCHEN consists, in essence, of a large kitchen table, with a stove and counters round it. And suppose, now, that in one corner there is to be an alcove. It is easy to see that this alcove may have to be a slightly unusual alcove; it may have to be part of the kitchen counter, or connect up with it in some way, and perhaps have a certain specific relation even with the kitchen table.

And suppose, further, that this slightly unusual alcove is now to contain a WINDOW PLACE and a WINDOWSILL, a place to sit, a low sill. Of course, again, this window place may have to take its character from the particular shape which the ALCOVE has; it may have less light, perhaps, because it is in the only corner not taken up by cooking things; it may have a higher ceiling than usual, because the kitchen needs more ventilation; it may have a tiled floor, or tiles on the wall, to counteract the steam and water in the kitchen.

In short, each part is given its specific form by its existence in the context of the larger whole.

369

This is a differentiating process.

It views design as a sequence of acts of complexification; structure is injected into the whole by operating on the whole and crinkling it, not by adding little parts to one another. In the process of differentiation, the whole gives birth to its parts: the parts appear as folds in a cloth of three dimensional space which is gradually crinkled. The form of the whole, and the parts, come into being simultaneously.

The image of the differentiating process is the growth of an embryo.

It starts as a single cell. The cell grows into a ball of cells. Then, through a series of differentiations, each building on the last, the structure becomes more and more complex, until a finished human being is formed.

The first thing that happens is that this ball gets an inside, a middle layer, and an outside: the endoderm, mesoderm, and ectoderm, which will later turn into skeleton, flesh, and skin, respectively.

Then this ball of cells with three layers gets an axis. The axis is laid down in the endoderm, and will become the spine of the finished person.

Then this ball, with an axis, gets a head at one end.

Later, the secondary structures, eyes, limbs, develop in relation to the spinal axis and the head.

And so on. At every stage of development, new structure is laid down, on the basis of the structure which has been laid down so far. The process of development is, in essence, a sequence of operations, each one of which differentiates the structure which has been laid down by the previous operations.

371

*The unfolding of a design in the mind of its creator,
under the influence of language, is just the same.*

A language allows you to generate an image of a building
in your mind, by placing patterns in space, one pattern at a
time.

At the beginning of a design process, you may have an
idea that the open space should be "more or less over
here," and the building "more or less over there." Neither
the pattern for "open space" nor the pattern for "building" is very precisely defined at this stage. They are like
two clouds, whose size is imprecise, and with imprecise
edges. It is not even perfectly certain, at this stage, that the
cloud called "open space" will be entirely open—nor that
the cloud called building will be entirely roofed. What is
happening, is that you place these two clouds, roughly, at
this stage of the design, with the full understanding that
the design is accurate only to within the order of magnitude of the clouds themselves, and that all kinds of details
which are smaller in scale, may be changed later.

Later in the process, you may be placing the "entrance"
to the building. Again, the pattern which you call the entrance is a cloudy volume, about the right size, clear
enough so that you can pin point its location, with respect
to other larger clouds, and to show its relations to the
things next to it, but no more exact than that.

And, yet another stage in the design process, you may
place a column. This column has a height, and a rough
size—but again, at the time you place it first, it has little
more. Later, you make the column more exact, by placing

the edges of the column, its reinforcing bars, its foundation, and so on.

Whenever we want to make one of these vague cloudy patterns more precise, we do it by placing other smaller patterns, which define its edge and interior.

Each pattern is an operator which differentiates space: that is, it creates distinctions where no distinction was before.

The operator is concrete and specific, insofar as it will always generate an instance of the pattern.

But the operator is quite general, because it specifies the operation in such a way that its performance interacts with the surroundings, to make a particular embodiment of the pattern which is unique.

And in the language the operations are arranged in sequence: so that, as they are done, one after another, gradually a complete thing is born, general in the sense that it shared its patterns with other comparable things; specific in the sense that it is unique, according to its circumstances.

The language is a sequence of these operators, in which each one further differentiates the image which is the product of the previous differentiations.

Since the patterns are arranged in order of their morphological importance, the use of the language guarantees that a whole is successively differentiated, so that smaller and

373

smaller wholes appear in it, as a result of the distinctions which are drawn.

When a pattern language is properly used, it allows the person who uses it to make places which are a part of nature, because the successive acts of differentiation which the patterns define, are ordered in such a way that at each step new wholes are born, infinitely various because they are adapted to the larger wholes in which they sit, and with the parts between the wholes themselves whole, because the acts of differentiation make them so.

Here is a simple example of a balcony whose shape grew by a differentiating process.

My house has a bay window looking out into a group of pine trees. I decided to build a balcony out there, six feet above the ground, at the same level as the living room itself. Here is the sequence of decisions which gave birth to the design.

TREE PLACES: I decided to use an old pine tree as the right-hand corner post of the extension. It is a beautiful old tree, which, as the corner of the balcony, spreads its branches to form a natural umbrella.

SUNNY PLACE: I put the left-hand post as far as it could be to the left, so as to catch a corner of sunshine that repeatedly falls on that spot during the day.

STRUCTURE FOLLOWS SOCIAL SPACES: I decided to place two other posts, not one, so that there would be two corner spaces created, each a useful social space, with a diameter of about 5 feet. One column would have split the thing, and made no spaces anywhere, since the corners would be too large.

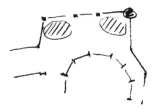

COLUMNS AT THE CORNERS: I wanted the corners to be large enough to function as social spaces, and therefore larger than the center span. On the other hand, since these columns would define the positions of intermediate beams, I wanted to make the central span as large as it could be—and not waste it by making it too narrow. As a result of these deliberations, I finally settled on 5½-3-5½. If the post had been equally spaced, at modular intervals, the corners would have been too small to live.

PERIMETER BEAM: The right-hand beam ran at an angle, so that it could run directly into the tree.

FLOOR SURFACE: The planks were cut, as needed, to fit the overall shape of the balcony.

Imagine what this balcony would have been like if I had tried to make it up from modular components.

Say, for the sake of argument, that there were some kind of prefabricated, concrete building modules available—each one four feet wide.

It would have been impossible to use the tree, because the modular piece has a prescribed way of connecting to a column—and there would, within the system, be no way to connect it to the tree because the tree slopes at an angle inconsistent with the modules.

It would also have been impossible to run the beam into the tree, because it runs in at an angle. It would have been necessary to make some awkward composition of squares, which would destroy the simple edge between the balcony and the bushes and trees below.

The width of the balcony would have had to be either 12 or 16 feet. The second of these is too large. The first does not make proper use of the site, and misses the patch of sunlight on the left.

It would not have been possible to use the corners as effective places: the even spacing of the columns would have made it impossible to make the corners large enough to use.

In short, this balcony—organic as it is—could not have been built up from modular components.

Only the process of differentiation, which guaranteed that each decision fit only the larger decisions which came before it, and could go unhampered by the details which were yet to come, allowed the balcony to become a natural living thing.

But of course, this process only works because the patterns in the language have a certain order.

Suppose, for instance, that I take a list of patterns for a house, in random order. I will not be able to build a coherent image from them, because the different operations will almost certainly contradict each other. To understand this clearly, imagine that someone is reading you a collection of patterns for a house, one at a time. You are trying to form a single coherent image of the house, as he goes along. And, suppose, for a moment, that he reads out the list of patterns in a random order. Thus:

OUTDOOR ROOM: The family room opens out onto a kind of outdoor room.

ALCOVES: There are alcoves all around the edge of the family room.

CAR HOUSE CONNECTION: The kitchen is near the entrance to the house.

CHILDREN'S REALM: The children's bedrooms are near the kitchen.

FARMHOUSE KITCHEN: The family room and kitchen are next to each other, with a half-open counter between them.

You cannot read this list of statements one at a time, in this order, and create a coherent image of a house, as you read them. When you come to the last statement, you will have to "go back." By the time you have read the first four statements, you have already placed the family room, garden, children's bedrooms, and kitchen in a certain relationship to one another—and it would be pure coincidence if this arrangement happened to include the fifth pattern—that kitchen and family room open into each other.

If the arrangement you are imagining at this moment has the kitchen and family room separated, you will have to change it—and to change it virtually means going back to the first statement again.

The patterns will only allow me to form a single coherent image in my mind, if the order that I take them in allows me to build an image of a design gradually, one pattern at a time.

And I shall only be able to do this if each pattern is always consistent with the total image which I have built from all the earlier patterns in the sequence.

This requires that the sequence of the patterns meets three simple conditions.

First, if pattern A is above pattern B in the network of the language, then I must take A before I take B. This is the most fundamental rule. For instance, if SITTING ROOM is above ALCOVE in the language (so that a sitting room contains an alcove as a part)—then, obviously, I cannot build ALCOVES into the image of my SITTING ROOM, until I have already got a rough and ready image of the SITTING ROOM itself.

Second, I must take all the patterns immediately above A, as close together in sequence as I can. If CIRCULATION REALMS and CAR HOUSE CONNECTION are both immediately above MAIN ENTRANCE, they both help to set the stage for the creation of the main entrance. They will only make a coherent framework for the entrance, in my mind, if they come close together, so that I can fuse them.

Third, I must take all the patterns immediately below the pattern A, as close together in sequence as I can. Thus, for instance, POSITIVE OUTDOOR SPACE and WINGS OF LIGHT, which both come immediately under BUILDING COMPLEX, must come close together. When you put a house on a lot you are *simultaneously* creating the open spaces which form the garden and shaping the building. You cannot help it. One defines the other. The building defines the open space and the open space defines the building. So you must use the two patterns as nearly at the same time as possible.

We have been able to show, experimentally, that the more a sequence of patterns meets these three conditions, the more coherent a person's image is.

When the sequence meets these conditions perfectly, any-one—even a so-called "lay" person—will spontaneously create a coherent image of a complete building in his mind, as he hears the patterns one by one. When he has heard all the patterns, he will be able to describe the com-plete design clearly, will be able to "walk" another person through it, describe what he sees from various angles, and so on . . . in short, his design is coherent and complete.

On the other hand, the more a sequence of patterns violates the three conditions, the more incoherent the person's image becomes.

For instance, if two patterns, both above a given pattern in the language, are widely separated in the sequence, it is very likely that the relationship between these patterns will be confused in the emerging design. Or, more ex-treme, if a small pattern comes before a large one in the sequence, and thus violates the first condition, it is very likely that all the patterns which lie in between the two in the sequence will be dropped out of the emerging de-sign, or even forgotten entirely.

And this is why a pattern language has the natural power to help us form coherent images.

For we can always use our language to produce a sequence

which is consistent with these three conditions. Suppose, for instance, that you want to use a language to design a house.

We know from chapter 16, that the language has the structure of a network, or cascade. Assume, for the sake of argument, that the language contains 100 patterns which are needed in the house. To get these 100 patterns, in the proper order, you must simply begin a kind of trip, in which you move through the network of the language, taking one pattern at a time, moving roughly downwards, and back and forth at the same time, following the three conditions as closely as you can.

The sequences which we obtain from language, will meet these three conditions almost automatically.

Of course, the particular sequence of patterns for any given project, will always be unique according to the details of the project.

This happens because, according to the context, the patterns have slightly different relations to one another . . . which will affect the sequence they have when we try to meet the three conditions. Thus, for example, in a house on a narrow city lot, the pattern SMALL PARKING LOT will exert a controlling influence on the design—and the pattern must therefore come early in the sequence. In another house, where there is more land, this pattern can come later in the sequence (since cars can be put almost anywhere without disturbance), but other patterns—for instance TREE PLACES—must come earlier because *they* now exert a controlling influence on the design.

But in every case, there is some sequence of patterns

which is the most appropriate for that design; and you can get this sequence more or less directly from your knowledge of the size of the morphological effect which each pattern has, compared with all the others.

The sequence of the patterns for a design—as generated by the language—is therefore the key to that design.

For once you find the proper sequence, the power to design coherent things follows from it almost automatically, and you will be able to make a beautiful and whole design, without any trouble. If the sequence is correctly formed, you can create a beautiful whole, almost without trying, because it is in the nature of your mind to do so. But, if the sequence is not correctly formed—if the sequence is itself incoherent, or the patterns in it incomplete—then no amount of trying will allow you to create a design which is whole.

Conventional wisdom says that a building cannot be designed, in sequence, step by step.

But the fact is that you cannot understand the morphology of a building, or create a design which has that morphology, until you understand which features are dominant, and which ones secondary—it is fundamental to your ability as an artist that you establish this morphological order in your mind. In this sense, the actual creation of the sequence, by the artist, is one of the most crucial aspects of the design task. You really understand what you are doing for the first time at that moment when the sequence of the patterns becomes clear to you.

Sequences are bad when they are the *wrong* sequences.

But the sequence which a language gives you works because it treats the building as a whole, at every step.

Each pattern is a field which spreads throughout the whole, and tinges it, distorts it, patterns it. We can take patterns, step by step, one at a time, because each pattern moulds the whole—and each pattern can mould the whole which is the product of the previous patternings.

In nature, a thing is always born, and developed, as a whole.

A baby starts, from the first day of its conception, as a whole, and is a whole, as an embryo, every day until it is born. It is not a sequence of adding parts together, but a whole, which expands, crinkles, differentiates itself.

A wave is shaped as a whole. It is part of the system of waves, and is a part of a legitimate well-formed living whole, as it starts, swells, crashes, and dies.

A mountain is shaped as a whole: the crust of the earth heaves, the mountain takes its form; and while it is growing, each rock, and particle of sand is also whole: there is nothing unfinished in it, during the thousands of years that bring it to the state we know today.

A building, too, can only come to life when it grows as a whole.

As we conceive the whole, in our minds, it starts as a whole, and continues as a whole, throughout our mental operations; and ends as a whole. Each mental operation differentiates it, makes it more elaborate: but treats it as a whole, and operates on the image we have of it, as a whole.

At every level, certain broad patterns get laid down: and the details are squeezed into position to conform to the structure of these broader patterns. Of course, under these circumstances, the details are always slightly different, since they get distorted as they are squeezed into the larger structure already laid down. In a design of this type, one naturally senses that the global patterns are more important than the details, because they dominate the design. Each pattern is given the importance and control over the whole which it deserves in the hierarchy of patterns.

And it follows, therefore, that when a pattern language is properly used, it allows the person who uses it to make places which are a part of nature.

The character of nature is not something added to a good design. It comes directly from the order of the language. When the order of the patterns in the language is correct, the differentiating process allows the design to unfold as smoothly as an opening flower.

We are ready now to find out the details of this process of unfolding.

CHAPTER 20

ONE PATTERN AT A TIME

*The process of unfolding goes step by
step, one pattern at a time. Each step
brings just one pattern to life: and the
intensity of the result depends on the
intensity of each one of these individual
steps.*

Suppose now, that for a given act of building, you have a pattern language, and that the patterns in this language are arranged in proper sequence.

To make the design, you take the patterns one by one, and use each one to differentiate the product of the previous patterns.

But how exactly, does each pattern work.

At any given moment in the unfolding of a sequence of patterns, we have a partly defined whole, which has the structure given to it by the patterns that come earlier in the sequence.

And we are now faced with the problem of injecting the next pattern into this whole, filling the whole with it, infusing the whole with the structure of this pattern, making just those differentiations in the whole, which will bring this next pattern to life, throughout the fabric of the whole.

How exactly does this work?

Suppose, for instance, that you want to create a WINDOW PLACE *which is alive.*

Start by remembering all the particular window places you have known: especially the ones which were most beautiful. Close your eyes, and concentrate on them—so that you get a direct instinctive knowledge of the pattern, rooted in your own experience.

And concentrate, also, on the particular aspects of the WINDOW PLACE which make it live: the light, the seat, the windowsill, flowers growing outside perhaps, the quietness and separateness, which make the window place a "place."

Ask yourself how this pattern would look if it were already in the place where you are wanting it.

To do this, you need only close your eyes, and imagine that you are coming through the door. Imagine that the room or place which you are shaping has a WINDOW PLACE in it.

Your knowledge of the pattern, interacting with your knowledge of the place, will speak to you, and tell you just what form the pattern takes, in this particular place.

To keep the pattern strong, it is essential that you don't yet put in any other details. You do not yet need to imagine the positions of the window panes, in detail, because that will be done by later patterns. You do not need to know, yet, what exactly is the height of window-sills, because the pattern LOW SILL does it for you, later. You do not need to know, yet, just exactly what the ceiling height is, there, because the pattern CEILING HEIGHT VARIETY will do it for you later.

The only thing you must have clear, at this stage, is the whole, the space of the WINDOW PLACE itself, how large it is, how the light comes into it, how people sit, so that they are related to the light and to the inside of the room, and, above all, just how the window place does indeed define a *place* which is identified, and light. These things you must know, because these are the ones which this pattern specifically deals with.

The most important thing is that you take the pattern seriously.

There is no point at all in using the pattern if you only give lip service to it.

For example, I remember one case where a man was designing a beach house, with two apartments one over the other—and an outdoor stair, leading to the upstairs one. He was telling me how the patterns he was using entered into his design: and he said that the stair landing at the top of the stair was the ENTRANCE TRANSITION for the upstairs room.

I said to him: Look, this little landing, which is maybe three feet by four, is not an ENTRANCE TRANSITION at all. You are calling it that and trying to pretend to yourself that you have created this pattern there. But it is just the top of the stair. An ENTRANCE TRANSITION is a place where the light changes, a place where the level changes, where you are suddenly filled with a sense of new experience, a change, a wiping clean, that happens just before you go inside.

If you really want to make an ENTRANCE TRANSITION there, at the top of the stair, you must close your eyes, and ask yourself: What would it be like, if this was the most wonderful entrance transition in the world?

Imagine. I close my eyes. I see a place from which there is a sudden view, which you can't see from the bottom of the stair. I see a place which is filled with the scent of jasmine in the summer. I hear my step as I reach this place up on top: it changes, because, perhaps, there is a creaking board. So now I begin to imagine a stair which is almost closed in, by wooden fretwork, the top placed with an opening which looks out on the sea; a trellis overhead with jasmine climbing on it; a seat across from the door, where I can sit, to smell the breeze; the stair made loosely, so that the boards creak as I begin to climb the stair . . . .

Now you have really done something.

Now this entrance transition is more than just a phrase; it is an actual living thing. But now, of course, it is a little strange, perhaps. How do I have to build the stair, to keep it closed in further down, with fretwork to let light in; how must I place the landing at the top, so that it looks back at the sea? It is no longer just the "top of the stairs" somewhere. It is a place which I will not forget, because it has a character. And this character is not created wilfully, by me—it has been generated, simply, by paying serious attention to the pattern.

Indeed, each pattern, when you really do it, creates an almost startling character.

When you insist, and genuinely form the pattern, and go

393

all the way with it, it generates a character: it looks almost strange; slightly startling. It is extreme; you know that someone has been working here. It is not bland, but full.

For instance, in the second picture of this chapter, the roof overhang of the SHELTERING ROOF *is immense.*

There is no lip service to the sheltering roof. The people who built this built it with all the courage and the certainty that it was really needed. There are no half measures; no compromises; this is a sheltering roof, in full.

In the third picture, the FILTERED LIGHT *is once again intense.*

This picture is important, because it shows that taking patterns seriously does not require money. Here, in the simplest hut, the people inside felt so strongly about FILTERED LIGHT that they strung beans on strings, across the window, in the most extraordinary way. They took the pattern seriously, and it created, for them, something unique.

It is the same intensity you may find in a rock or tree which grows under extraordinary circumstances. When a tree grows in a corner, wind from one angle, rocks beneath it, it may take on a wild character, intense, created by the interaction of the special circumstances, with its genes. When the patterns are given their full in-

394

tensity, and allowed to interact freely with circumstances, we get the same.

And in the first picture, we see LIGHT ON TWO SIDES OF EVERY ROOM *as intense as possible.*

Almost everyone has some experience of a room filled with light, sun streaming in, perhaps yellow curtains, white wood, patches of sunlight on the floor, which the cat searches for—soft cushions where the light is, a garden full of flowers to look out onto.

If you search your own experience, you can certainly remember a place like this—so beautiful it takes your breath away to think of it.

Look at the great room from the Topkapi Palace in this first picture. It is almost as though the room itself is one great window. You can make a room like that, if you pay enough attention, are serious enough about the windows, look to see where the light is, place the room, not in some place where it just gets light on two sides, but in the best place, where it can get light from all around, and the best and most beautiful light there is on the site. Then it can happen.

You may not believe that you can make a place as beautiful as that.

So, when you come to this pattern, LIGHT ON TWO SIDES OF EVERY ROOM, you check in a halfhearted, perfunctory manner, to see if every room has two walls to the outside, and that there are a couple of windows, more or less in the right place.

But that produces nothing. It is only when you pay attention, in the full belief that every room you make can be as beautiful as the most beautiful light-filled room which you have ever seen—then you are serious enough. At that moment it will happen. All it requires is the will.

To do it you need only let it happen in your mind.

Say to yourself: I am coming into that room, I am not in it yet, but I come in through the door, and there, to my surprise, is the most beautiful room that I have ever been in. The pattern LIGHT ON TWO SIDES is there, as intense and beautiful as in any room that I have ever known, as intense as in the picture of the Topkapi Palace . . . you say all this to yourself, before you walk in through the door. And then, with your eyes closed, in your imagination, you walk from the next door room, throw open the door, and step inside . . . and there it is.

And there it is. Suddenly, without your making any conscious effort, your mind will show you how this light on two sides is, in that particular place, as beautiful as you have ever known it anywhere.

Do not consciously try to create the pattern. If you do this, the images and ideas in your mind will distort it, will begin to take over, and the pattern itself will never make its way into the world: instead there will be a "design."

Get rid of the ideas which come into your mind. Get rid of pictures you have seen in magazines, friends' houses . . . . Insist on the pattern, and nothing else.

The pattern, and the real situation, together, will create the proper form, within your mind, without your trying to do it, if you will allow it to happen.

This is the power of the language, and the reason why the language is creative.

Your mind is a medium within which the creative spark that jumps between the pattern and the world can happen. You yourself are only the medium for this creative spark, not its originator.

I remember once, sitting in Berkeley, trying to work out a site plan on paper, for our houses in Peru. One of the LOOPED LOCAL ROADS into the site was not yet properly in place, and we could not find a suitable way of fitting this pattern road into the design, the way the patterns told us to—so I decided to take a walk around the site in my imagination.

I sat in my chair, in Berkeley, 8000 miles from the real site in Lima, closed my eyes, and began to take a walk around the market. There were many narrow lanes, covered with bamboo screens to shade them, with tiny stalls opening off them, and fruit sellers selling fruit from carts. I stopped by one old woman's cart, and bought an orange from her. As I stood there I happened to be facing north. And then I bit into the orange—in my imagination. And just as I bit into it, I suddenly stopped and asked myself, "Now, where is that road?" And, without thinking, I knew exactly where it was, and what its relation to the market was—I knew it must be over *there*, towards the right, from the direction I was facing. I knew that to be natural; it must come sweeping towards the market, and touch it over there.

Then I stopped, and came back to my room, and my chair, and my effort to make the design. I realized at once that this position of the road, which had come to me so naturally, was quite different from all the ones we had been trying on paper in those last few days—and that it was exactly right, and satisfied the demands of all the patterns perfectly.

It was the vividness of being there, and biting into that orange, that allowed me to know, spontaneously, the most natural place for that road to be.

You may find this way of letting patterns form themselves, unusual.

To do it, you must let go of your control and let the pattern do the work. You cannot do this, normally, because you are trying to make decisions without having confidence in the basis for them. But if the patterns you are using are familiar to you, if they make sense to you, if you are confident that they make sense, and that they are profound, then there is no reason to be afraid, and no reason to be afraid of giving up your control over the design. If the pattern makes sense, you do not need to control the design.

You may be afraid that the design won't work if you take just one pattern at a time.

If you take one pattern at a time, what guarantee is there that all the patterns will fit together coherently? What happens if you put the patterns together, one at a time, and then, suddenly, with the ninth or tenth, you find that it is quite impossible, because there is a conflict between the design which has emerged so far, and the next pattern in the sequence?

The greatest fear we experience in the process of design is that everything will not work out. And yet the building will become alive only when you can let go of this fear.

Suppose, for instance, you are trying to decide where to place the entrance to your house. As you are doing it, images of other problems flit through your mind. Will I be able to fit the dining room in if I put the entrance here? But on the other hand, if I put it over there, maybe I won't have room to put the bed alcoves in properly; . . . what shall I do? How can I place the entrance so that all these problems will work themselves out when the time comes?

But you cannot create a pattern at full intensity, so long as you are worrying and thinking about other patterns, which you will have to deal with later in the sequence.

399

This frenzy will always kill the pattern. It will force you to create artificial, "thought out" configurations, which are stiff and lifeless. This is the thing which prevents people, most often, from creating a pattern at full intensity.

Suppose, for example, that we are trying to build a house which has fifty patterns in it. It seems almost inconceivable that these fifty patterns will not somehow conflict: and it seems essential, therefore, to work out some overall scheme in which enough compromises are made to allow each of the patterns to be present to some extent.

This frame of mind destroys the patterns.

It destroys all possibility of life, because as soon as you begin to compromise the patterns there is no life left in them.

But there is no need for this frame of mind. It is not necessary to make compromises between the patterns.

When you start to think about compromises between patterns, you are not taking account of the fact that every pattern is a *rule of transformation.* The fact that every pattern is a rule of transformation means that each pattern has the power to transform any configuration by injecting a new configuration into it, without essentially disturbing any essentials of the configuration which was there before.

Suppose that I want to create a MAIN ENTRANCE.

The character of the MAIN ENTRANCE as a rule means that I can take any configuration, which lacks this pattern—it may be a real building which exists already, or a partly thought out building in my mind—and apply this pattern to it—that is, inject a MAIN ENTRANCE into it, in the most beautiful and extreme form possible—without disturbing the essentials of what I have already.

There is no reason to be timid.

If I am going to create a beautiful MAIN ENTRANCE, there is no point in worrying about whether I will later be able to create a beautiful ENTRANCE TRANSITION there.

At this time when I inject MAIN ENTRANCE into the design, I need think only about the MAIN ENTRANCE pattern, in all its fullness and extremity—in the certain knowledge that when I come, later, to the ENTRANCE TRANSITION pattern, I will once again be able to inject *that* pattern, in all its fullness and extremity also.

The order of the language will make sure that it is possible.

For as we have seen in Chapter 19, the order of the language is the order which the patterns need to operate on one another to create a whole. It is a morphological order, similar to the order which must be present in an evolving embryo.

And it is this very same order which also allows each

pattern to develop its full intensity. When we have the order of the language right, we can pay attention to one pattern at a time, with full intensity, because the interference between patterns, and the conflicts between patterns, are reduced to almost nothing by the order of the language.

Within the sequence which the language defines, you can focus on each pattern by itself, one at a time, certain that those patterns which come later in the sequence will fit into the design which has evolved so far.

You can pay full attention to each pattern; you can let it have its full intensity.

Then you can give each pattern just that strange intensity which makes the pattern live.

CHAPTER 21

SHAPING ONE BUILDING

From a sequence of these individual patterns, whole buildings with the character of nature will form themselves within your thoughts, as easily as sentences.

We are ready, now, to see just how a sequence of patterns can create a building in our minds.

It happens with surprising ease. The building almost "makes itself," just as a sentence seems to when we speak.

And it can happen as easily within an ordinary person's mind, or in a builder's mind. Everyone, builder or not, can do this for himself, to make a building live . . . .

Assume, to start with, that we have a language for a house.

Look at the patterns in the order they come in, one at a time.

Add nothing, except just what the patterns demand.

Slowly, you will find that an image of a house is growing in your mind.

Here are the rough notes I wrote down during the week it took to design a small cottage in this way.

I decided to build a small cottage/workshop at the back of our office. A place large enough to live in; a place where guests might stay; and a place where someone could live and work, as a workshop; and a place we could rent to a friend, when it wasn't occupied by one of us.

There is a large house in front; another cottage behind; an old garage; outside stairs leading to the upstairs of the large house. I decided that it would not be practical

407

to spend more than about $3000 for materials. At $8 per square foot for materials (I knew that we would build it ourselves so labor was to be free), we could build a cottage of 400 square feet.

Here is the language I chose for the building:

WORK COMMUNITY
THE FAMILY
BUILDING COMPLEX
CIRCULATION REALMS
NUMBER OF STORIES
HOUSE FOR ONE PERSON
SOUTH FACING OUTDOORS
WINGS OF LIGHT
CONNECTED BUILDINGS
POSITIVE OUTDOOR SPACE
SITE REPAIR
MAIN ENTRANCE
ENTRANCE TRANSITION
CASCADE OF ROOFS
ROOF GARDEN
SHELTERING ROOF
ARCADE
INTIMACY GRADIENT
ENTRANCE ROOM
STAIRCASE AS A STAGE
ZEN VIEW
TAPESTRY OF LIGHT AND DARK
FARMHOUSE KITCHEN
BATHING ROOM
HOME WORKSHOP

408

SHAPING ONE BUILDING

LIGHT ON TWO SIDES OF EVERY ROOM
BUILDING EDGE
SUNNY PLACE
OUTDOOR ROOM
CONNECTION TO THE EARTH
TREE PLACES
ALCOVES
WINDOW PLACE
THE FIRE
BED ALCOVE
THICK WALLS
OPEN SHELVES
CEILING HEIGHT VARIETY

The first thing was repair.

The existing cottage is disconnected. The garage is a bit derelict; the trees and grass at the very back need pruning and are very overgrown. Above all, the people who live upstairs in the main house, and at the back, have no over-all sense of connection to one another. Also the most beautiful part of the garden—which faces south, and is under the locust tree, is unused, because there is nothing near it or around it, and no paths which naturally go to and fro to make it naturally usable.

To solve all these problems, I tried, first of all, to make a building which created SOUTH FACING OUT-DOORS *and* POSITIVE OUTDOOR SPACE.

409

For SOUTH FACING OUTDOORS, I imagine a nice big terrace, out towards the back of the main house, in the sun. If we put it to the south and west of the cottage, it will be in the other opening in the trees, and get plenty of sun: a good place to work, make things; perhaps we can put a workbench out there in good weather; and a place for a couple of chairs and a table, where we can sit and have a drink. We need to spend a day on the site, watching the sun, to identify the exact places where sun falls (SUNNY PLACE); it is tricky, because the sun comes through the trees, only in a few special places, and we must be very accurate about placing them.

All this puts the cottage as far to the north as possible. To form POSITIVE OUTDOOR SPACE, I also place the building well back into the site, so that it leaves a well-formed space between the garage and the trees in front. In that position, there is space for a cottage, running north-south, up to about 13 feet wide, and up to about 25 feet long. As far as connections with the existing cottage are concerned (BUILDING COMPLEX, CONNECTED BUILDINGS), there is no bathroom in the existing cottage, so it will be a great help if we build a bathroom which the two cottages share. There is a natural place for that, right between the two buildings.

Next NUMBER OF STORIES, CASCADE OF ROOFS, SHELTERING ROOF, ROOF GARDEN *give me the overall shape of the building.*

Mostly it will be a one-story building; but we want to try the two-story structure, and it would be nice to have a sleeping loft upstairs. This two-story part of the thing should naturally be to the north end, so that it forms a ROOF GARDEN to the south. Given its position, it makes sense to think of this sleeping loft as about 8 x 13, opening out to a flat roof to the south, over the one-story part of the cottage. This goes some way towards creating the CASCADE OF ROOFS. So that our neighbor to the north doesn't have a high wall right next to his garden, it makes sense to imagine lower, alcove roofs falling off to the north. And the same somewhere to the south perhaps, and the same again where the entrance is, there might be an entrance porch. This will make a number of lower roofs, low enough to touch, around the edge of the building (SHELTERING ROOF and CASCADE OF ROOFS).

Within this overall shape, CIRCULATION REALMS *and* WORK COMMUNITY *tell me how to complete the site.*

CIRCULATION REALMS is not good; and the connection with the main house needed by WORK COMMUNITY isn't good enough. The main trouble is this. There are two paths to the back: one up the driveway; the other through dark bushes. The one up the driveway is OK, but not a direct connection; and the main house's back porch goes out sideways to it; not direct. To make the connection clear, and the circulation, we will open up the back of the back porch, so it connects directly to the terrace of the cottage. It will only be a few feet, then, from the back porch, to the coffee, umbrella, chairs, workbench—or whatever else we put on the terrace—and it will be natural to go back and forward all the time. We can lay tiles into the earth, to make the connection; also, looking at the bushes under there, which are so dark—we need to prune them, cut out dead wood, to bring more light in along that path. We might even prune out enough dead wood so grass could grow there, with the trees just standing in the grass.

SITE REPAIR *tells me exactly what to protect around the building*.

The tree to the north is down, as our neighbor wanted; in exchange we will, I hope, be able to build up to his fence—since he can get sunlight all the way onto his lawn now. It is a shame cutting down a tree: but the trees at the back grew too thick; one less and the others will grow stronger; and, most important, it helps to repair his garden to the north of ours, by giving him SOUTH FACING OUTDOORS too.

In clearing the site, the little apple tree next to the garage seems more beautiful than ever; and the wild onions, with their white flowers, growing around the foot of it are lovely. We have put stakes around them, to protect them while we build: they get trampled very easily (SITE REPAIR).

Combining SITE REPAIR and ROOF GARDEN, I imagine the roof garden about eight or nine feet up, beautifully framed and surrounded by the lower branches of the trees to the east and west: on the site I stake out the rough position of this roof garden, so that it will fit just right into the trees.

Now I begin more carefully to work with my eyes closed, to imagine how the patterns will be, in their best, most natural, most simple form, as the building comes to life.

MAIN ENTRANCE *gives me the approach to the building, and the position of the entrances.*

There are two ways to approach the cottage—either from our back porch of the main house, or up the driveway. Where is the entrance and what is it like, to make these two approaches work? In both cases I come across the terrace in front, to reach the entrance. I had originally thought of an entrance with a porch or arcade: but it seems too dark in there. As I close my eyes, I see a front door, standing forward a little from the main room of the cottage, just behind the bramble bush, and next to the acacia which is still standing. I imagine a small seat on either side of it: a natural place to sit in the sun: and the entrance frame elaborated, perhaps carved or painted, not much, just slightly, perhaps bulging forward. Since I know that the bathroom will be to the back, next to the existing cottage, towards the north, and I assume there will be a short arcade connecting the two buildings, and giving access to this bathroom, I am not certain of the relation between the main entrance and this arcade behind it. Also I am not certain if the entrance is at a slight angle, to face the driveway more, or if it faces due west. Before I thought it ought to be west, but clearing the site has made the diagonal seem possible. Somehow it seems natural that it should occupy the little diagonal between the apple tree and the acacia. There is also the question of the stair. Shall it be near the entrance going up—perhaps even outdoors—or shall it be back in the far corner, tucked away (OPEN STAIRS, STAIRCASE AS A STAGE)?

INTIMACY GRADIENT *and* INDOOR SUNLIGHT *give me the overall layout of the inside.*

INTIMACY GRADIENT doesn't mean much in such a small building, except perhaps for the following ideas. (1) A small seat or window seat inside the front door, (2) the stairs far enough back so it is a secluded "bed" area, and (3) the stairs placed so a person can go out to the bathroom without coming through the front door—in other words a kind of back access out to the little arcade that gives onto the bathrooms. INDOOR SUNLIGHT tells me that main usable spaces are towards the terrace, towards the garage, towards the main house—and that the north side, over towards our neighbor, is kept for dark closets, storage. It may make sense to place a whole row of storage alcoves over on the north side—this will also help to accomplish NORTH FACE. This may include kitchen counter and stove if they are added later.

STAIRCASE AS A STAGE, ZEN VIEW, TAPESTRY OF LIGHT AND DARK *give me the position of the stair to the upstairs.*

Standing inside the main room of the cottage, it feels as if the stair could go up on the side opposite the entrance.

414

This makes the most sense; it helps form the room then, and its roof, which will stick up slightly, at the back of the roof terrace, and form a nice angle with the two-story section—a beautiful corner, facing south-west, nice to sit in to enjoy the roof. This means that the stair will go up, perhaps towards a window at its top, which looks out onto the neighbor's garden to the north (new view—the only place from which one can see out that way); and gives LIGHT TO WALK TOWARDS. Other aspects of TAPESTRY OF LIGHT AND DARK—there should be light, where the back area (kitchen area) opens out to the door which leads to the arcade—perhaps a little fountain or court there, forming light, inviting us out towards the small existing cottage. And, of course, from inside the main room, looking out towards the front door onto the terrace, is also looking towards light.

ARCADE *tells me how to connect the building to the cottage west of it.*

As far as the little arcade at the back is concerned, between the "kitchen" and the old cottage, with the bathroom off it, I talked to Susie in the cottage: we looked at the window of her bedroom, where I had hoped to make a door, and it was clear to both of us that if we made a door, it would ruin the inside of the room—it is so small, the second door would make it like a corridor. So, I suggested we leave the window frame where it is, and put a step on the inside, and two steps on the outside, like a stile. We will put a casement window in the window frame, perhaps make the windowsill 3 inches lower; and she can get out to the bathroom by going over the stile, down the two steps, into the arcade.

SLEEPING TO THE EAST *helps shape the roof in detail, because of light.*

I looked at the light through that window. There is a danger our new cottage may take away her morning light; so we will place bamboos to mark the roof line we expect, and move it, until there is still plenty of morning light coming in through that window. Looking out of the same window, it seems more important for the roof to pitch to east and west, with gable ends at north and south, so that the slope of it allows the light to come down easier into her cottage. The gable end makes more sense for the sleeping loft anyway—it can open directly onto the roof garden (SHELTERING ROOF).

ENTRANCE TRANSITION *shows me how to arrange the area in front of the building.*

I haven't been careful enough with this pattern—have left it a little too late. I have been thinking about the possibility of a TRELLISED WALK, or TRELLIS anyway, to help close off the terrace to the south, and help protect it a little from the big house to the south. This will also make the terrace more of an OUTDOOR ROOM, and help to make the direct connection to the house more important than the one from the driveway. So I close my eyes, and imagine coming up the driveway, passing under a jasmine-covered trellis, which ties into the garage, through into the brighter light of the terrace, which forms a kind of anteroom to the main entrance. Then this whole terrace becomes a kind of room. The trees, which form its corners, also help to emphasize its character as an OUTDOOR ROOM.

FARMHOUSE KITCHEN *gives me the character of the main room inside.*

Even though the cottage will be a workshop, and place to live, it makes most sense to think of the inside as a FARM-HOUSE KITCHEN, with a big table in the middle, chairs around it, one light hung over the center, a couch or armchair off to one side . . . . When I start to imagine this, and imagine entering it, I realize that it is more important than I realized to keep it back, slightly, from the door, to make something out of the ENTRANCE ROOM that lies between—even though, in a building as small as this, this ENTRANCE ROOM may be shrunk to almost nothing. I imagine coming in, between two seats, into a glazed place, with light coming in, and then passing through a second doorway, perhaps a LOW DOORWAY, into the main room of the FARMHOUSE KITCHEN proper.

CONNECTION TO THE EARTH *and* TERRACED SLOPE *help me to complete the way the building's outer edge is formed.*

Of course, the terrace gives the connection to the earth. But I have been trying to imagine how to make the edge of the terrace, where it meets the earth. If the terrace itself is made of tiles (laid either in earth, or grout—not sure yet), the edging could be a SITTING WALL—but that seems too formal, too enclosed—or perhaps better, it could be made by a simple concrete block surround. This seems a bit stark. I close my eyes, and see the slight step, with blocks that are filled with rock-garden flowers—these form the edge except at the few particular places where there is an actual step to the path beyond.

The slope of the ground is not enough to need a TERRACED SLOPE; but there is a definite fall of a few inches from the back of the site to the front of the terrace. We decide to place a natural step, along the contour line, wherever it makes sense—so that we do as little earth moving or filling as possible, and the house sits just the way the land is.

As far as the connection to the earth goes, there are still two big unanswered questions. What exactly happens around the little apple tree to the south? And what exactly happens along the west wall of the building, between the entrance area and the bathing room arcade? It is possible that the place under the acacia tree might be blocked completely by a WINDOW PLACE which forms part of the entrance, or falls just inside it. In this case one would not be able to walk along this edge of the building, and could only get to the bathroom arcade by going into the building. Not sure if this is right; perhaps too tight.

WINDOW PLACE *and* ENTRANCE ROOM *fix the detailed arrangement of the entrance.*

In order to make progress on all this, we went out to the site, and looked around, trying to imagine all this more concretely on the land. We started especially with the front door. Should it be angled, to face the terrace, or facing west (into the acacia tree, or facing south, towards the garage)? Although facing south is less direct than when it is angled, it seems best—it creates a slight sense of ENTRANCE TRANSITION, doesn't allow such a complete view of the inside from the terrace—it uses the little apple tree very nicely, to one side: and it leaves the WINDOW PLACE to the west, just perfect, inside the front door, helping to form the ENTRANCE ROOM. We staked it out, with seven-foot-high stakes, so we could begin to feel its presence. There is a need to protect the apple tree and wild onions, from trampling—so it will be natural to make a low wall at a slight angle, perhaps curving out, to form the approach into the door—this will make the FRONT DOOR BENCH.

ALCOVE *then generates a further differentiation of the inside room.*

Now we stood inside the room, looking towards the door, towards the counter area at the back, to make the actual shape of the room work out just right. The WINDOW PLACE to the right of the door works beautifully. Another ALCOVE to the left of the door, on the left-hand side of the apple tree seems just right too.

Now STAIRCASE BAY *shows us how to stake out the four corners of the stair, so that we get a realistic look at its effect on the room.*

419

I imagine it very steep (7 feet horizontal run, for a climb of 8′6″), and no more than about 2 feet wide—since it only leads to a sleeping loft. We fix the top of the stair, by knowing that the back counter of the kitchen will come in three feet from the north face of the building, and that the upper story will rise directly from that line. If the sleeping loft is 7 feet north-to-south, enough for a bed—and the stair comes up inside it, with a 3 foot landing at the top, this allows us to fix the top of the stair 6 or 7 feet south of the property line—and the bottom of the stair 14 feet south of the line. When we look at the stair, it blocks the south-east alcove a bit—so we splay the alcove, around the apple tree, to connect it better with the main room. A splay of two feet makes an enormous difference. We stake it out also, and imagine a window in it, looking west towards the apple tree (WINDOW PLACE).

THICK WALLS *helps me define the inside edge of the farmhouse kitchen.*

Now, standing in the middle of the room which is to be the FARMHOUSE KITCHEN, I imagine another seat or closets under the stair; perhaps a window under the stair too, looking towards the garden to the east: small windows over the counter to the north which forms the main THICK WALL. Talking about the second story, we realize that the load of its southern wall will fall right over the vault which forms the FARMHOUSE KITCHEN: it will probably need a rib in the middle, and this rib can give us a nice center to the room, a place to hang a light (POOLS OF LIGHT).

CEILING HEIGHT VARIETY *completes the upstairs and the downstairs.*

This pattern is satisfied almost automatically by what has gone before. For the main room, I imagine one big vault, perhaps 8′6″ high at the center. The back wall, where the kitchen counter is, the main alcove to the south, and the window place by the door, all spring off the perimeter beam, which will be at about 6′6″—going down to 5′6″ or 5′0″. Upstairs the sleeping room is low anyway, under the roof; and it has a still lower section, over to the west, where the bed is in an alcove which has no more than a 4′6″ to 5′0″ ceiling.

All in all, the design took about a week of continuous on-and-off thought.

I mulled each group of patterns, in turn, as the notes show. Sometimes, I spent as much as an hour thinking about one pattern. In these cases, I didn't actively think how to do the pattern for an hour. I did all kinds of other things, drove the car, played music, ate an apple, watered the garden, etc., waiting for the pattern to form itself in my mind, by taking on shape appropriate to this particular site and problem. In many of these cases, I got the key insight by walking into the design, so far as it was completed, and then asking, what would I see over there if this pattern I am now thinking about were in the building? Very often, the answer came almost immediately. But it only came if I was really there, could touch and smell what was around me.

And I never made a drawing of the building.

The design was done completely in my mind.

Only in the fluidity of your mind can you conceive a whole. As the design unfolds, and the new patterns are brought into play, according to the order of the language, the entire design has to shift and resettle itself in your mind with every new pattern. Each new pattern in the sequence transforms the whole design created by the previous patterns—it transforms it as a whole, it shakes it up, and realigns it.

This can only happen if the design is represented in an utterly fluid medium; it cannot happen in any medium where there is the slightest resistance to change. A drawing, even a rough drawing, is very rigid—it embodies a commitment to details of arrangement far beyond what the design itself actually calls for while it is in an embryonic state. Indeed, all the external media I know—sand, clay, drawings, bits of paper lying on the floor—are all far too rigid in this same sense. The only medium which is truly fluid, which allows the design to grow and change as new patterns enter it, is the mind.

Representation there is fluid: it is an image, yet an image which contains no more than essentials—and it can change, almost of its own accord, under the transforming impact of a thought about a new pattern. Within the medium of the mind, each new pattern transforms the whole design, almost by itself, without any special effort.

Imagine trying to build sentences by shuffling words around on a piece of tracing paper.

What terrible sentences. The act of speech is a spontaneous, and immediate response to a situation. The more spontaneous it is, the more directly related to the situation, and the more beautiful. This spontaneity is governed by the rules of English which are disciplined and ordered; but the use of these rules, and the creation of a totality from them, takes place in the immediacy and fluidity of your own mind.

Just so with a pattern language. The patterns are disciplined; and the order of the language is disciplined. But you can only use these patterns in that order if you are willing to combine the discipline they give you, with the spontaneity and immediacy of direct experience. You cannot create a design by patchwork, on pieces of tracing paper. You can only create it, as if it were a real experience of a real building: and that you can only do in your mind.

It is only in the mind's eye, eyes shut, not on paper, that a building can be born out of the vividness of actual experience.

In the cottage I have been describing, we even built the building without the use of drawings—simply by staking out the building, as I saw it in my mind's eye, and then using a pattern language for construction, in the way described in chapter 23.

Of course, this little experimental building is still immensely far from the great beauty and simplicity of the houses which are shown at the beginning of the chapter.

It will take years more of experiment, with ways of building, before we can do that.

It is too loose, too informal, the construction patterns which control its detailed shape are not harmonious enough, not disciplined enough . . .

Yet still, this building has just the beginning of a spirit, a hint of a touching quality, which is at least a few steps down the road.

Anyone can use a language to design a building in this way.

No matter who does it, the buildings which are made like this will be ordinary and natural, because each part in the design is formed by its position in the whole.

It is a primitive process. The primitive farmer spends no time "designing" his house. He thinks briefly where and how to build it, and then sets about building it. The use of the language is like that. The speed is the essence. It takes time to learn the language. But it takes no more than a few hours or days to design a house. If it takes longer, you know it is tricky, "designed," and no longer organic.

And it is just like English.

When I speak English, the sentences form themselves in my mind as fast as I can say them. And this is true of pattern languages also.

The quality that makes a building feel as though it has been there for a thousand years, the quality that makes it feel that it has flowed like writing from a pen, comes almost automatically when I relax my mind, and let the language generate the building freely there.

I still remember the first time I used a pattern language in this way. I found myself so completely caught up in the process that I was trembling. A handful of simple statements made it possible for my mind to flow out and open, through them—and yet, although the house which came was made by me, born of my feelings, it was at the same time as though the house became real, almost by itself, of its own volition, through my thoughts.

It is a fearsome thing, like diving into water. And yet it is exhilarating—because you aren't controlling it. You are only the medium in which the patterns come to life, and of their own accord give birth to something new.

CHAPTER 22

SHAPING A GROUP OF BUILDINGS

*In the same way, groups of people can
conceive their larger public buildings, on
the ground, by following a common pattern language, almost as if they had a
single mind.*

We know from chapter 21, that an individual person, can create a building in his mind simply by letting a sequence of patterns generate it, on the site.

Now we go one step further, and see how a group of people, also on a site, and with a common language, can use the same process to design a larger building.

It is often said that no group of people can create a work of art, or anything which is whole, since different people pull in different directions, and make the end product a compromise which has no strength.

The use of a shared pattern language solves these problems. As we shall now see, a group of people who use a common pattern language can make a design together just as well as a single person can within his mind.

Here is an example of a clinic.

It is a psychiatric clinic to serve a rural population of about 50,000 in California. The building has about 25,000 square feet of internal space, and sits on a piece of land whose area is about 40,000 square feet in the middle of an existing hospital. The building was designed by a team which included the director of the clinic (Dr. Ryan, a psychiatrist), several of his staff members who had years of experience working with patients, and two of us from the Center for Environmental Structure.

Again the process begins with a pattern language.

We sent Dr. Ryan a sequence of patterns from the printed pattern language which we thought might be useful.

We asked him to pick those he thought were relevant; get rid of those which were irrelevant; and asked him to add whatever special patterns or new "ideas" which seemed to be missing, including, of course, those special parts or "patterns" specific to a clinic. Those new ones which he added are marked with asterisks below.

After our first discussion, we had a language of some forty patterns:

BUILDING COMPLEX
NUMBER OF STORIES
SHIELDED PARKING
MAIN GATEWAY
CIRCULATION REALMS
MAIN BUILDING
PEDESTRIAN STREET
*ADULT DAY CARE
*ADOLESCENT DAY CARE
*CHILDREN'S DAY CARE
*OUTPATIENT
*INPATIENT
*ADMINISTRATION
*EMERGENCY
FAMILY OF ENTRANCES
SOUTH FACING OUTDOORS
WINGS OF LIGHT
POSITIVE OUTDOOR SPACE
HALF-HIDDEN GARDEN
HIERARCHY OF OPEN SPACE

433

COURTYARDS WHICH LIVE
CASCADE OF ROOFS
SHELTERING ROOFS
ARCADES
PATHS AND GOALS
PEDESTRIAN DENSITY
INTIMACY GRADIENT
COMMON AREAS AT THE HEART
ENTRANCE ROOM
TAPESTRY OF LIGHT AND DARK
FARMHOUSE KITCHEN
FLEXIBLE OFFICE SPACE
SMALL WORK GROUPS
RECEPTION WELCOMES YOU
A PLACE TO WAIT
SMALL MEETING ROOMS
HALF-PRIVATE OFFICE
LIGHT ON TWO SIDES OF EVERY ROOM
BUILDING EDGE
OUTDOOR ROOM
THE SHAPE OF INDOOR SPACE
CEILING HEIGHT VARIETY

Gradually this language changed.

As more discussion took place, people's ideas about the patterns which the clinic should contain, changed. They decided that INPATIENT was unimportant, since the nearby hospital would take care of overnight patients. Then it turned out that the clinic needed a single area for occu-

434

pational therapy—and that this would become the MAIN
BUILDING.

Dr. Ryan decided that there ought to be a GREEN-
HOUSE *as part of this* MAIN BUILDING: *patients could
help plants to grow, and then transplant them into the
gardens, and look after the gardens.*

Then the discussion of the GREENHOUSE made the HALF-
HIDDEN GARDENS seem much more important, and they
became an essential part of the conception of the building.

Later, when we realized the importance of the CHIL-
DREN'S HOME, a place at the entrance of the clinic where
parents could leave children while they were being treated,
we introduced STILL WATER, and a FOUNTAIN where the
children could play and splash about.

There was some debate about COMMUNAL EATING;
finally it was agreed that this pattern should be included,
because the advantages of staff and patients eating lunch
together regularly seemed so essential. Only the fact that
each person should cook for the others in turn was not
included, since it seemed impractical.

*Every aspect of the clinic's life, was discussed, and set-
tled, in the medium of patterns.*

The language has the medium in which people worked
out their disagreements, and in which they built a common picture of the building and the institution as a whole.

Usually people have a great deal of trouble when they

435

try to define the future of an institution—because they have no language, no medium, in which they can forge their definitions, no way of gradually building up agreements, no way of gradually settling disagreements.

But with the pattern language as a base, the group of people gradually come to see themselves, and their activities, and their environment, as one thing—as a whole.

And finally, when everyone agreed about the pattern language, we were ready to begin design.

At this stage, the people who were going to run the clinic, had a shared vision, a vision not only shared in its intentions, in its broad outline, but shared in the details too. As a community, they knew, now, just exactly what they wanted, how it was going to work, what kind of places there would be in it, . . . everything in short, they needed to know, in order to begin design.

Then we began the design itself.

It took a week, Monday to Friday, out on the site itself, walking around parked cars and obstacles, overcoats against the fog, walking, walking all day long, cups of coffee, crazy dancing around, as the building took shape, chalk marks on the ground, stones to mark corners. People wondered what on earth we could be doing out there in the fog, walking around, all day long, for so many days.

We began with BUILDING COMPLEX.

436

The first pattern. We sat, at first, around a table in the nearby health center. How is this particular clinic going to reflect the building complex pattern? The pattern requires that any building be made up of visible components, which correspond to social groups: and—if the complex is at a low density—that the components actually be separate, connected by arcades and passages.

First of all, Dr. Ryan said, I see many many little cottages, each one individual and personal. How many do you see? Well, perhaps 30 separate cottages.

The entire building complex will have 24,000 square feet. I point out that if there are 30 cottages, each one will on the average have about 800 square feet—perhaps 25 × 30—and that some of them will be even smaller. This didn't sound right. There was some discussion among the staff. Then he said, Well, let's perhaps say 6 or 8 separate buildings, clustered and connected, but identifiable and separate.

With this idea clear in our minds, we went outdoors to the site itself.

Next we placed the MAIN GATEWAY *and* MAIN EN-TRANCE *to the building complex.*

437

All the next patterns we took on outdoors. We walked out into the fog in overcoats, and looked around. I asked: Suppose there is one main entrance to this building complex: Where is it? Close your eyes; imagine; where do you see it?

Is it along the main street? Is it on the corner? Dr. Ryan said: I see it half way along the driveway which leads back from the road to the main hospital. I asked then: Well, let's decide exactly where it is. The pattern says that it must be immediate and visible from all possible lines of approach. If it is in this position, then there are two lines of approach—one from the main road, walking back; one from the hospital parking lot, if you have driven in, parked your car, and are now walking forward, towards the road again. Let us go to both these places and try to imagine the best position for it.

First, all six of us stood at the road end of the driveway, and looked back. I walked to the halfway point and said: Imagine that I am at the entrance—is it right now? I moved a few feet—now? moved again . . . now? They said stop, go back, forward a bit—there was very great agreement—and I made chalk marks at the nearest and the farthest points. They were about 10 feet apart only, in a total length of 200 feet.

Then we went to the other end—the parking lot, and did the same thing. Again I made chalk marks which now showed the best place to make the entrance feel good, for someone coming to it from his car. The two sets of chalkmarks were about ten feet apart: less than the size of the entrance itself.

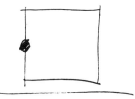

Now the position of the main entrance was fixed. I explained that we would now mark that, and that from now on it would be a given about the design—that we would no longer think about moving the entrance, in view of later things—but would let the design grow outward from this decision. A little frightening—what if things don't work out?

Next, with the main entrance fixed, we started to define the CIRCULATION REALMS.

I explained that this pattern required a single, simple pedestrian area, opening directly from the main entrance, and, further, a series of individual pedestrian realms opening off this one main path.

We stood at the main entrance, and wondered how this might be.

At the far end of the site, opposite the entrance, were four magnificent trees. It seemed natural, then, to make the main path go down towards those trees. And, with several small buildings opening off this path, some to the left, some to the right, it was easy to imagine a series of smaller paths, more or less at right angles to the main path, opening off it.

439

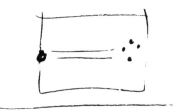

Within the circulation realms we placed the MAIN
BUILDING.

This pattern calls for a main building, in any group of
buildings, to act as a heart and focus: and requires that this
building have paths, tangent to it, with views into the inside, so that everyone who moves about the building complex is connected to it all the time.

We spent some time discussing what part of the clinic
might most naturally function as a main building. Finally,
we agreed that the so-called occupational therapy building
—where patients do various kinds of creative work—
would make the best "heart," and decided to make a large
building, with a specially high roof, right in the middle,
for this reason.

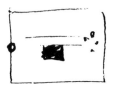

Then, outside the main building, an ACTIVITY NODE.

If there was to be a node of activity, inside the building complex, it seemed natural to place it just at one of the places where the main "street" is crossed by two of the wide "streets"—and where several important buildings meet around it. We decide to open this crossing, to have a fountain there, and to make doors from the main building, from the administration building, and from the child care, with children playing, all open into this node.

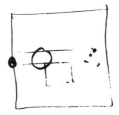

Around the activity node at the key points in the circulation realms, we placed RECEPTION, ADMINISTRATION, OUTPATIENT, ADULT DAY CARE, ADOLESCENT DAY CARE, CHILD DAY CARE.

Now we placed the various different buildings on the site. Dr. Ryan had rather clear ideas already, about the positions of these buildings. He showed us where he felt they

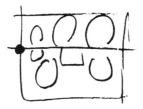

441

ought to go, and we discussed it, walking about the site.

One question came up. There were going to be two outpatient teams—Dr. Ryan had placed them to the right, after, just after the entrance, since that seemed to him the most natural position for the buildings which would be used most.

Since there were to be two teams, each with its own identifiable place, we thought about the circulation realms. We all stood at the activity node and asked ourselves how they might be placed, so that they would be clearly different—so that a patient would know which one was "his."

Several of the staff stood, with their eyes closed, and suggested that if there were a courtyard, and the two teams opened off this courtyard to the left and right respectively, it would be clear and simple.

Then, in a special place, near the main entrance, COMMUNAL EATING.

Dr. Ryan agreed that the process of sharing food is one of the most fundamental in any human group. We discussed the various ways this might happen, and might help patients to become more emotionally stable.

He and the chief administrator for the clinic decided finally that it would make most sense to place a kind of café, in the first garden on the left, attached to the library and administrative services, visible from the activity node and fountain at the main cross roads within the project.

Now, within the individual building areas, we made
SOUTH FACING OUTDOORS, WINGS OF LIGHT, POSITIVE
OUTDOOR SPACE.

Now came the most difficult part of the process. At this
stage, we had some rough idea of where the various buildings were; and some rough idea of the main paths and
movement between buildings. Now came the moment
when the actual position of buildings, and the shape of
the outdoors had to be fixed. This is always one of the
most difficult moments in the layout of a large group of
buildings. It is tense, and rather nerve-racking. Until this
has been accomplished, there is a diagrammatic quality
about the things which have been laid out: the people
walking about ask themselves whether there is any actual,
concrete way of laying out the buildings which gives them
sensible shapes, and which gives sensible shapes to the outdoor spaces too.

As always, everyone became rather nervous. Indeed, in
this particular case it was especially difficult. We spent an
afternoon, not knowing exactly how to arrange the buildings, went home and slept on it; and the next morning,
finally found a way of doing it which made it seem simple
and workable.

I thought, first, that every garden, in between the
buildings, needed to be cupped towards the south. This
made the left-hand side and the right-hand side, which
so far had seemed symmetrical, become asymmetrical.

It was complicated by the fact that all these gardens, or
courtyards, needed to be connected to the main pedestrian

path—so there would be views of flowers, and trellises, glimpsed from the path, inviting people into the back spaces.

We realized, finally, that the double effect of the connection to the main path, and the facing south, coupled with the idea of buildings which were not too wide at any point, so that they would give natural daylight in all rooms, led us to a series of rough T-shaped buildings placed to the north of south-facing courtyards. At this moment, when, for the first time, we had a layout of the building space and open space, we finally knew we had a group of buildings that could be built.

There was no doubt, at any stage, that these patterns would make something buildable. But it is worth recording the fact that to those people who had not seen the process in action, it was very remarkable that the issue would resolve itself within the loose and slightly irregular array of buildings which had been formed so far.

This is an extreme example of the fear, the fear of plunging in, which people must live with, when they are letting their language generate a building for them. It was only because of the confidence that it would work, that everyone allowed the thing to remain fluid for so long.

Of course, it would have been possible to make some formal arrangement of buildings and open space—some formal geometrical arrangement, very much earlier. A formal arrangement would have guaranteed that there would be some feasible way of placing the buildings.

But it would have killed the spirit of the buildings.

It would have killed that subtle, rambling balance of coherence, and incoherence, which comes from the fact that every building is unique, according to its position in the whole.

Within the individual buildings, and in the proper places in the circulation realms, we placed a FAMILY OF ENTRANCES.

Finally, to make these buildings coherent, not only with respect to space and volume, but also for the person coming in, we dealt with the family of entrances: the patterns which require that, in some fashion, all the different buildings have similar entrances, which are clearly visible, as a group, from the main pedestrian paths, and which are also members of a family, so that one sees "at a glance" the way they span the full range of possible entrances.

We walked about the site, which was by now laid out in some detail, with chalk marks and stones, and asked ourselves what we would like to see from various points, what we would like to see of entrances. I talked about the FAMILY OF ENTRANCES pattern: then asked everyone to stand in different places in the site, with their eyes closed. Imagine, now, that the FAMILY OF ENTRANCES pattern is solved as perfectly as you can imagine—it is ideal; it is

445

what you dream about when you think this pattern is there, in the most beautiful form it can be.

One person suggested "a whole lot of porches"; each one with its seats, so people can wait, outdoors, for appointments, a couple of steps up. Nice wood columns—each one sticking forward from its respective building.

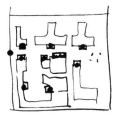

At this stage, the basic layout of the building complex, as a complex, was complete.

The decisions which had been made on behalf of the clinic "as a whole" were finished. Now it was time to go down into the details of the individual buildings, and the individual gardens.

For this, we asked the doctors and the staff to rearrange themselves, in small groups, each one responsible for one of these buildings—so that the individual buildings could be designed by the people who knew most about them, most about what was going to happen there.

Now different specialists on the clinic staff worked out the details of each different building.

446

The doctors concerned most with children designed the building for child treatment and for adolescent treatment; the social workers most concerned with outpatients designed the outpatient areas; the administrative officer of the clinic designed the administrative building.

The director of the clinic himself designed the details of the large central building.

He put child care at one end, just inside the entrance, so that playing children would be visible, and children coming to it would feel comfortable and unafraid (as specified by VISIBLE CHILD CARE). He placed a large greenhouse at one end of the main social hall, with the idea that patients could learn to take care of plants, and might, in the end, take care of all the plants in the clinic's gardens (OCCUPATIONAL THERAPY). He made alcoves inside the main social hall where small groups can gather to talk (FAMILY ROOM ALCOVES again); and an arcade outside, along the main street, to create a zone of social space neither entirely private nor entirely public (as directed by ARCADE).

Each part of the building was designed, in detail, by a process like the process described in chapter 21.

The patterns which affected the design included, for example, SHORT CORRIDORS, which explains how long corridors in buildings make people feel inhuman; RECEPTION WELCOMES YOU, which says that a building for patients should not have a formal reception counter, but instead a more informal arrangement with comfortable chairs, a

447

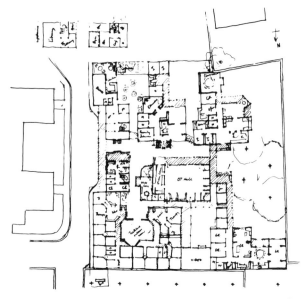

fireplace, and coffee where people can be made to feel at home; FARMHOUSE KITCHEN, a pattern most relevant to houses, which shows how a kitchen with a big table is one of the most comfortable places for communal discussion—this pattern was used in three of the day treatment programs; FLEXIBLE OFFICE SPACE, which requires a large number of small workrooms and alcoves, instead of the continuous open workspaces typical of modern office buildings. FAMILY ROOM ALCOVES, also most often used in houses, shows how small, low-ceilinged alcoves off the edge of larger rooms give people a chance to sit alone, or in twos, and be quiet, without leaving the larger group altogether.

And we see then how a group of people can design a complex building.

448

Once they agree about the language, the actual emergence of the form is simple and fluid. When a group of people try to do something together, they usually fail, because their assumptions are different at every stage. But with a language, the assumptions are almost completely explicit from the start.

Of course they no longer have the medium of a single mind, as an individual person does. But instead, the group uses the site "out there in front of them," as the medium in which the design takes its shape. People walk around, wave their arms, gradually build up a common picture of the building as it takes its shape—and all, still, without making a drawing.

And, it is for this reason, that the site becomes so much more important for a group.

The site speaks to the people—the building forms itself—and people experience it as something received, not created.

And they are able to visualize the building, right before their eyes, as if it were already there.

The idea that "ordinary" people cannot visualize a building is completely false.

The building grows, and comes alive, before their very eyes.

A few sticks in the ground, or stones, or chalk marks, are enough to bring the image to mind.

And then the building can be built directly from these marks.

Of course, this building, like the experimental building in chapter 21, is still immensely shallower than the buildings in the photographs which start this chapter.

It has great beauty of layout. But in its details of construction it still falls far behind. Indeed, in its construction it is completely spoiled.

For reasons outside our control, it was necessary that this particular building, once laid out, was then "detailed" by ordinary processes. It was taken to the drawing board, by people who had not laid it out, far from the site, and given mechanical "drawn" details, quite inappropriate to its design . . . until it became, in the end, no different from a thousand ordinary buildings of our time.

In short, it was almost destroyed, because it was not built in the right way. At first I hesitated, I was not sure whether to write this, or whether to include the picture, because it is so sad and so depressing. But then I realized how essential it is to include it: because many people may

451

be willing to lay out a building in the way I have described, and will then try to get it built from drawings.

The life, pulse, substance, subtlety of the building can only be retained, if it is built, in the same way that it has been designed—by a sequential and linguistic process, which gives birth to the building slowly, in which the building gets its final form during the actual process of construction: where the details, known in advance as patterns, get their substance from the process of creating them, right there, exactly where the building stands.

In short, a building laid out by a pattern language process, and which comes to life because of it, will die again, quite certainly, when it is built, unless the process of construction is the same—unless, that is, the same spirit which generated rooms that are just right, entrances where they should be, light coming from the right directions . . . is carried on into the details, and also shapes the columns, and the beams, the window frames, the doors, the vaults, the colors and the ornament as well.

In the next chapter we shall see how such a construction process works.

Yet even this clinic, crude as it is in its construction, already touched the hearts of the people who laid it out.

In earlier chapters I have described, in theory, why the active use of a language is so important to a person. It is because it is the only process in which he is able to make his picture of the world solid and actual—his feelings are embodied in the active concrete manifestation of his language: he feels his world as whole; it comes from within him, and is then around him, physically.

In the case of this clinic, we observed this process in fact.

Dr. Ryan told us, after his clinic was built, that this one week he spent with us, shaping the building, was the most important week he had spent in five years— the week in which he had felt most alive.

Now, years later, seeing the building made real—even though he has since moved—he remembers that week, standing in the fog, making chalk marks on the ground as we laid the building out, talking about the place for the entrance, the place for the greenhouse, the places where people could sit, the fountain, the small gardens, the rooms, the arcades—he remembers this week as the best week in five years of his working life.

The simple process by which people generate a living building, simply by walking it out, waving their arms, thinking together, placing stakes in the ground, will always touch them deeply.

453

It is a moment when, within the medium of a shared language, they create a common image of their lives together, and experience the union which this common process of creation generates in them.

CHAPTER 23

THE PROCESS OF CONSTRUCTION

*Once the buildings are conceived like
this, they can be built, directly, from a
few simple marks made in the ground—
again within a common language, but
directly, and without the use of drawings.*

Suppose now, that you have the layout of a building done, according to the processes described in the last two chapters. It happens, as we have seen, with very great ease.

Now we come to the actual building of the building.

Again, just as before, the process is sequential. Only now the patterns operate not on a mental image, but on the building itself, as it is being built. Each pattern defines an operation, which helps to differentiate, and to complete, the building as it grows: and when the last patterns are introduced into the growing fabric, the building is complete.

Again, the patterns operate upon the whole: they are not parts, which can be added—but relationships, which get imposed upon the previous ones, in order to make more detail, more structure, and more substance—so the substance of the building emerges gradually, but always as a whole, at each stage of its growth.

Suppose, to start with, that we have used a pattern language to lay out a rough scheme of spaces for a building.

And suppose that we have captured this rough scheme on paper, with a rough pencil sketch, or on the ground, with stakes, or sticks and stones.

In order for the building to be alive, its construction details must be unique and fitted to their individual circumstances as carefully as the larger parts.

459

This means that, like the larger parts, the details must be very carefully shaped according to their position in the larger whole; and, although similar parts will have a similar shape, no two of them will ever be exactly identical.

Look, for instance, at these drawings. According to the room you start with, the exact spacing of the columns, and hence the exact size of panels which form the walls, are different in each case.

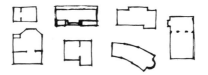

The rooms become alive because the details of the column spacing fit the whole. Any kind of irregularity in the room can be accommodated without trouble by the building process. The exact size and spacing of the building details, governed by the process, adapts itself to the nature of the room.

The details of a building cannot be made alive when they are made from modular parts.

Suppose, for example, that the building system contains a panel which is four feet wide, which fits together with other panels on a four-foot grid. None of the many rooms which I have described could be built, exactly as they are, with these four-foot panels.

To build these rooms out of modular four-foot panels, each of the rooms would have to be made into a perfect square, sixteen feet by sixteen feet.

460

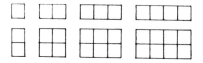

The modular panels tyrannize the geometry of the room.

If the builder wants to build the room from modular four-foot panels, he must change the size of the rooms, and change their shape, to fit his panels.

In such a building system, it is impossible for a person to create a plan which reflects the larger subtleties of site or plan. Each plan will always be chopped and disfigured to make it fit the building details.

And the beautiful variety in which a hundred or a thousand rooms can all be roughly fifteen by sixteen, yet no two alike, is destroyed, and replaced by an endless repetition in which hundreds and thousands of rooms are exactly and identically the same.

And, for the same reason, the details of a building cannot be made alive when they are drawn at a drawing board.

The details of a building cannot be alive when they are specified in the form of working drawings, because these drawings always assume, for the sake of simplicity, that the various manifestations of a given part are all identical.

The person who draws a working drawing cannot

draw each window, or each brick, differently, because he has no basis for knowing the subtle differences which will be required. These only become clear when the actual building process is already under way. So he draws them the same, because he has no reason, sitting at the drawing board, to make them different. But if the builder builds according to a detailed drawing, and is constrained by his contract to make the building exactly like the drawing, he then makes the detail identical, to follow the drawing—and in the actual building this becomes dead and artificial.

To make the building live, its patterns must be generated on the site, so that each one takes its own shape according to its context.

Consider, for instance, patterns like COLUMNS AT THE CORNERS or FINAL COLUMN DISTRIBUTION, which give the proper column spacing so that columns act as stiffening for walls, in the most efficient way.

To create these patterns correctly the builder makes a room by placing columns at the four corners, and then places extra columns along each wall, at equal spacings, to make column intervals somewhere between 4 and 6 feet, according to the length of the wall, then finally places a beam along each wall, over the columns.

This process is an active representation of the patterns. Each time the process is used, it will create a slightly different configuration, according to the plan of the room.

Each room will have in it the skeleton of columns and beams which embody the same patterns. Yet, no two rooms will have exactly the same panel sizes.

It is essential, therefore, that the builder build only from rough drawings: and that he carry out the detailed patterns from the drawings according to the processes given by the pattern language in his mind.

This is commonplace in nature. When the spider builds its web, the process is standardized; but the parts which are created are all different. Each web is beautiful, unique, perfectly adapted to its situation. Yet it is created by a standard process: and there is just one process. It is very simple. Yet this simple process interacts in an infinite variety of ways with different circumstances to produce different particular webs.

And just so in the building process which I shall now describe. The individual processes are standardized, and very simple. But the actual parts which are produced are infinitely various—they are infinitely different manifestations of the patterns which the processes define.

The process for making vaults is standard—but the individual vaults which it produces are unique.

What is standard is the process of weaving the basket, placing the strips of wood, covering with cloth, stiffening the cloth with resin, covering the resined cloth with lightweight concrete . . . . But the actual product, which this process produces, is different each time, according to the local circumstances.

And the process for making columns is standard—but again the individual columns which it produces are unique.

Nailing the boards, placing in position, nailing on the beam, filling with concrete—these are standard operations. But each column that is made this way is different—it is made by a different person, and reflects that fact. Perhaps one is carved, another colored in an individual fashion— and each is in a different position, has different connections to its surroundings, and is therefore different because of that.

For concreteness' sake, I shall now give a sequence of construction processes which will produce a building in this manner.

Of course, the sequence of these processes is just an example: it depends on a particular combination of materials. But some similar sequence, with just the same increasing definition, starting rough, and getting more precise as the building gets finished, is necessary.

First, stake out the corners of the ground-floor rooms and spaces.

To make sure these stakes are right, it is often helpful to

use large stakes, bamboos, or old bits of wood, so that several people can visualize the exact form and size of the rooms, their relation to one another, and their relation to the outdoors around them.

Wherever there are outdoor spaces near the building—terraces, paths, entrances, balconies, arcades, trellises, garden walls . . . stake them out as well, so that you can feel the indoors and the outdoors together.

It is very likely—almost certain—that you will modify the building as you have so far conceived it. The stakes are so vivid that you will almost certainly begin to see all kinds of subtlety, which you could not imagine before, now that the stakes and rooms are actual, right out there on the ground.

Modify the position of the stakes, a foot here, a foot there, until they are as perfectly placed as you can imagine; and until the layout of the rooms seems just exactly right.

Erect the corner columns, and place stiffening columns as nearly as possible at equal spacings, within the framework given by the corner columns.

For buildings of different heights, and on different stories, also according to the building height, these intermediate columns need different spacing, because the forces coming down are different. But on any one floor, their spacing will be roughly constant.

However, on any one floor the spacing is only roughly constant. The different rooms have walls of different lengths. Because they are not modular, the spacing of the intermediate columns is relaxed and natural; it will vary with the exact spacing of the corner columns.

Tie the columns together, with perimeter beams.

These beams then form the upper edge of every room. They make it possible to visualize the space of the rooms, very clearly; make it possible to put the window frames and door frames in position: and most important, they provide the tension ring around each room, which forms the basis for the springing of the individual vaults.

Make the beams lowest around alcoves; higher around ordinary rooms, and highest of all round the big and public rooms.

This will start the process of creating ceiling height variety. The alcoves can have beams as low as 5 feet or 5 feet 6 inches; the ordinary rooms as low as 6 feet or 6 feet 6 inches; the larger rooms perhaps 7 feet, 8 feet, or 9 feet.

In every case, the belly of the vault will add a foot or two, or even more to the perimeter beam height; accordingly, the extent of the addition will depend on the span of the vault.

Put in the window frames and door frames.

You already have some rough idea of where you want to put the doors and windows, from the conception of the building you have worked out in your mind.

But now the framing of the rooms is up, you can see

466

just exactly where the openings should go. By mocking them up, with bits of rough wood, you can modify them, and adjust them, until they create the perfect relationship between the inside and the outside, give the right views, the right amount of light in the right places, the right sill heights, the right heights for the doors, and the proper breakdown of the larger openings into smaller ones.

Now weave the baskets which will form the basis for the vaults above each room.

Each room, no matter what its shape, can be roofed with a simple vault, whose formwork can be woven out of thin strips of flexible wood, perhaps a foot apart. This basket can adapt to all the small irregularities of the room, and can even go round corners if it has to.

And shape the belly of the vault; it can be shaped to give each room just the ceiling height it needs. For structural reasons the vault needs to be roughly one sixth of the span of the vault. But this sixth is quite variable, and you may now adjust the exact curve of the vault to make the room feel right for just exactly what you will be doing there.

Put in the walls between the columns and the window frames.

These walls can be made of any simple sheet material: tiles, wood planks, hollow blocks, lightweight sheets and boards, cut and placed so they fill the gaps between the columns and the window frames.

467

Make half vaults for the stairs, so that each stair goes up at just the proper angle in the bays reserved them.

The stairs can be conceived as lying over vaults. The steps will be filled in, over a vault, or pair of vaults, or series of vaulted arches. These vaulted arches now give the position of the stair.

Trowel the concrete for the vaults onto the basket forms, and fill the walls to make them solid.

Using perhaps a lightweight fill, or ultralightweight concrete, trowel a one-inch vault onto the basket forms, after they have been covered with a simple cloth and stiffened; and do the same to fill the walls and columns in one continuous mass, so that the building becomes three dimensionally rigid.

Now start the second story, by the same procedure as the first.

Place columns in between the columns which are already there, and place the bottom of these columns on the vault, where they will be filled by the fill which forms the floor.

Fill the floor, to make it horizontal.

Make up the form boards on the outside of the building, to contain a horizontal floor, poured in above the vaults: and fill the space with voids—jugs, bottles, anything which will form roughly spherical bubbles in the concrete, and reduce its mass without reducing strength.

Complete the second story, just as you have built the first, then do the same for the third if there is one.

Make the terraces and seats and balconies around the building.

Treat them as part of the building, and yet part of the earth.

Use terracotta tiles set simply in the earth, with small plants growing in between them. Set the tiles in mud, keep it as wet as possible, so that it grips the tiles quite firmly, and yet makes the possibility of movement over time, and allows plants to grow between them.

Plant a few small flowering plants, between the tiles, while you are setting them in mud, so that after a few months, the flowers are yellow, purple . . .

Build individual doors and windows, as cheaply as you can, but each one shaped, and subdivided right according to the frame.

Because of the procedure you have followed in laying out the window frames and door frames, all the openings in the building are of slightly different sizes now.

This is essential, and it means that you cannot use standard doors or windows.

Now nail together simple doors and windows. They can be made of simple planks just nailed and glued to-

gether, with small strips to form the subdivision of the window panes, routed out to make a rebate for the window glass.

Carve decorations in the panels round the doors, and in the other places where you want some emphasis or gaiety.

You can carve simple scrolls and lines and hearts and dots into the boards which form the outside of the walls. Later, when the building is almost finished, you can fill these scrolls with plaster.

Paint the walls white; leave the columns visible.

Plaster in between the splines of basketwork which formed the basis for the vaults, and are still visible below the vault in every room.

Plaster in the ornaments which you have carved.

Plaster into the holes in those panels where you have cut holes for ornaments.

Oil the wood; wax the floor.

Then, finally, the finished building will have a rhythm of the same patterns repeated hundreds and thousands of times, but different every time that they occur.

There are not only roughly equal columns, column spacings, arcades, windows, doorways, dormers, roofs, and terraces. These are the larger patterns which repeat. But there is also a wealth of mouldings, tiles, drips, gutters, panels, brickwork, edges, door sills, ornaments, small strips, small squares, small cornerstones, column heads, column feet, rings cut in columns, braces, bracing details, nail-heads, handles, spacers, sparsely placed, just where they have to be, but visible, so that the building is completed by these smallest structures, and formed by the rhythm of their almost regular irregularities.

The picture on the last two pages shows an example of a building built like this.

This picture is a photograph of a model. The building is a four-story apartment building, for twenty-seven families, in which the members of each family have designed their own apartments, using a common pattern language, and the building is then intended to be built, floor by floor, using the system of columns and beams and vaults which I have just described.

Although the model is very rough, it is already possible to see the way that the discipline of the construction process interacts with the informality of plan, to produce a building which goes much further towards the quality without a name, than either of the actual buildings shown in chapters 21 and 22.

A building built like this will always be a little looser and a little more fluid than a machine-made building.

Its doors and columns, windows, shelves, wall panels, ceilings, terraces, and balustrades are shaped exactly to take their part in the larger whole: they fit it perfectly. And because they fit it perfectly, they are therefore a little rougher in appearance than the slick machine-smooth quality of buildings made of factory materials.

But the beauty of the building lies in the fact that it is whole.

The essential thing is this. Each process (given by a pattern) takes the configuration which has been produced by the previous processes, and adapts itself to them. No matter where the columns are, the process of weaving a vault can form the vault *according to* the position of the columns. No matter where the edges of a window are, the process of making a window forms the window and its panes *according to* the size and shape of the window frame.

And it is this which makes the building whole.

The building, like the countless buildings of traditional society, has the simplicity of a rough pencil drawing. Done in a few minutes, the drawing captures the whole—the essence and the feeling of a horse in motion, a woman bending—because its parts are free within the rhythm of the whole.

And just so with the building now. It has a certain roughness. But it is full of feeling, and it forms a whole.

474

CHAPTER 24

THE PROCESS OF REPAIR

*Next, several acts of building, each one
done to repair and magnify the product
of the previous acts, will slowly generate
a larger and more complex whole than
any single act can generate.*

We know now, how a single act of building works.
We know that any person can lay out a building for
himself; that any group of people can do the same;
and we know how the builders can then carry out a
process of construction, which will make a unified or-
ganic whole, out of the stakes marked on the ground.
   Now we shall see how several acts of building, in
a row, will generate an even more coherent and more
complex whole, piecemeal—by making sure that every
act contributes to the order of the previous acts.

In theory, according to chapter 18, every act of building
is, with respect to its larger context, an act of repair: a part
of the much larger process in which several acts together
generate the larger wholes from which a building complex
or a town is made.

   But so far we have not had an opportunity to see this
clearly—because in chapters 19-23, we have been paying
attention to the individual creative act as an act which
makes something new.

   Now we shall change the focus, and pay attention to
each act, as an act of repair, within the larger whole.

No building is ever perfect.

Each building, when it is first built, is an attempt to make
a self-maintaining whole configuration.

   But our predictions are invariably wrong. People use
buildings differently from the way they thought they
would. And the larger the pieces become, the more serious
this is.

The process of design, in the mind's eye, or on the site, is an attempt to simulate in advance, the feeling and events which will emerge in the real building, and to create a configuration which is in repose with respect to these events.

But the prediction is all guesswork; the real events which happen there are always at least slightly different; and the larger the building is, the more likely the guesses are to be inaccurate.

It is therefore necessary to keep changing the buildings, according to the real events which actually happen there.

And the larger the complex of buildings, neighborhood, or town, the more essential it is for it to be built up gradually, from thousands of acts, self-correcting acts, each one improving and repairing the acts of the others.

Suppose, for instance, that some corner of your house is not as alive as you would like.

For example, suppose I look at the house, and realize that its garden is not working properly as a HALF-HIDDEN GARDEN, because although it is to one side of the house, there is not enough protection between the garden and the street. It needs some kind of wall.

And, suppose that I go further, and bearing in mind that work needs to be done to mend the barrier between the garden and the street, I examine the garden from the point of view of PRIVATE TERRACE ON THE STREET, and find it missing. Suppose that I decide I need to build a small brick terrace, at one side of my house, where it touches the garden, in order to repair this gap.

Now, if I have already decided that some kind of wall needs to be built to protect the garden where it is too open, it is only natural that I shall try to make the missing terrace in some way to link it to this missing wall.

In short, when I get a chance to start mending the garden, I can mend both these defective patterns with the same act of building. And the repairs I make are not just "repairs," but new designs, complex themselves, between the crevices of the first design.

Or suppose that you have built a small laboratory building.

It has a kitchen, a library, four labs, and a main entrance. You want to add a fifth laboratory to it, because you need more space.

Don't look for the best place right away. First, look at the existing building, and see what is wrong with it. There is a path where tin cans collect; a tree which is a beautiful tree, but somehow no one uses it; one of the four labs is always empty, there is nothing obviously wrong with it, but somehow no one goes there; the main entrance has no places to sit comfortably; the earth around one corner of the building is being eroded.

Now, look at all these things which are wrong, and build the fifth lab in such a way that it takes care of all these problems, and also does, for itself, what it has to do.

Can you see how rich and various the parts of the building will be, when they are built like this?

The fifth lab will be unique, unlike any of the other labs. But not because you try hard to make it subtle, or beautiful, or arty. It comes about in the most obvious way, just because you are trying to be practical. Can you imagine how hard it is to make one little laboratory, about 20 feet by 20 feet, repair all these different problems at once?

It isn't impossible; but to do it you will have to stretch it here, extend it there, give it a special window here to make the tree more useful, bring the path around it here, to make the path with the tin cans less deserted, give it a door at just this spot, to help create a pleasant corner in the entrance, where people can wait.

So the richness and uniqueness of this little addition comes about in the simplest and most practical way possible. It happens almost by itself, just because you pay attention to the defects in the present building, and try hard to repair them.

Each act of building, which differentiates a part of space, needs to be followed soon by further acts of building, which further differentiate the space to make it still more whole.

This is commonplace in nature: and indeed, it is just this which always manages to make the parts of nature whole.

Consider the leaves on a tree. At first sight it seems as though the leaves are solid, and the air between the leaves is merely space. But the air between the leaves is as much a part of nature as the leaves themselves: it takes on shape as strongly as the leaves themselves; and like the leaves, it is given its shape by the influences which work on it.

Each leaf has a shape which is determined by the need for strength, the growth of the material, and the flowing of the sap within the leaf. But the air between two leaves is given its shape as definitely. If the leaves are too close together, the air between the leaves cannot act as a channel for the sunlight which the leaves need; and there may not be enough breeze there to ventilate the leaves; if the leaves are too far apart, the distribution of the leaves on the twigs and branches is inefficient, and the tree will not get enough sunlight to support it. Every part you look at is not only whole itself, but is part of a larger whole, has wholes around it, and is itself made up entirely of wholes.

This is essential to the way that nature works: and all of it is generated by the processes of successive differentiations, each one helping to fill gaps, and mend gaps in the whole.

When things are first built, the gaps between the parts are often left unwhole.

In the kind of world we have today, almost half the places in a building or a town are places "in between" the places where you are meant to be.

The dark narrow space between two houses, the corner of the kitchen which no one can reach, the area between the train tracks and the next door industry—these are obvious examples of places which are literally forgotten and left over.

And there are more remarkable examples, where spaces are actually intended to be left over.

Think about streets with cars parked on them, parking lots, long corridors, waiting rooms, the path between the front door and the street, the garage, the closet underneath the stairs, the bathroom, the windowless front hall of the house. All these places are made with the mistaken notion that you are only there in limbo, in between the moments of living—as if they were way-stations between the few places where you are actually meant to be alive.

But these gaps must be healed and made as whole as the parts on either side of them.

In a town or building which is whole, there are no places like this; and in a life which is truly lived, there are no moments like this either.

In a life which is truly lived, there are no moments which are "in between" or "out of life"—every moment is lived fully. The Zen master says "when I eat, I eat; when I drink, I drink; when I walk, I walk." A building or a town which is alive, has the same quality.

In a building or a town which is alive, and which supports a life that is fully lived, there are no places which are way-stations between moments of living; every place is made in such a way that life can be savored fully there. Every square inch of it has some valuable purpose, and is able to support some moment in a person's life which is truly lived; and for this reason every part of it is whole, and every place between two wholes is also whole.

Slowly, as the "process of repair" repairs the gaps between the wholes, the structure becomes complete and whole at every level.

This goes vastly beyond the normal conception of repair.

In the commonplace use of the word repair, we assume that when we repair something, we are essentially trying to get it back to its original state. This kind of repair is patching, conservative, static.

But in this new use of the word repair, we assume, instead, that every entity is changing constantly: and that at every moment we use the defects of the present state as the starting point for the definition of the new state.

When we repair something in this new sense, we assume that we are going to transform it, that new wholes will be born, that, indeed, the entire whole which is being repaired will become a different whole as the result of the repair.

In this sense, the idea of repair is creative, dynamic, open.

It assumes that we are constantly led to the creation of new wholes, by paying attention to the defects in the existing wholes, and trying to repair them. It is still true that every act helps to repair some larger, older whole: but the repair not only patches it—it also modifies it, transforms it, sets it on the road to becoming something else, entirely new.

In this framework, we gain an entirely new view of the process through which a sequence of acts of building generates a whole.

Broadly, what is happening is that there is, at each stage in the life of any part of the environment, a wholeness which is specific to that moment in its life: and that each new act of building, provided that it is done with an eye to making the overall whole still more whole, more alive, will transform that whole, and gradually give birth to new wholes.

In this sense, then, the idea of repair explains both how we can mend past defects in things, and also, at the same time, how it is possible to make and remake the world so that the cooperation of a number of acts of building, in sequence, also creates wholes which are complete, and live, at every moment of their history—yet always giving way, under the process of repair, to even newer wholes, which once again remake themselves at the next stage of the repair.

In order to see this clearly, let us imagine that there is somewhere a building complex, growing, over time.

Step by step, each act of building, which contributes to the growing whole, is also helping to repair or heal what is already there.

Specifically, let us imagine a cluster of houses growing over time.

Each house starts with a small beginning—no more than a family kitchen, with a bed alcove off one end, and a kitchen counter.

All in all, no more than 300-500 square feet to start with.

Then, for the first few years, people add 100-200 square feet more each year.

First a bedroom perhaps; another bedroom; a workshop; a garden terrace; a full bathing room; arcades and porches; studio; a bigger sitting room, with a big fireplace; a garden shed.

And, at the same time common things are also built; they plant an avenue of trees; a small gazebo; a shared outdoor room; paving on the paths; closed-in garages; a communal workshop; a small fountain or a swimming hole. . . .

As the buildings reach maturity, the increments get smaller.

A bench; a sitting wall; a roof over the entrance; a railing on the terrace upstairs; a stair to the roof; a fishpond; a baywindow; an extra gate; a vegetable patch; a wall of shelves; a garden seat around the trunk of a growing tree. . . .

487

*Yet, at the same time, collectively, the houses begin
to generate the larger patterns which define the
cluster.*

Each person begins to work with his neighbor, first the
neighbor on one side, then the neighbor on the other side;
and together they try to make the space between their
houses beautiful. Of course, they start by eliminating obvious conflicts between windows, or cases where one house
takes the sun from the next man's garden; but they also
work out details according to the detailed patterns. For
example, one group of people decide to make their entrances open off a small public garden, with a tree, and
with an outdoor seat in it, facing the sun, and from which
people can watch the distant outdoor room, according to
the patterns TREE PLACES, OUTDOOR SEATS, and PUBLIC
OUTDOOR ROOM.

For example, path shape says that a path must be a
place, almost like a room, partly enclosed, with a middle,
so that people feel comfortable staying there, not just
walking through. Each group uses this pattern to make
the paths outside their houses better shaped, with seats in
them; and the pattern even affects the exact shape of the
boundary wall where the houses meet the paths.

And PRIVATE TERRACE ON THE STREET says that each
house should have a private terrace, near its living room,
but placed so that one can see from it, into the public
space of the street beyond, and wave or say hello to someone out there, without the privacy of the house being dis-

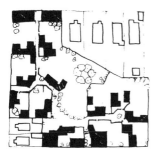

The slow growth of twelve houses

489

turbed. Each of the houses has such a terrace, and the way these terraces make the paths alive is also discussed and modified by the groups at each end of the cluster.

Slowly, at every level, the arrangement of wholes becomes so dense that there are no gaps between the wholes: every part, and every part between two parts, is whole.

In a house, the garden round the house is positive; the boundaries between house and garden are again positive. The thickness of the walls is positive; the wall which forms the enclosure between terrace and garden is again positive; a seat; while the interior walls are places too (shelves, niches, etc.); within the house, each room is, of course, a place; but to make this happen, each one has windows on two sides—with the result that the rooms take on an odd configuration, in plan—and every place between the rooms is once again a place. At the level of construction, we find the same. Every room has its corners marked by columns. Each column is again a visible coherent thing; the columns which stand free have places around them once again; each column is itself made in such a way that the places where it joins other entities, are once again entities: columns and feet.

So, the houses get their form, both as a group, and separately, as individuals, from the gradual accretion of a number of small separate acts.

The bench is placed, to form a terrace; the extra bed-room helps to shield the garden from the neighborhood; the paving on the path is placed in such a way that it defines the entrance transition, and forms a contour edge to help prevent erosion from the rain; the extra growing house helps to form common land outside the house; the avenue of trees helps to form a park in the common land; the garages not only shield the cars, but also help to form gateways into the cluster. . . .

Every small act helps not only to increase the space, but also makes a contribution to the larger patterns which are needed there.

And finally, the common character of the cluster of houses grows, without control, simply from the accumulation of the individual acts—because each act of building is conceived as something which not only does good for itself, but also has the obligation to help generate the whole.

In chapter 19 I argued that an organic whole could only be created by a differentiating process.

I explained that only a process of differentiation, because it defines the parts within the whole, can generate a natural thing; because only this kind of process can shape parts individually, according to their position in the whole.

We see now that there is a second, complementary process which produces the same results, but works piecemeal, instead.

491

When a place grows, and things are added to it, gradually, being shaped as they get added, to help form larger patterns, the place also remains whole at every stage—but in this case the geometric volume of the whole keeps changing, because there is an actual concrete aggregation of matter taking place.

This process, like the simple differentiating process, is able to make wholes in which the parts are shaped according to their place.

But this process is still more powerful: because it can make groups of buildings which are larger and more complex.

And it is more powerful, above all, because it leaves no mistakes: because the gaps get filled, the small things that are wrong are gradually corrected, and finally, the whole is so smooth and relaxed, that it will seem as though it had been there forever. It has no roughness about it, it simply lies there stretched out in time.

CHAPTER 25

THE SLOW EMERGENCE OF A TOWN

Finally, within the framework of a common language, millions of individual acts of building will together generate a town which is alive, and whole, and unpredictable, without control—this is the slow emergence of the quality without a name, as if from nothing.

Finally, then, we come to the town itself.

We have seen how a few dozen acts of building, done within a common pattern language can gradually generate a whole; and that the larger patterns which are needed to define that whole, can be created piecemeal, by the slow concrescence of the individual acts.

Now we shall see how this same process can be extended to a town.

For we now face at last, the deepest and the most far-reaching postulate of all—namely: the postulate that it is possible for all the large-scale order of a town to be created purely by means of incremental piecemeal acts.

The first thing to recognize is that for any system as vast as a town there is a fundamental problem.

When a single human mind or a group of minds together conceive a building, they naturally conceive it as a whole, and its parts then fall into place, both to support that whole, and also to be whole themselves.

But when a town grows, it does not grow in one human mind, nor in any coherent group of minds. A town is made from millions upon millions of individual acts of building. How can we be sure that the town will be whole, and not a rambling, incoherent chaos, if it is built from millions upon millions of individual acts?

The question is: can the structure emerge, simply from the spontaneous interaction of the parts?

Can it be created by a free process, in which the people locally do what they want, and still create the whole successfully?

Or must it be planned, by a hidden hand, according to a blueprint or a master plan?

Must there be some kind of control, some kind of totalitarian order, imposed from above, which restricts the freedom of the individual acts, and forces them into a large-scale order?

To put this question in perspective I should like to compare it to a question that arose in the early years of biology: "How does an organism get formed?"

Consider your hand, for example. Hold it out in front of you. Do you realize that this complex shape, this intricate structure of bones, and muscle, fingers, thumb, fingernails, joints, wrinkles, subtle curves, has come into being entirely without the background of a blueprint or a master plan?

Do you realize, fully, that the cooperation of the cells has formed this hand, guided only by certain rules which direct the growth of the individual cells, according to their interaction with each other?

Or consider another example. As I look out of my window, I see a few square yards of flowering bushes there, with grass below them, a tree or two sticking out, and a few other plants, sitting among them.

If I look at these bushes, down to the details of their individual leaves, the grains of soil below them, the twigs, the petals of the flowers, the insects sitting on the leaves, the gaps between the leaves, where lower leaves are open to the sky, do I have to believe that there is a hidden designer who has created this?

At first biologists thought that there must be a hidden designer.

They believed that this miracle could not be happening without something to guide it, a spiritual master plan, which told the cells just where to place themselves. Up until the seventeenth century, some biologists even believed that every cell in a man contained a little man, who was a model of the larger man.

Yet now it has become clear that the organism is formed purely by the interaction of its cells, guided by the genetic code.

Recently, our experiments have begun to make it clear that this seeming miracle is not a miracle of guidance from above, but instead a miracle of subtle organized cooperation between the parts: that the growing cells alone, communicating with each other, and guided only by the instructions programmed into them by the genetic code, act correctly, with respect to one another, in such a way that they create an entirely individual whole, not predictable in detail, but recognizable in species.

And this is true for a town too.

At one time people believed that a town had to be planned by a planner who made a plan or blueprint. It was said that if the order of the town is not created from above, there will just not *be* an order in the town. And so, even in spite of the most obvious evidence of all the beautiful towns and villages built in traditional societies without master plans, this belief has taken hold, and people have allowed themselves to give up their freedom.

As in biology, though, it is becoming clear now that the structure of a town can be woven much more deeply, more intricately, from the interaction of its individual acts of building within a common language, than it can from a blueprint or a master plan—and that indeed, just like your hand, or like the bush outside my window, it is best generated by the interaction of the rules which govern the construction of the parts.

Let us see in detail, how a process of interacting rules can work to generate a town.

The essential fact, which makes it possible, is that the patterns are not generated, suddenly, completely, but that instead each larger pattern comes into being as the end product of a long sequence of tiny acts—and that these tiny acts themselves have the power to create the pattern, if they are repeated often enough.

This is commonplace, in the growth of an organism,

499

where all the larger patterns are generated, merely as the end products of tiny, daily transformations.

At any given moment, in a growing organism, there is no sense of the "end" or of the final "goal" of growth. There is, instead, a process of transformation, which is able to take the present state of the organism, and move it slightly, in the next minute of growth—in such a way that when the same process is then repeated in the minute after that, and in the minute after that, slowly, inexorably, the necessary patterns come into being—not according to some plan, but as the product of a sequence of transforming steps.

In detail, this happens through the action of certain chemical fields, created by the hormones. These fields encourage and inhibit growth, at different parts of space—and this differential growth process then slowly generates the growing whole. According to the state of these fields at any one moment, the growth process creates a certain minute growth, which transforms the existing structure, just slightly, according to a certain rule.

As the growth occurs, the chemical fields change, so that the "same" transformation, guided by the "same" rule, has a slightly different effect each time that it occurs. Thus, the repeated application of the transformation, guided by the changing concentrations in the chemical fields which tell the organism how close it is to reaching equilibrium, guide it towards the finished pattern. But the finished pattern is merely the end product of the succession of tiny transformations.

And just this too, must also happen in a town.

In this case, the "chemical fields" are replaced merely by people's consciousness of the larger scale patterns, which provide the rules of growth. If people have agreements about these larger scale patterns, then they can use their knowledge of the patterns, and the degree to which these patterns have been attained, or not, to guide the growth and the assembly of the smaller patterns.

Slowly, under the impact of this guidance, the sequence of small-scale transformations will, of its own accord, create the larger patterns, piece by piece: without any individual person necessarily knowing just exactly how or where these larger patterns will be in the finished town.

Here, for example, is the way a process of this kind can generate a very large-scale pattern like CITY COUNTRY FINGERS.

At any given moment, the actual boundary between the town and the country is a rough uneven curve. Suppose that the town gives local communities incentives which encourage growth just where these curves bulge outwards; which inhibit growth on the outside of the places where the curve bulges inwards; and which even encourage destruction of buildings, and the re-creation of open space, on the inside of the curve at those points where the curve bulges inwards.

Under the impact of these incentives, the bulges will grow outwards gradually, to form city fingers; the "non-bulges" will stay where they are, or even grow backwards into the town, maintaining and creating country fingers.

Of course, in any one month, the actual progress is minute. But that does not matter. Under the impact of this growth process, slowly but inexorably the pattern CITY COUNTRY FINGERS will come into being.

On a slightly smaller scale, the same can happen in a community to generate a PROMENADE.

Suppose, for instance, that there is the beginning of a PEDESTRIAN STREET, and PROMENADE, between some corner where there is an ice cream store, and another corner where people gather in the evenings.

The community now makes it clear to all the individual neighborhoods around the line between these points, that they want to encourage the removal of car traffic from the paths along this line, that they hope to see new community activity locate along the emerging promenade, and so on.

Each neighborhood, then, formulates the way in which it can best help the slow creation of this PROMENADE—

and does so because it will gain from the incentives which the larger community has in its power. Suppose, for instance, that one neighborhood sees that it can create a GATEWAY, with a little SPORTS ACTIVITY, in a place where the PROMENADE might run. In order to create the promenade, they will then build a path, which might run in that part of the community, past the gateway which leads into the neighborhood, and past the table tennis and local sports. Gradually the promenade emerges from the piecemeal efforts of the different neighborhoods.

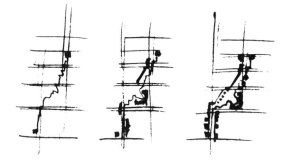

And the same kind of process can also generate the patterns in a local neighborhood.

Consider two patterns which are the responsibility of the local neighborhood: MAIN GATEWAYS and NETWORK OF PATHS AND CARS.

The neighborhood creates incentives, which encourage the house clusters, and work communities, and individual house owners, to generate these patterns slowly, piece by piece.

One year the people in one cluster take down a back fence, and so a path begins from one street, in between two clusters, and towards another street. The next year, a different cluster connects its common area with that same path, acting again under the incentive which the local neighborhood provides, knowing that it is in their interest to help to generate this larger pattern which the neighborhood needs.

Another year, the people who live near the boundary of the neighborhood decide to bridge the street with a pair of small buildings which help to form a gate. Of course, they build this gate in such a way that it connects with the emerging NETWORK OF PATHS AND CARS. This act does not, in itself, form a complete MAIN GATEWAY. But the narrowing of the street, where the two buildings have been built, is clearly the precursor of a gate: other smaller acts will follow it, to make the gateway complete. But meanwhile, the neighborhood has allowed these two buildings to encroach on the street, because they recognize that the narrowing which this creates will gradually move that corner of the neighborhood towards a state where it does have the MAIN GATEWAY which the whole neighborhood needs in that quarter.

Each of these processes requires a large group, and a group of smaller groups.

In this respect they are just like the example of the houses and the cluster of houses, in chapter 24, but extended to a larger scale. There the houses act individually, to generate the larger patterns which the cluster needs. And just so here, but at a larger scale. The clusters act together, to generate the patterns which the neighborhood needs. The neighborhoods act together to create the patterns, which the community needs. And the communities act together to generate the patterns which the whole town needs.

In order for these processes to cover the whole structure of a town, it is therefore necessary that the town be made up from a hierarchy of groups and land, each one responsible for its own patterns.

At the lowest level, each individual person owns his own private space: and is responsible for helping to create the patterns there, according to his needs.

At the second level, the family has its own land, and its own common space: and the workgroup has the same. The families, and workgroups are responsible for all the larger patterns which are needed for the common space.

At the third level, each cluster of families or workgroups is a well defined legal entity—a legally defined group—which owns its own land (that land, which the families all use together, but which is not private to any one of them)—and is responsible for all the patterns which are needed there.

At the fourth level, the neighborhood, made up of clusters, is again a well-defined, legally constituted human group, which once again owns that land which is common to its members—local roads, local parks, local kindergartens—but does not own the smaller common lands the clusters own. The neighborhood, as a group, is responsible for the patterns in its common land.

At the next level again, there are communities, made up of neighborhoods—again well defined, and legally constituted—again with their own common land, including larger roads, large public buildings, again responsible for all those patterns which are needed to serve the whole community.

Finally, at the level of the town, there is again a legal entity, again owning common land—*not* owning, as a town does now, *all* the streets, *all* the parks, but owning only those which are specifically used by everyone—the very largest ones, and responsible for just those largest patterns which are needed in this largest common land.

And, in order for the larger patterns to come into being, piecemeal, from the aggregation of the smaller acts, it is then necessary that each group is made responsible for helping the next larger group, create the larger patterns which the larger group requires.

Thus, when a person forms his room he is given specific incentives to help to form the larger patterns of the household, or workshop in which his room is placed: so COMMON AREAS AT THE HEART, A ROOM OF ONE'S OWN, INTIMACY GRADIENT, BUILDING EDGE, POSITIVE OUTDOOR SPACE, WINGS OF LIGHT, will gradually emerge.

And when members of a family build or modify their house, they are given specific incentives by the cluster, which makes them responsible for improving the environment around them—above them, below them, and to the side: so BUILDING COMPLEX, CIRCULATION REALMS, HALF-HIDDEN GARDEN, SMALL PARKING LOTS, SHIELDED PARKING, FAMILY OF ENTRANCES, will gradually emerge under the responsibility of the cluster.

When each cluster modifies its overall form, or builds on, it is responsible to the neighborhood for bringing larger neighborhood patterns into being: NEIGHBORHOOD BOUNDARY, MAIN GATEWAY, GREEN STREET, POOLS AND STREAMS, CHILDREN'S HOME, LOOPED LOCAL ROAD, HOME WORKSHOPS, SCATTERED WORK, QUIET BACKS. The neighborhood can give money, or other incentives, to encourage those small acts which help to bring these larger patterns into being.

The larger community can in the same way give both money and permission to those neighborhoods which help bring its even larger patterns into being: ACCESSIBLE GREEN, PARALLEL ROADS, PROMENADE, SHOPPING STREET, MOSAIC OF SUBCULTURES, SUBCULTURE BOUNDARY, SCATTERED WORK, SACRED SITES, HOLY GROUND, HEALTH CENTERS. Again, these larger patterns will emerge according to the voluntary cooperation of the neighborhoods. ECCENTRIC NUCLEUS, DENSITY RINGS . . .

Even at the very largest levels, the region and the city can provide incentives which will encourage these communities to modify their own internal structure in a way which helps the largest patterns to appear: NETWORK OF TRANSPORTATION, RING ROADS, CITY COUNTRY FINGERS, LOCAL TRANSPORT AREAS, AGRICULTURAL VALLEYS, ACCESS TO WATER, SACRED SITES . . .

Under these circumstances, it is certain that every pattern will appear at the level where it is needed.

The small patterns produced directly by the individuals, and repeated over and again. The large patterns generated indirectly, by the gradual incremental repetition of the smaller patterns.

But it is never certain just exactly where a given pattern will appear.

Nor is it certain just what form any one pattern will take, in any one particular place.

We know, ahead of time, what general form it has.

But we do not know its exact form, its exact dimensions, its detailed character, until it has grown to maturity —because it forms itself, in the process of growth, and it is only growth itself, in response to the details of its surroundings, which can shape it correctly.

In this sense it is like the natural order of an oak tree.

The final shape of any one particular oak tree is un-predictable.

When the oak tree grows, there is no blueprint, no master plan, which tells the twigs and branches where to go.

We know in general that it will have the overall form of an oak, because its growth is guided by the pattern language for an oak tree (its genetic code). But it is un-predictable, in detail, because each small step is shaped by the interaction of this language with external forces and conditions—rain, wind, sunlight, the composition of the earth, position of other trees and bushes, the thickness of the leaves on its own branches.

And a town which is whole, like an oak tree, must be unpredictable also.

The fine details cannot be known ahead of time. We may know, from the pattern language which is shared, what kind of town it will be. But it is impossible to predict its detailed plan: and it is not possible to make it grow accord-ing to some plan. It must be unpredictable, so that the individual acts of building can be free to fit themselves to all the local forces which they meet.

The people of a town may know that there is going to be a main pedestrian street, because there is a pattern which tells them so. But, they cannot know just where this main pedestrian street will be, until it is already there. The street will be built up from smaller acts, wherever the opportunity arises. When it is finally made, its form is partly given by the history of happy accidents which let the people build it along with their own more private acts. There is no way of knowing, ahead of time, just where these accidents will fall.

This process, exactly like the emergence of any other form of life, alone produces a living order.

It is a process by which the small acts of individuals, almost random, are sieved and harnessed, so that what they create is orderly, even though the product of confusion.

It creates order, not by forcing it, nor by imposing it upon the world (through plans or drawings or components) : but because it is a process which draws order from its surroundings—it allows it to come together.

But of course, by this means far more order can come into being, than could possibly come into being through an invented act.

It is vastly more complex than any other kind of order. It cannot be created by decision. It cannot be designed. It cannot be predicted in a plan. It is the living testament of hundreds and thousands of people, making their own lives and all their inner forces manifest.

And, finally, the whole emerges.

CHAPTER 26

ITS AGELESS CHARACTER

*And as the whole emerges, we shall see
it take that ageless character which gives
the timeless way its name. This character
is a specific, morphological character,
sharp and precise, which must come into
being any time a building or a town
becomes alive: it is the physical embodiment, in buildings, of the quality without a name.*

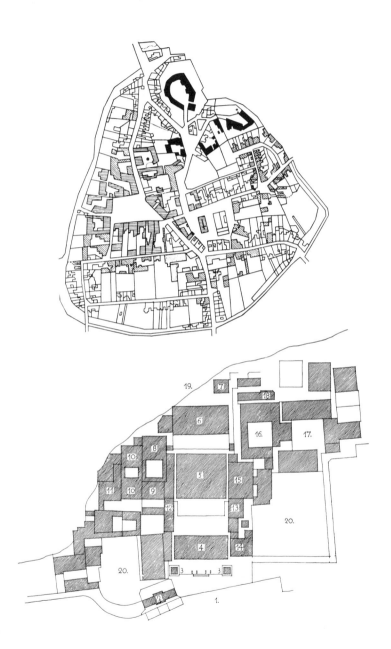

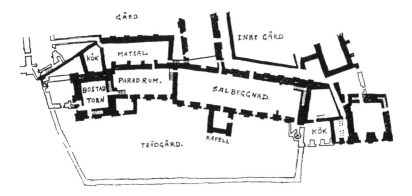

GÅRD

INRE GÅRD

KÖK   MATSAL

PARAD RUM.

BOSTAD

TORN

SALBYGGNAD.

KÖK

TRÄDGÅRD.   KAPELL

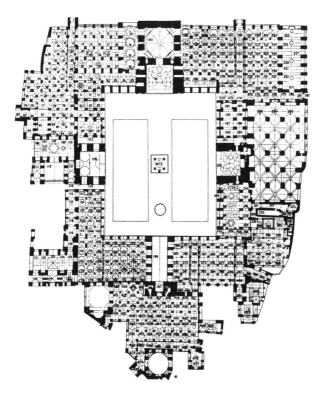

If you follow the way of building which I have described in the last twenty-five chapters, you will find that the buildings which emerge will, gradually, and of their own accord, take on a certain character.

It is a timeless character.

Look at the drawings of buildings which people have made with pattern languages on this page and the next. They could be Roman, Persian, from Mohenjo Daro, from medieval Russia, Iceland, Africa. They might be five hundred years old, or five thousand, or built five thousand years from now.

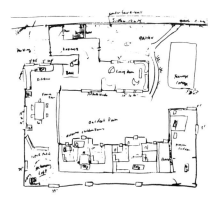

Willy nilly, without realizing what they are doing, without knowing its significance, people make buildings which are far more like the countless towns and buildings of vanished cultures, and ages past, than any of the buildings which are being built today.

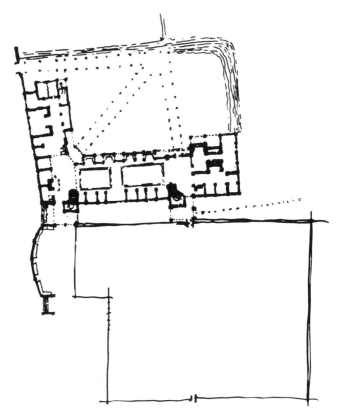

In short, the use of languages does not just help to root our buildings in reality; does not just guarantee that they meet human needs; that they are congruent with forces lying in them—it makes a concrete difference to the way they look.

In order to make this precise, let me distinguish two different morphologies.

Imagine that we sort the buildings of the world into two piles. In the one pile, all those traditional buildings, built for thousands of years, in traditional societies all over the world. And, in the other pile, all those buildings built in the last hundred years, built by totalitarian technology, by industry.

Although the buildings and towns in the first pile have vast variety of different forms—brick houses, straw huts, stone vaults, timber framing, thatched roofs, log cabins, piled dry stone walls, stone columns, steep roofs, flat roofs, arched windows, straight windows, brick, wood, stone, white, blue, brown, yellow, narrow streets, wide streets, open compounds, closed courtyards—still compared with the other pile, they have something in common.

It is a particular morphological character. And when buildings are made in the framework of the timeless way, they always have this special character.

This character is marked, to start with, by the patterns underlying it.

Low buildings; open stairs leading to upper floors; long tables with communal eating; roofs which are either pitched or domed, large and visible, or else used as terraces; rooms placed so that the light floods into them from two sides at least; gardens made for smelling and touching flowers not only seeing them; water still and moving; arcades along the edge of buildings; porches between buildings and gardens; small public and private squares, with arcades and porches at their edges; galleries at upper levels; columns at the corners of the rooms and spaces; ceilings at different heights according to the intimacy of rooms; small alcoves at the edges of rooms; trellises covered by roses and vines; walls in which possessions and decorations show the character of life and fill the room with it; communities separated from one another by substantial boundaries, so that each one can live in its own way, unhampered by the others.

It is marked by greater differentiation.

If we compare these buildings with the buildings of our present era, there is much more variety, and more detail: there are more internal differences among the parts.

There are rooms of different sizes, doors of different widths, columns of different thickness according to their place in the building, ornaments of different kinds in different places, gradients of window size from floor to floor.

There are small rooms opening off larger rooms; there are swellings at the places where paths meet; there are enlargements of the connection where a column meets a beam; there are more highly differentiated kinds of wood pieces in a window to correspond to the divisions between large panes and small.

Though most of the rooms are rectangular, there are a few circular, or elliptical, or odd-shaped polygons, mixed in among the rectangles. Edges between adjacent places are always places in themselves; they have a thickness, there is a crinkled character to them; it is almost never just a plane between two voids. There are openings between each space, and the ones next to it; and these openings occupy a fairly large percentage of the wall area. Curved lines and surfaces are rare; but they occur occasionally, at points of emphasis. Columns are thick, and often bunched or clustered. Paths are often slightly crooked, streets often taper, with minor bends in them. The character is marked, in short, by greater differences, and greater differentiation.

But it is marked, above all, by a special balance between "order" and "disorder."

There is a perfect balance between straight lines and crooked ones, between angles that are square, and angles that are not quite square, between equal and unequal spacing. This does not happen because the buildings are inaccurate. It happens because they are more accurate.

The similarity of parts occurs because the forces which create the parts are always more or less the same. But the slight roughness and unevenness among these similarities, comes from the fact that forces are never exactly the same.

The straight lines which are roughly straight, will come about because the boundary of a space must always have a space which is alive on both sides of it. A curved wall forms a concavity of space on its outside, which tends to destroy space. But the straight walls are not perfectly straight, because there is no reason for them to be perfect.

The angles which are roughly square will come about because few angles in a room, or in the edges of an outdoor area are comfortable if they are acute. But they are not perfectly square, because there is no reason for them to be perfect.

And it is marked, in feeling, by a sharpness and a freedom and a sleepiness which happens everywhere when men and women are free in their hearts.

A few cups and glasses standing on a rough table, a handful of flowers freshly picked from the garden on the table, the notes of an old piano, children playing in the corners.

It is not necessarily complicated. It is not necessarily simple.

Many students, when they first try to create this character, create a tortured intricacy. But this is almost the opposite of the true character. In order for a place to have this character, it does not necessarily have hundreds of small angles, funny corners, and so on. Sometimes, it is perfectly regular.

It comes simply from the fact that every part is whole in its own right.

Imagine a prefabricated window which sits in a hole in a wall. It is a one, a unit; but it can be lifted directly out from the wall. This is both literally true, and true in feeling. Literally, you can lift the window out without doing damage to the fabric of the wall. And, in your imagination, the window can be removed without disturbing the fabric of what surrounds it.

Compare this with another window. Imagine a pair of columns outside the window, forming a part of the window space. They create an ambiguous space which is part of the outside, and yet also part of the window. Imagine splayed reveals, which help to form the window, and yet, also, with the light reflected off them, shining in the room, they are also part of the room. And imagine a window seat whose back is part of the window sill—not a seat leaning against the window sill, but a seat whose back is indistinguishable from the window sill, because it is continuous.

This window cannot be lifted out. It is one with the patterns which surround it; it is both distinct itself, and also part of them. The boundaries between things are less marked; they overlap with other boundaries in such a way that the continuity of the world, at this particular place, is greater.

This character emerges whenever any part of the world is healed.

Each thing is made of parts, but the parts overlap and interlock to such an extent that the oneness of all things becomes more marked. There are no gaps between the parts, because each gap is just as much a part itself. And there are no clear divisions between levels in the structure, because, to some extent, each part reaches down, and is continuous and integral with smaller units of structure, which, once again, cannot be lifted out, because their boundaries overlap, and are continuous with larger units.

It is therefore the most fundamental mark of health and life in our surroundings.

Under the guidance of a process which allows wholes to form, at the scale of individual persons, families, gardens, trees, forests, walls, kitchen counters, each part becomes whole in its own terms, because it is adapted to the larger wholes which it is part of, and because it is adapted to the smaller wholes which are a part of it.

Then the world becomes one—there are no rifts— because each part is part of larger wholes, and smaller, there is a continuum of order, which leaves the parts indistinct, and unified.

Outwardly this character reminds us of the buildings of the past.

You can see this in the historical plans at the beginning of the chapter. They too, all have this inner relaxation. They too all have the balance of order and disorder; the gentle rectangles, distorted slightly, wherever the building or the land require it; they too all have the subtle balance of small spaces and open spaces; the unity which happens when each part, inside or outside, is a part with its own solid shape; they all have the slightly rambling, innocent appearance, which shines through the tighter order, and lets us feel at peace.

If we think carelessly, we may imagine that this gentle character comes merely from the fact that they were made informally, without machines, and slowly over time. But the truth is that this character arises in these buildings not because of history, or because the processes which built them were so primitive. These buildings have this character because they are so deep, because they were made by a process which allowed each part to be entirely one with its surroundings, in which there is no ego left, only the gentle persuasion of the necessities.

Yet this character cannot be generated by a person yearning for the ancient past.

It happens simply because when you understand as much about the forces which surround us as a person with a living pattern language does, and when you build according to these forces, the kinds of buildings which you make, are simply more like ancient buildings than like modern ones.

What looks at first sight like an accidental quality which marks the towns and villages of the past, turns out to be the most fundamental physical property of the world we live in.

It is simply the character of buildings which reflect the forces in them properly.

The prismatic buildings of our own time, the buildings built with the simple geometry of cubes, and circles, spheres, and spirals, and rectangles; this geometry is the naïve order, created by the childish search for order. We happen to think of this order as the proper order for a building, because we have been taught to think so; but we are wrong.

The proper order for a building or a town, which comes about when buildings are correctly fitted to the forces in them, is a much richer order, with a far more complex geometry. But it is not merely rich and complex; it is also very specific. And it will show itself, under any circumstances, where buildings are actually correct. Whenever anyone manages to make a building which is alive, it will have this specific character, because that is the only character which is compatible with life.

When I myself first started to make buildings with this character, the character amazed me.

At first, I was afraid that I must really be a conservative at heart and that I was unconsciously striving to re-make the past.

But then I read a passage in an ancient Chinese painting manual—the Mustard Seed Garden manual of painting—which made the situation clear to me.

The writer of that manual describes how, in his search for a way of painting, he had discovered for himself the same central way that thousands of others like him had also discovered for themselves, throughout the course of history. He says that the more one understands of painting, the more one recognizes that the art of painting is essentially one way, which will always be discovered and rediscovered, over and over again, because it is connected with the very nature of painting, and must be discovered by anybody who takes painting seriously. The idea of style is meaningless: what we see as a style (of a person or of an age) is nothing but another individual effort to penetrate the central secret of painting, which is given by the Tao, but cannot itself be named.

The more I learn about towns and buildings, the more I feel the same thing to be true. It is true that many of the historic styles of building have some quality in common—they have it not because they are old, but because man has, over and over again, approached the secret which is at the heart of architecture. In fact, the principles which make a building good, are simple and direct— they follow directly from the nature of human beings, and the laws of nature—and any person who penetrates these laws will, as he does so, come closer and closer to this great tradition, in which man has sought for the same thing, over and over again, and come always to the same conclusions.

And it is because this same morphology, underlying all things, will always arise in the end—that the timeless way of building is a truly timeless one.

As you learn to make buildings more and more alive, and thereby more and more true to their own nature, you will inevitably approach this timeless character.

These are the forms which man has found, time and

time again, as he approaches the heart of building. As the acts of building in a community are governed more and more by a common pattern language, they will more and more closely create and re-create the body of timeless forms which have been part of architecture since society began.

The timeless character of buildings is as much a part of nature as the character of rivers, trees, hills, flames, and stars.

Each class of phenomena in nature has its own characteristic morphology. Stars have their character; oceans have their character; rivers have their character; mountains have their character; forests have theirs; trees, flowers, insects, all have theirs. And when buildings are made properly, and true to all the forces in them, then they too will always have their own specific character. This is the character created by the timeless way.

It is the physical embodiment, in towns and buildings, of the quality without a name.

THE
KERNEL OF
THE WAY

And yet the timeless way is not
complete, and will not fully generate
the quality without a name, until we
leave the gate behind.

CHAPTER 27

THE KERNEL OF THE WAY

Indeed this ageless character has nothing, in the end, to do with languages. The language, and the processes which stem from it, merely release the fundamental order which is native to us. They do not teach us, they only remind us of what we know already, and of what we shall discover time and time again, when we give up our ideas and opinions, and do exactly what emerges from ourselves.

From what you have read so far, it may seem as though the life of buildings, and the timeless character they have when they are living, can be created simply by the use of pattern languages. If the people have a living language, it seems that what emerges from their acts of building will be alive; it seems as though the life of towns can be created simply by the use of languages.

And yet, we wonder, can it be so simple? Can any process really generate the nameless quality which stirs the heart of nature? Can any theory be so powerful?

These doubts are right. There is a kernel at the center of the timeless way, a central teaching, which I have not described till now.

The essence of this kernel is the fact that we can only make a building live when we are egoless.

Imagine, for example, blue tiles, white fountains, birds nests under the arcades, yellow paint, fresh scrubbed woodwork.

Ornaments around the edge of the roof, red flowers in bushes round the entrance, great windows, filled with cushions, flower pots where seedlings are growing, and a broom hanging on the wall . . . pinnacles high in the sky, the vaults of the building catching the light of the sun, deep shadows in the alcoves around the building edge.

The beauty of this place, the quality in it which touches us, the thing which makes it live, is, above all, that it is carefree, that it is innocent.

This innocence will only come about when people honestly forget themselves.

It goes without saying that the vast steel and glass and concrete structures of our famous architects do not have this quality.

It goes without saying that the mass-produced development houses, built by big developers, do not have this quality.

But it is true that even the more "natural" architects, like Frank Lloyd Wright and Alvar Aalto, also do not reach this quality.

And it is also true that the "funky" relaxed hippy-style architecture, with irregular redwood facades, and old-fashioned country style interiors, also does not reach this quality.

These places are not innocent, and cannot reach the quality without a name, because they are made with an outward glance. The people who make them make them the way they do because they are trying to convey something, some image, to the world outside. Even when they are made to seem natural, even their naturalness is calculated; it is in the end a pose.

In case you think that I am simply rejecting my own time, and searching for the past, I should like to tell you about two places I know which are entirely of the twentieth century, and have this innocence.

One is a fruit stand, on a country road, not far from here. It is a simple shelter, made of corrugated iron and plywood—it has no purpose whatsoever, except to protect the fruit.

The other is the deck of a fishing boat, in the North Sea. It is a simple diesel-engined fishing boat, perhaps a 40-foot boat. Three Danish brothers fish from it. In one corner there is always a huge pile of empty beer bottles, perhaps 3 or 4 feet high; they drink continuously while they are at sea, and while they are in port.

These two places have a little of the innocence and egolessness which is necessary to the quality without a name. And why? Because the people who made them simply do not care what people think of them. I don't mean that they are defiant: people who defiantly don't care what other people think of them, they still care at least enough to be defiant—and it is still a posture. But in these two cases, the fruit stand, and the deck of that fishing boat, the people did not care what other people thought; and they also do not care about the fact that they don't care. It means nothing to them. They only do exactly what they have to do to take care of their situation.

And of course, there are larger examples too.

A concrete yard, or a steel mill, where there is no desire to impress at all, only the need for things to work . . . that sometimes has this quality. A farmyard has it often, for the same kind of reason; or a new café, where the owners have too little money to do anything to impress, and concentrate only on making their customers feel comfortable, in the true sense, with a bare minimum.

And, of course, sometimes it exists too in a house, built

some time ago, the flowers round the house, the rambling trellises, looked after with patience, hidden behind a great wall, not visible, done only out of love and out of the desire to live, and let the roses bloom.

To make a building egoless, like this, the builder must let go of all his willful images, and start with a void.

Architects sometimes say that in order to design a building, you must have "an image" to start with, so as to give coherence and order to the whole.

But you can never create a natural thing in this state of mind. If you have an idea—and try to add the patterns to it, the idea controls, distorts, makes artificial, the work which the patterns themselves are trying to do in your mind.

Instead you must start with nothing in your mind.

You are able to do this only when you no longer fear that nothing will happen, and you can therefore afford to let go of your images.

At first, when you are still unsure that a pattern language will genuinely generate forms inside your mind, you hang on, tight, to all the images you have, because you are afraid that without them, there may be nothing left. Once you learn that the pattern language and the site together, will genuinely generate form inside your mind, from nothing, you can trust yourself to let go of your images entirely.

For a person who is unfree, the language seems like mere

information, because he feels that *he* must be in control, that *he* must inject the creative impulse, that *he* must supply the image which controls the design. But once a person can relax, and let the forces in the situation act through him as if he were a medium, then he sees that the language, with very little help, is able to do almost all the work, and that the building shapes itself.

This is the importance of the void. A person who is free, and egoless, starts with a void, and lets the language generate the necessary forms, out of this void. He overcomes the need to hold onto an image, the need to control the design, and he is comfortable with the void, and confident that the laws of nature, formulated as patterns, acting in his mind, will together create all that is required.

At this stage, the building's life will come directly from your language.

A man who is not afraid to die, is free to live because he is open to what happens next, and is not always killing it by trying to control it.

In the same way, the language and the building it creates begins to come to life when I begin to be relaxed about what happens next. I can work within the order of the language, without worrying about the patterns which are coming later, because I am sure that, no matter what happens, I will always be able to find a way of bringing them into the design, when I come to them. I don't need to take precautions in advance. Why am I so sure that I can always find a way of bringing in the smaller patterns? Because I don't care what shape the finished building or its details have—provided only they are natural. I have no preformed mould that I am trying to pour the patterns into; I don't mind how strange, how curious, the building turns out to be, if I can only satisfy the patterns.

Sometimes a willow tree which grows in an awkward corner of a garden, ends up bulging and twisted, as it fits itself to the forces in the garden. But it is no less natural, no less free. If a building which I make turns out bulging and twisted it will be no less free than the willow tree. And it is because of this, because I am not afraid of these deformities, that I can always take the patterns in the order of the language; and because of this that I can always make a building which is natural and free, like the wild willow.

Yet, at the very moment when you first relax, and let the language generate the buildings in your mind, you will begin to see how limited your language is.

Once you realize that the only thing which matters is the reality of the situation which surrounds the building, and not your images of it, you are able to relax, and allow the patterns of the language to combine themselves freely in your mind, without trying to impose an artificial image on their combination.

But at the same moment, you will begin to realize that the reality of the situation is not only more important than your images, but also more important than the language too. The language, no matter how useful or how power-

ful, is fallible, and you cannot accept its patterns automatically, or hope that they will ever generate a living
thing mechanically—because, once again, it is only the extent to which you yourself become ordinary and natural,
that in the end determines how natural, and free, and
whole the building can become.

*One place can have "good" patterns in it, and yet be
dead.*

For instance, it so happens that there is a little square in
San Francisco which has four patterns in it. The square is
small; there is a BUILDING THOROUGHFARE; there are
ACTIVITY POCKETS in it; and there are STAIR SEATS. But
each of these patterns is subtly wrong. The space is small
—yes. But it is placed in such a way that it will never be
used, so the density of pedestrians will still be too low—the
point of the SMALL PUBLIC SQUARE, to make the place feel
full, is missing. There is a BUILDING THOROUGHFARE
through the place, leading into a building—yes. But there
are no places for involvement along this path, so the path
becomes irrelevant, and helps nothing come to life. There
are ACTIVITY POCKETS—yes—there are small corners
placed around the edge of the square. But they are so
placed that no activity could ever gather in them—they
have the wrong relationship to the paths of access. And the
places where people *would* naturally gather, if they could,
are obstructed by stairs, and barriers.

The square has these patterns in it—but it still fails—because in each case the point of the pattern, the spirit of the

pattern, is missing. For the man who made this square, these patterns were empty formal tools, which didn't help the place to come alive at all.

Another place can be without the patterns which apply to it, and yet still be alive.

For the same square could also *not* have these patterns in it, and yet be whole.

Suppose the square is large—part of it could be treated like a park—and the corner of it where people are most likely to gather, made into a small, partly enclosed space. This would be in the spirit of SMALL PUBLIC SQUARE, but without following the letter.

Suppose there is no way of making a path go through the square for BUILDING THOROUGHFARE—then it would be possible to put a children's playground, or a grove of trees, at the back, and two activity pockets, right on the street. This would be in the spirit of BUILDING THOROUGHFARE, by using the street itself as a tangent thoroughfare—but again without following the letter of the pattern.

So long as you are using patterns slavishly, mechanically, they will interfere with your sense of reality, as much as any other images. You will be able to use them properly, only at that moment when you have the proper disregard for them.

So paradoxically you learn that you can only make a building live when you are free enough to reject even the very patterns which are helping you.

542

And, in the end, the buildings will become alive only when the person who uses the language is himself egoless and free. Only then will he be able to recognize the forces as they really are, instead of being overawed by images.

But at that moment he no longer needs the language. Once a person has freed himself to such an extent, that he can see the forces as they really are, and make a building which is shaped by them alone, and not affected or distorted by his images—he is then free enough to make the building without patterns at all—because the knowledge which the patterns contain, the knowledge of the way the forces really act, is his.

It may seem to you that pattern languages are useless then.

If it is true that you cannot make a building live, even with the help of a pattern language, unless you are first egoless and free; and if it is also true that once you have reached this state of freedom, you will be able to make a living thing, no matter how you do it; it seems to follow then that the pattern language is useless.

But it is just your pattern language which helps you become egoless.

The patterns in a living language are based on fundamental realities, which everyone already knows, in his innermost self. You know that small alcoves, arcades, low ceilings, opening windows, sheltering roofs, make funda-

543

mental sense—and you forget it only because our society has filled your mind with other distorting images. The language only shows you what you yourself already know. The language is able to awaken you to your own innermost feelings, and to what is true. Gradually, by following the language you feel free to escape from the artificial images which society has imposed upon you. And, as you escape from these images, and the need to manufacture things according to these images, you are able to come more into touch with the simple reality of things, and thereby become egoless and free.

The language frees you to be yourself, because it gives you permission to do what is natural, and shows you your innermost feelings about building while the world is trying to suppress them.

One student of architecture, here in Berkeley, his mind filled with the images of steel frames, flat roofs, and modern buildings, read the ALCOVE pattern, then came to his teacher and said, in wonderment: "I didn't know we were allowed to do things like this." *Allowed!*

The more I watch our pattern language being used, the more I realize that the language does not teach people new facts about their environment. It awakens old feelings. It gives people permission to do what they have always known they wanted to do, but have shunned, in recent years, because they have been frightened and ashamed by architects who tell them that it is not "modern." People are afraid of being laughed at, for their ignorance about "art"; and it is this fear which makes them abandon their own stable knowledge of what is simple and right.

A language gives you back your confidence in what seemed once like trivial things.

The first things—the innermost secret likes and dislikes we have—are fundamental.

We give them up, and try to be important, and clever—because we are afraid that people will laugh at us.

The SHELTERING ROOF, for instance, is so full of feeling, that many people daren't admit it.

A language will allow this inner thing, which carries feelings, to guide your acts.

At this final stage, the patterns are no longer important: the patterns have taught you to be receptive to what is real.

It is no longer the pattern ALCOVE which tells you to create alcoves. It is because you see reality in a particular case. And the reality you see shows you that a particular alcove is the right thing to do.

The pattern ALCOVE—which first functioned as an intellectual crutch—is no longer necessary to you. You see reality directly, like an animal. You make the alcove as an animal might make an alcove—not because of the concept—but directly, simply because it is appropriate.

545

At this stage, you work directly with what is real.

But do not think, casually, that you can do this now, and that you therefore do not need a language to enable you to do it. At this moment, you cannot see the reality: because your mind is full of images and concepts. And while you are at the stage where you rely on images and concepts (style, flat roofs, sheets of glass, white painted steel, thick redwood trim, shingles, rounded corners, diagonal lines) you cannot face reality directly—you cannot tell the difference between what is real, and what unreal. And in this state, the only way you can escape these images, is to replace them with more accurate images—that is what patterns are. But finally, you can release yourself from images entirely.

And in this sense, the language is the instrument which brings about the state of mind, which I call egoless.

It is the use of pattern languages which after patient use, will allow you to come back to that part of yourself which has always been there, and is there now, but is obscured by images and ideas and theories, which make it impossible for you to be yourself, or act as nature does.

The impulse to make windows overlooking life, to make ceilings vary in height, columns thick enough to lean against, small window panes, sheltering steeply sloping roofs, arcades, seats by the front door, bay windows, alcoves, is already part of you. But you have been told so much, that you no longer value these inner impulses. You curb them, because you think that someone else knows better. You are perhaps afraid that people may laugh at you for being so ordinary.

A pattern language does nothing really, except to wake these feelings once again.

It is the gate which leads you to the state of mind, in which you live so close to your own heart that you no longer need a language.

It is utterly ordinary. It is what is in you already. Your first, most primitive impulses are right, and will lead you to do the right thing, if you will only let yourself.

There is no skill required. It is only a question of whether you will allow yourself to be ordinary, and to do what comes naturally to you, and what seems most sensible, to your heart, always to your heart, not to the images which false learning has coated on your mind.

This is the final lesson of the timeless way.

Imagine yourself building a simple porch outside your room: a column to lean against; a gusset to strengthen its connection to the beam; decorated with fretwork, so that the light falls softly, without glare from the sky; a rail to lean on easily, so that you can walk out and lean and smell the summer air; and the yellow sunlight, lit by the yellow grass, warming the unpainted wooden planks.

Imagine that you have reached the point, in your life,

where you are making such a porch. You are a different person now. The fact that you have understood the importance of these details, in your life, that you have understood how much they influence your life, means that you are now alive in a more simple sense.

So finally you learn that you already know how to create this ageless species which is the physical embodiment, in buildings, of the quality without a name, because it is a part of you—but that you cannot come to it until you first master a pattern language, and then pass beyond the language, once it has taught you to allow yourself to act as nature does.

To act as nature does is the most ordinary thing in the world. It is as ordinary as a simple act of slicing strawberries.

One of the most moving moments in my life, was also one of the most ordinary. I was with a friend in Denmark. We were having strawberries for tea, and I noticed that she sliced the strawberries very very fine, almost like paper. Of course, it took longer than usual, and I asked her why she did it. When you eat a strawberry, she said, the taste of it comes from the open surfaces you touch. The more surfaces there are, the more it tastes. The finer I slice the strawberries, the more surfaces there are.

Her whole life was like that. It is so ordinary, that it is hard to explain what is so deep about it. Animal almost, nothing superfluous, each thing that is done, done totally. To live like that, it is the easiest thing in the world; but for a man whose head is full of images, it is the hardest. I learned more about building in that one moment, than in ten years of building.

When we are as ordinary as that, with nothing left in any of our actions, except what is required—then we can make towns and buildings which are as infinitely various, and as peaceful, and as wild and living, as the fields of windblown grass.

Almost everybody feels at peace with nature: listening to the ocean waves against the shore, by a still lake, in a field of grass, on a windblown heath. One day, when we have learned the timeless way again, we shall feel the same about our towns, and we shall feel as much at peace in them, as we do today walking by the ocean, or stretched out in the long grass of a meadow.

ACKNOWLEDGMENTS

During the fourteen long years that it has taken me to write this book, I have been helped by three people, above all. First, by my beloved Ingrid, who inspired me always, who understood so clearly what I was trying to do, who was always ready to talk, to look at it again, to help me see exactly what feelings were created by a passage in it, and who found many of the most beautiful photographs. Second, by my dear friend Sara, who came, year after year, at a moment's notice, to discuss a chapter, or a page, or a sentence . . . but most often, during our work together, helped me in our discussions of the theory as a whole. And third, by Peter Mailloux, who spent almost a year, the most difficult year of all, helping to see me through the final editing.

As for the photographs, many of them come from books and magazines long out of print, and it has not always been possible to find the names of the photographers. However, both in the few cases which follow where I *have* been able to identify the photographer, and in all those other cases where I have not, I am immensely grateful to the photographers for their wonderful pictures, which do so much to explain the central meaning of the book.

ACKNOWLEDGMENTS

6	Erik Lundberg	190	Ed Allen (drawing)
20	E. O. Hoppe	194	Werner Bischof
24	Augustin Myska	196	David Vestal
42	Marvin Bolotksy	197	John Durniak
44	Henri Cartier-Bresson	212	Erik Lundberg
46	Ernst Haas	213	Eugene Atget
56	Bernard Wolf	214	Luc Joubert
57	Bernard Wolf	278	Henri Cartier-Bresson
58	Henri Cartier-Bresson	280	Bruce Davidson
59	André Kertesz	281	Henri Cartier-Bresson
60	André Kertesz	366	Lennart Nilsson
61	Henri Cartier-Bresson	388	Ursula Pfistermeister
76	Henri Cartier-Bresson	389	Eugene Atget
102	Roderick Cameron	406	Erik Lundberg
138	K. Nakamura	408	Erik Lundberg
142	David Sellin	480	Eugene Atget
158	Kocjanic	518	Prip Moller
170	Bernard Rudofsky	535	Henri Cartier-Bresson
189	Ed Allen (drawing)	536	Werner Bischof